Y0-CIR-725

PICTORIAL GUIDE TO
THE MAMMALS
OF
NORTH AMERICA

Text and Photographs by

LEONARD LEE RUE III

THOMAS Y. CROWELL COMPANY, NEW YORK

Established 1834

Pictorial Guide to

THE

MAMMALS

OF

NORTH AMERICA

1487
PROPERTY OF
LINCOLN COUNTY SCHOOL DISTRICT
NEWPORT, OREGON
PLEASE RETURN

Drawings of tracks by Charles Gottlieb. The drawings of the tracks of the nine-banded armadillo, coatimundi, and sea lion are adapted from *A Field Guide to Animal Tracks* by Olaus Murie (Houghton Mifflin Company).

Copyright © 1967 by LEONARD LEE RUE III

All rights reserved. Except for use in a review, the reproduction or utilization of this work in any form or by any electronic, mechanical, or other means, now known or hereafter invented, including photocopying and recording, and in any information storage and retrieval system is forbidden without the written permission of the publisher.

Designed by Mort Perry

Manufactured in the United States of America

L.C. Card 67-12408

DEC   '74

4 5 6 7 8 9 10

To My Son
JAMES KEITH RUE

Acknowledgments

It is a great personal satisfaction to me to see this book in print. As far back as I can remember, I have been studying, observing, photographing, and reading about wildlife. Truthfully, I can not recall a time when I was not interested in the subject.

Today I make my living from photographing, and writing and lecturing about, wildlife. I enjoy all three activities equally. They enable me to stimulate an interest in wildlife and the out-of-doors among others. This is essential if we want to be sure that our natural resources will be provided for in the future. Of the three activities, nevertheless, I must admit that I enjoy photography the most, because it gives me a reason to be outdoors working with wildlife. My favorite subjects are mammals. While I enjoy the basic comforts of civilization, I have willingly spent many uncomfortable hours, days, and even weeks studying and photographing wildlife on their conditions and in their own environments. I find it infinitely more rewarding to observe the small secrets that enable a creature to survive than to visit a huge metropolis to see what man has wrought. I spend more of my time with wildlife than with people, and I do so by choice.

This book contains essays on sixty-five different species belonging to nine of the eleven mammalian orders that are found in North America. They are representative of the larger and better-known species that you have a good chance of seeing for yourself. Many of the small mice, rats, ground squirrels, and voles have an extremely restricted range or are seldom seen and are unknown owing to their diminutive size and secretive natures. I hope to be able to see more of our country's mammals and to photograph them.

Special thanks are due to Mary Irving, who helped to whip this book into shape, to Eddie Schelenberger, Bill Shipley, Fred Space, and Joe Taylor. I am also indebted to my eldest son, Lenny IV, who helped me both with the mammals and the photography. And to my typist, Elizabeth Rue, thanks. Because this book is the result of some fifteen years of work, it is impossible to give recognition individually to the many people who have helped me on it. Most of my personal friends have contributed both time and knowledge to the project. To attempt to list them all would be to forget to list a few. I thanked them at the time, and I wish to thank them again now.

LEONARD LEE RUE III

Contents

Introduction

What are mammals? Mammals are animals, but they differ from the birds, reptiles, insects, and other creatures in a number of ways. All mammals have a backbone, a four-chambered heart, a single bone in each half of the lower jaw, three bones in the middle ear, a diaphragm that varies the shape of the chest cavity, some hair on the body; they are warm-blooded, give birth (except the monotremes) to their young alive, and nurse their young. The name mammal derives from the Latin *mammae,* for the mammary glands of the female that supply its young with milk. Mammals have better-developed brains than any of the other animals and have been more successful in adapting to a wide variety of natural conditions.

The first mammals appeared in North America about 75,000,000 years ago. These prehistoric creatures were so different from the modern mammals with which we are familiar that they would be almost unrecognizable. Compared with fish, reptiles, insects, and birds, mammals are real Johnny-come-latelies. Man is the most recently developed of the mammals.

On a world-wide basis, there are approximately 900,000 known species of insects, 232,000 species of invertebrates, 30,000 species of fishes, 20,000 species of birds, 12,000 species of mammals, 6,000 species of reptiles, and 1,500 species of amphibians. In North America, there are about 650 known species of mammals. Approximately 375 of these are found north of the Rio Grande, in the United States and Canada.

Mammals are found all over the world, in all types of climate and habitat. Some have a wider distribution than others; some are common, others are extremely rare. They range in size from the tiny pygmy shrew to the 125-ton blue whale, and are divided unequally among nineteen groups, or orders. Each order is further divided into families, which in turn are made up of closely related genera containing even more closely related individuals, or species. An example of this is: Order Carnivora (meat-eaters), Family Canidae (dogs, foxes, wolves), Genus *Canis* (dogs, wolves), Species *lupus* (gray wolf).

All mammals have basically the same body structure, which is modified to fit the form of life of the individual family and species. Teeth of different sizes and shapes are adapted to gnawing, grinding, piercing, grasping, or cutting. Tails serve to grasp, steer, feel, bludgeon, or signal. Claws are used for digging, fins for swimming, hoofs for running. Other anatomical adaptations permit mammals to swim underwater, climb trees, fly, glide, jump, and burrow.

The young of the placental mammals (in contrast with those of the other two groups, the monotremes and the marsupials) develop and are nourished in the female's body. In some mammals (bats, bears, otters, to name a few), fetal development is retarded through delayed fertilization of the egg cell (ovum). The advantage of delayed implantation, as this is called, is that these mammals may breed at various times of year and the development of the embryo (or gestation period) will not be completed until the proper time, so that the young can be born in the spring. It occurs usually among mammals that are solitary and not numerous, and thus is nature's way of making sure that the females are bred. Most mammals breed at a time of year that will ensure complete development of the embryo by spring, to provide the newborn with the advantages of warm weather and its accompanying bountiful supplies of food.

Mammal	Gestation Period	Average Number of Young
Opossum	13 days	8–18
Eastern Cottontail Rabbit	28 days	5–7
Porcupine	2 months	2–4
Peccary	4½ months	2
Black Bear	7 months	2
Fisher	12 months	3

During the winter, when the food they eat is not available, certain mammals hibernate. They store up body fat or food, then retire to a snug den and fall into a deep, deathlike sleep. Heartbeat, temperature, breathing rate, all decrease markedly. Woodchucks, chipmunks, some bats and mice are true hibernators. Bears, raccoons, skunks, and various other mammals that sleep through the winter remain dormant but do not hibernate. They can be awakened quickly, and their temperatures, breathing, and pulse rates remain almost normal.

Mammals are important to man as sources of food, clothing, and transportation. Man's superior intelligence enabled him to gain ascendancy over his fellow mammals. Dogs, horses, cattle, sheep, and goats were domesticated and adapted to human uses and purposes. There are still many people in North America who depend upon wild game as a major food source. In most cases, however, hunting today is done for sport and recreation. Millions of fur-bearing mammals provide pelts for the fur industry, and countless mammals are kept strictly as pets. The purely esthetic value of just looking at and watching animals cannot be underestimated. Increasingly we are becoming aware that we are our wild brothers' keepers. Call it stewardship, if you will, but as human population increases and the number of wild mammals decreases, man will have to take better care of the mammals that remain or they will be erased from the face of the earth, as many species already have been.

PICTORIAL GUIDE TO
THE MAMMALS
OF
NORTH AMERICA

1

❧ ❧ ❧

Marsupialia—

Pouched Mammals

After the primitive, egg-laying monotremes—the platypus and echidna—the marsupials are the most ancient of mammals. Their origins go back to the Mesozoic era.

The order Marsupialia contains many different species. The pouched mice and rats, phalangers, koalas, wombats, wallabies, kangaroos, and opossums are all marsupials. Numerous species inhabit the Australian region and Central and South America, but the only marsupial found in North America above the Rio Grande is the opossum (*Didelphis,* or those with two reproductive tracts).

Some marsupials glide about in the treetops, some hop and bound about on the ground, some live in the water. Still others, like the native North American opossum, feed on the ground but readily climb trees. The one common denominator is that the female carries and nourishes its young in a *marsupium,* or pouch, on the lower abdomen. In some species the pouch opens to the front and is formed by a fold of skin, while in others it opens to the rear.

Despite the fact that its hairless tail, ears, and feet often freeze off in cold weather, the indefatigable opossum is steadily increasing its range northward into southern Canada. Only time will tell whether it has reached its limit of expansion or whether it can adapt to even hardier climes by gradually becoming a hibernator or by growing hair on its exposed and vulnerable appendages.

Opossum
(Didelphis marsupialis)

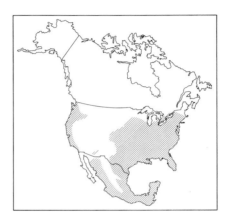

SIZE: *36 inches long, including 13-inch tail.*
WEIGHT: *Up to 12 pounds.*
HABITS: *Nocturnal; plays possum when frightened.*
HABITAT: *Wooded and farm areas.*
FOOD: *Meat, fruits, berries, nuts, grain.*
BREEDING: *2–3 litters of 8–18, April to September. Gestation 13 days.*
ENEMIES: *Dogs, cats, coyotes.*
LIFE SPAN: *7 years.*

The only marsupial in North America, the opossum is also the only animal that can hang downward by its tail. But the tip of the long hairless tail often freezes off in cold weather.

Captain John Smith is said to have named this member of the Didelphidae family back in the the seventeenth century by borrowing the Algonquin Indian word for it, *opossom*. Whatever name it goes by, and it is commonly called possum, the opossum is one of the stupidest of mammals. Its tiny brain is only about one-sixth the size of a raccoon's. It is not exceptionally swift or agile. Yet today there are more opossums than ever before. The opossum seems to be well on its way to proving the biblical statement that the meek shall inherit the earth.

From Texas northward to the Canadian border, the dim-witted possum is found in almost every type of habitat, except open plains and high elevations. It is partial to wooded and farm areas, where it makes its den in a hollow tree,

After they leave her pouch, young opossums ride around on the mother's back, clinging fast to her fur.

burrows beneath the foundations of an old farm building, or takes over a woodchuck's abandoned burrow. The opossum is found chiefly east of the Rockies and in Mexico.

About the size of a large house cat, the full-grown opossum may weigh as much as twelve pounds and measure up to thirty-six inches in length, including its naked, scaly thirteen-inch tail. Mice, rats, and various other mammals wrap their tails around a branch for support while climbing, but only the opossum is able to sustain its entire weight with its tail when the occasion demands. It is the only animal found in the United States capable of using its tail as a hand. All four feet of the opossum have five toes. Because the hind foot closely resembles the human hand, except that the thumb has no nail, opossum tracks are easily recognized. Like its tail and feet, the opossum's ears are hairless. Its white face terminates in a piglike snout, and its long jaws have fifty teeth—more than any other North American land mammal. The opossum's body is covered with long, coarse, silvery-white guard hairs over darker underfur.

In the period from April to September, the female opossum often has two or three litters. Her fur-lined abdominal pouch serves as an incubator for the eight to eighteen young that are always born prematurely just thirteen days after conception. At birth they are about the size of the eraser on a lead pencil; sixteen newborn opossums do not fill a teaspoon. Their eyes and ears are undeveloped, and their hind legs and tails are mere stubs. The front legs, however, are fully developed, with functional nails on the toes. This is fortunate for, small as the tiny opossums are, they must make their way to the maternal pouch by themselves. Once inside the pouch, each attaches itself to one of the mother's teats and does not let go for more than a month. If the mother has more young than teats (which may vary in number, but average about thirteen), the superfluous offspring die and are expelled from the pouch. The young do not have to nurse, but are force-fed by the mother.

The young stay in the pouch until they are about six weeks old, when they begin to venture forth. They get about by riding on their mother's back, clutching fast to her hair. Drawings that show the young opossums hanging by their tails from the mother's tail as she walks about are using artistic license to perpetuate an untruth. Usually the opossum is active at night, when its poor eyesight is offset by its keen hearing and sense of smell, so few people have had a chance to see for themselves how the mother really carries her young.

Sometimes one or more of the babies falls off the mother opossum's back and is lost as she forages for food. By the time they are eight weeks old, however, baby opossums are the size of small rats and can fend for themselves. With luck, a possum lives about seven years.

The opossum eats anything it can find or catch. Meat, fruits, berries, nuts, and grain are consumed. This dietary versatility explains why the simple possum is in the process of extending its range while other more intelligent mammals are being forced back. In the fall the opossum gorges itself and grows very fat. It does not hibernate during extremely cold weather but may remain in its den for several days at a time.

Perhaps the opossum is best known for its habit of playing possum—feigning death to escape from its enemies. Although Didelphis is regarded as the chief practitioner of this art, the hyena, grouse chick, spider, and hog-nosed snake also practice it.

Some experts claim that playing possum is an involuntary act, similar to a fainting spell in a human being. Others believe that it is a conscious act performed by the animal when danger threatens. In this state, the opossum falls on its side and lies limply, its mouth hanging open. This appearance of death has value, for the dog, cat, coyote, or other predator loses interest after giving the carcass a few half-hearted shakes. It has been my personal experience that opossums rarely play possum. Of the thousands of opossums that I have handled, only ten or twelve ever collapsed as expected. The others tried to escape by running away or by turning around and biting.

The opossum figures prominently in the folklore of the Indians, Negroes, and whites of the southern United States. One story tells how the opossum lost the hair off its tail when it was burned over a fire. According to another version, the hair was skinned off when the opossum, stealing corn near a graveyard, was surprised by a ghost. A joke it played on its fellow mammal, the deer, is said to be responsible for the opossum's big, grinning mouth.

In the rural South, opossum meat is enjoyed in such combinations as sweet potatoes and possum. Pelts seldom bring more than 35 cents each. They are used for inexpensive garments and trimmings. Opossums also are widely used in laboratory research.

2

❧ ❧ ❧

Insectivora—Insect-Eaters

Generally speaking, the insect-eaters are small bodied, with long, narrow snouts, and five-clawed toes on each limb. In the burrowing species, the eyes are rudimentary. Their body covering consists of short, dense fur, and occasionally spines. They live on the ground, following a burrowing or semi-aquatic existence. Most insectivores are active only at night, and many consume great quantities of food. Some are carnivorous.

Members of the order Insectivora are found everywhere in the world, with the exception of Australia, most of South America, Greenland, and Antarctica. The only members of the order in North America are the moles and shrews. Their relatives include such diverse creatures as the Madagascan tenrec and the spiny European hedgehog. Both Talpidae (moles) and Soricidae (shrews) live in tunnels and burrows, in the leaf mold of forest areas, or beneath the surface of the earth. All moles and shrews have a strong, musky odor produced by a glandular secretion that makes them generally unpalatable to their predators.

Common Mole
(Scalopus aquaticus)

SIZE: *6–8 inches, not including 1-inch tail.*

WEIGHT: *2–5 ounces.*

HABITS: *Digs subterranean tunnels; active day and night.*

HABITAT: *Underground.*

FOOD: *Earthworms, grubs, spiders, centipedes.*

BREEDING: *1 litter of 3–5 per year. Gestation 42 days.*

ENEMIES: *Hawks, owls, cats, dogs, foxes, weasels, snakes.*

LIFE SPAN: *2–3 years.*

The common mole spends nearly all its life in its underground network of tunnels. The five strong claws on each of the forefeet are especially effective for digging.

The common, or Eastern, mole spends most of its life underground, tunneling through well-drained soil in meadows and woodlands throughout the eastern United States and southern Ontario. The adult mole weighs two to five ounces, measures about six to eight inches in length, not including its tapering, almost hairless one-inch tail. As an adaptation to its subterranean life, the legs are exceptionally short. The huge, shovel-like forefeet appear to be fastened directly to the heavy shoulders. This shortening of the bone structure has had the effect of shortening and strengthening the muscles. The mole's hind feet resemble those of a rat. Some people carry a mole's foot as a charm to prevent rheumatism and toothache.

Linking the five digits of each foot are small areas of skin-covered tissue or webbing. Although all moles can swim when necessary, the Latin word *aquaticus* in the common mole's scientific name refers to this digital webbing. The mole also appears to swim through the soil when tunneling.

One recent summer a mole was caught at the camp where I was working. Hoping to get some photographs, I took it out onto the camp's parade field. The earth on the field had been packed down by tens of thousands of marching feet and by countless vehicles over a thirty-eight-year period. Furthermore, drought had baked the soil into hardpan so firm a pick could hardly dent it. When the mole was placed down on the field, it was unable to touch the ground with both stumpy forefeet at the same time. To move forward, the mole pushed with its hind feet, then rocked its body sideways, so that each forefoot in turn touched the ground. The mole made a sweeping movement with each foot as it briefly made contact with the ground, digging its long, strong claws into the earth. Dirt and pebbles began to fly faster and faster. After it had the hole started, the mole stopped its sideward rocking and concentrated on digging. In less than three minutes it had loosened enough earth to hide completely from sight. If I had not seen this feat I would have declared it impossible. We recaptured the mole with ease because it was still digging through rock-hard soil. But if the ground had been soft forest humus we never would have been able to catch it.

The mole has eyes so small they cannot be distinguished without close examination. The ears are all but invisible. After centuries of disuse, these sense organs have degenerated to their present state, for neither is of much use to a creature that lives most of its life underground. The mole's sense of smell, on the other hand, is highly developed, and it uses its elongated nose in locating the worms and insects that make up its diet. The mole also has a good sense of touch, and is alert to any vibrations or tremors of the earth. This tactile sense not only helps the mole to locate its prey, it helps it to escape from its enemies.

Another adaptation to tunnel life is the mole's soft, dense fur, which may be grayish or brownish in color and is highly valued. This velvety fur's most remarkable feature is the tapering of each strand at the point where it enters the skin. There is no rubbing a mole's hair the wrong way—it lies flat in any direction. If the mole's hair were not so flexible, it would catch against the side of the narrow tunnel and prevent the mole from backing out. When a mole goes into reverse, its fur does also, permitting its bearer to scoot backward with ease. The tail guides the mole in its backward journey, in much the same way that a blind man's cane helps him feel his way.

The shallow tunnels dug by moles in their search for food often cause their creators' death by the hand of the irate landowner whose beautiful lawn has been defaced. It is useless to try to make the lawn's owner understand that these tunnels are beneficial because they help to aerate the soil, or get rainwater underground where it belongs.

Many gardeners erroneously believe that the mole causes further damage by eating the roots and bulbs of plants and flowers. Earthworms, grubs, spiders, centipedes, and the larvae and pupae are the food staples of the mole. Daily it consumes about its weight in food, and in the process does a lot of good by eating many harmful insects. However, its tunnels often are invaded by meadow mice, which do eat roots and cause considerable damage.

Man is not the mole's only enemy. It is also preyed upon by all the predators that feed on mice, including the hawk, owl, cat, dog, fox, weasel, and snake. Frequently a predator does not actually see the mole, but closely observes its passage through a tunnel. The predator pounces on the tunnel, pinning the mole in the passageway beneath, and then digs out its quarry. In periods of drought or in winter, the mole is free from predators. At such times the mole follows right behind the earthworm as it burrows deeply into the earth below the parched topsoil or frost line.

Moles mate in March. The average litter of three to five young per year is born after a gestation period of about forty-two days. The fully furred little ones are miniature copies of their parents. Their nest of dried vegetation lies in a chamber in a deep, underground tunnel. About one month after birth the young are weaned; at the age of two months they are almost full grown. Males are slightly larger than females.

The common mole is active day or night throughout the year. Except during the breeding season or when the mother is with her young, the mole leads a solitary existence. Its life span is from two to three years.

Star Nose Mole
(Condylura cristata)

SIZE: *Body and head 6 inches; tail 3 inches.*
WEIGHT: *3 ounces.*
HABITS: *Active all year and at all hours.*
HABITAT: *Damp or boggy soil.*
FOOD: *Insects, worms, small fish.*
BREEDING: *1 litter of 2–7 per year.*
ENEMIES: *Hawks, owls, snakes, foxes, raccoons, dogs, cats.*
LIFE SPAN: *2–3 years.*

The star nose mole may not have much in between, but it has two unusual features at opposite ends of its body. In front it has twenty-two pink fleshy feelers from which it gets its name. Its tail serves as a storeroom, building up a reserve supply of food for times of scarcity. Here, drawing its feelers inward, the mole devours an earthworm.

The star nose mole owes its name to the twenty-two pink, fleshy appendages that ring the end of its long nose. These little feelers, called rays or tentacles, measure between one-quarter and one-half inch in length, and help the mole in locating its food. As the mole seeks earthworms among leaf mold on the forest floor, aquatic life in marshy areas and on lake and stream bottoms, the two top central rays are held forward while the others are in continual motion. When the mole consumes its food, all the rays are drawn inward.

This mole also has a distinctive tail. More than half as long as the mole's body, it is constricted at the base and is covered with bristly hair. The most interesting feature about this tail is that it is used as a storeroom. In both sexes during winter and early spring it builds up with fatty tissue, increasing in diameter to about the size of a lead pencil. Moles share this feature with several different types of mammals that store excess body fat in their tails when food is abundant, utilizing it later as a reserve supply of food in times of scarcity or as a reserve source of energy during the breeding period.

The star nose mole makes its home in damp or boggy soils from Manitoba southward to Georgia and northeastward to Labrador. It is active throughout the year and at all hours. Occasionally in wintertime the star nose mole is found wandering about in the snow. This usually happens in swampy areas, where warm springs prevent the ground from freezing to any extent. Sometimes this mole even travels under the ice.

Although this mole digs tunnels, as evidenced by the many "molehills" it deposits on the surface, it spends so much more time above ground and in the water that it is seen more frequently than the common mole. It also is exposed to greater danger from such predators as hawks and owls, snakes, foxes, raccoons, dogs, and cats. Both the common mole and the star nose mole are about the same size, but the latter has long legs, a much longer tail, and its eyes are better developed. Its ears are barely visible, and it has a glossy coat of waterproof blackish-brown fur.

Not surprisingly, the star nose mole is an excellent swimmer and diver. It seeks open water, where it dives to the bottom to hunt for the aquatic insects, crustaceans, and small fish that make up a large part of its diet, which also includes worms. The mole's broad forefeet and strong hind legs push it through the water in good style, and it uses its tail as a rudder.

The star nose mole begins to breed when it is about ten months old. Like all moles, it breeds once a year, in March. Although this species is more sociable than the common mole, most moles lead a solitary existence. Only rarely are several moles found inhabiting the same tunnel, and these usually are the female and her young of the year. The female does not even tolerate the male after breeding, but raises her family by herself.

The mother gives birth to her young in a special chamber dug in a tunnel deep underground, thus assuring them maximum protection until they are able to take care of themselves. The two to seven young moles are born about six weeks after conception and are remarkably well developed, even to the fleshy "star" on their noses. A month after birth the young moles, dark gray in color and almost full grown, go off on their own.

BUILDING MEDIA CENTER
Newport High School

Short-Tailed Shrew
(Blarina brevicauda)

SIZE: 4–5 inches, including tail.

WEIGHT: Less than 1 ounce.

HABITS: Builds runways through plant debris, moss, and snow. Poisons and feeds on animals often larger than itself.

HABITAT: Woodlands, especially forest leaf mold.

FOOD: Insects, snails, salamanders, frogs, snakes, mice, birds, other shrews, vegetation.

BREEDING: 2–3 litters of 3–6, April to September. Gestation 17–21 days.

ENEMIES: Other shrews.

LIFE SPAN: Rarely lives longer than two winters.

The short-tailed shrew is one of the commonest mammals of eastern North America. It is one of the most ferocious creatures on earth. The shrew's basic body metabolism is so high that it must hunt almost constantly to satisfy its tremendous appetite. Every twenty-four hours the shrew eats and burns up about three times its weight in food. Because of this frantic pace, it rarely lives more than two winters. The salvation of the world is that the shrew weighs only a fraction of an ounce and is about the size of a mouse. If it were any larger, books would be written about shrews instead of about man-eating lions and tigers.

The adult short-tailed shrew measures between four and five inches, including its tail. It has a long, pointed snout, tiny eyes, almost invisible ears, and a soft coat of silvery-gray fur. Like all shrews, it has five digits on each foot.

The shrew has a voracious appetite and consumes about three times its weight every day. Here a shrew kills a garter snake by injecting poison which affects the snake's nervous system.

This tiny terror feeds on anything it can find, even other shrews. In addition to insects of all kinds, it avidly consumes snails, salamanders, frogs, small snakes, mice, the young of ground-nesting birds, and some vegetation. Frequently the shrew's gluttony serves as a useful check on such destructive insects as the larch sawfly.

The short-tailed shrew is able to feed on mice much larger than itself because it has a secret weapon in the form of poison glands in its mouth. When this shrew bites its prey with its thirty-two black-tipped teeth, its poisonous saliva enters the wound. The quick-acting poison causes paralysis of the nervous system, but rarely death. If the shrew permits too much time to elapse between biting and eating the mouse, the poison loses its toxic potency, and the mouse may recover.

I stumbled onto this fact when watching a short-tailed shrew attack a white-footed mouse. The mouse was bitten repeatedly. I could actually see paralysis occur, as the victim's body began to quiver and then stiffen. Instead of finishing its attack, the shrew then began to dash about wildly. In about ten minutes the mouse appeared to regain consciousness and the control of its limbs. At that moment the shrew returned to its quarry and proceeded to devour it. I am convinced that a shrew could never catch a mouse under ordinary circumstances, unless it cornered one in an underground passageway. The mouse is too alert and active and the shrew is badly hampered by its diminutive eyes and limited eyesight.

The shrew does not secrete enough poison to make it dangerous to man. On the many occasions when I have been bitten by a shrew, I have felt nothing more painful than a nasty little mouse-like bite. Although the early settlers in eastern North America knew about the poison, later generations relegated it to the category of an old wives' tale. Only within the last few decades have scientific tests proved the existence of this poison, which is produced by no other North American shrew.

The shrew finds that forest leaf mold provides an ideal habitat and contains quantities of food. Using its strong feet and nose, the shrew makes surface and subsurface runways through plant debris, moss, and snow. These runways are used for foraging and also serve as shelters. Nests of dried leaves and grasses may be placed under a log or stump or in a shallow burrow about six inches below the surface.

The female short-tailed shrew gives birth to a litter of from three to six young after a gestation period of seventeen to twenty-one days. The babies are pink, almost hairless, and smaller than a honeybee. Within a month they are furred out, their teeth have developed, and their eyes have opened. They are now weaned and are forced to leave the nest to search for their own food, while the mother prepares for the next of the two or three litters she may bear in the period from April to September.

3

❧ ❧ ❧

Chiroptera—

Winged Mammals

Bats, which belong to the order Chiroptera (from *cheiron*, hand, and *pteron*, wing), are flying mammals. Other mammals may glide, but only bats are able to equal the bird's accomplishment of free, sustained flight.

There are almost 2,000 species of bats in the world. No other order of mammals, except the rodents, has so many species. The greatest number of bat species is found in the tropics. In North America there are three families of bats—the free-tailed (Molossidae), leaf-nosed (Phyllostomidae), and insect-eating bats (Vespertilionidae). Most of the thirty-eight North American species, including the little brown bat and the red bat, belong to the family Vespertilionidae, "the evening ones."

In all bat species, male and female usually look alike and have scent glands that produce a musky odor. Bats mate in the fall and sometimes in the winter and spring as well.

The bat's forearm has been lengthened and modified into a wing. In some instances the fingers are longer than the forearm. The thumb is short and protrudes from the forward part of the wing, where it serves as a hook for grasping. Arm and fingers are covered with a leathery, elastic membrane that also is fastened to the body, legs, and tail. The membrane between the legs and tail can be bent forward to form a funnel-like net that is used by the bat as it flies to scoop insects out of the air. The bat also achieves some steering control by dragging its feet. This increases air resistance and helps to turn the body.

The hind feet are small, have sharp claws, and are used mainly for grasping. On the ground the feet are rather ineffective, and the bat moves by hitching itself forward with its wings and pushing with its feet. While resting or hibernating, a bat hangs by its hind feet. It spends eighty per cent of its life hanging upside down. The bat must rest in this position because its knees bend backward, making it impossible for the bat to hang in any other position.

The old saying about being blind as a bat has no basis in fact. Bats have good eyesight and can see in daylight, but commonly fly at night. According to the sixth-century B.C. Greek philosopher Aesop, avoidance of creditors was the bats' motivation for night flying, and there have been various other explanations. Bats feed mainly at night because they can find more moths at that time, and moths make up the bulk of the little brown bat's diet.

Bats fly more by ear than by eye. Many experiments have been carried out to test the bat's use of echolocation, which operates on the same principle as sonar used in submarines and allows it to fly through all sorts of obstacles without hitting them. Scientists have constructed various types of wire mazes and have sealed the bat's eyes, but the little creature flew as unerringly as before. When they sealed its sensitive ears, however, the bat lost its way and blundered into the wires.

Our improved technology now permits us to hear what the bat has been hearing for years. In flight the bat emits sounds of such high frequency—up to 100,000 cycles per second—that they cannot be heard by the human ear. These supersonic sounds are uttered at a rate of from thirty to sixty per second until they bounce off an object and are echoed back to the bat's ear and tragus (a projection rising from the inside base of the external ear). The echoes form a picture in the bat's brain, allowing it to "see" what lies ahead and avoid it if necessary.

The bat also uses sound waves to locate its prey. When the sound echoes from a moth, the bat sets out in pursuit. Not to be outdone, the moth has a countermeasure, an anti-bat sonar of its own. When this sonar warns of a bat homing in, the moth takes evasive action. Often it tumbles to the ground, where the bat's sonar cannot distinguish the moth from the background. In turn, the bat uses its fluttering or swooping flight to "scramble" the moth's sonar until it is close enough to the moth to pursue it in direct flight.

As creatures of the night, bats have long been associated with Halloween witchcraft and have been popular subjects of folklore in most parts of the world. Some species, such as the leaf-nosed, mastiff, and others, present a decidedly weird appearance, which often is enhanced by bright colors—orange, tan, white. Only the vampire bats of the tropics lap human blood, however. Some bats eat fruit, such as guavas, bananas, mangoes, and figs. Some eat fish, and others feed only upon insects. In Ireland the bat is a symbol of death, but in China it is a symbol of long life and happiness.

Little Brown Bat
(*Myotis lucifugus*)

SIZE: *3½ to 4½ inches, including tail. Wing span 10 inches.*
WEIGHT: *½-ounce.*
HABITS: *Nocturnal; hibernates October–March.*
HABITAT: *Caves, hollow trees, buildings.*
FOOD: *Small insects, eaten on wing.*
BREEDING: *Delayed implantation, birth of single offspring in spring. Gestation 56 days.*
ENEMIES: *Hawks, raccoons, foxes, other bats, snakes, birds of prey.*
LIFE SPAN: *10½ years.*

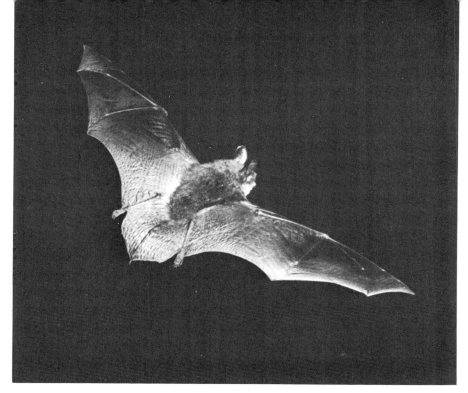

The only mammal capable of flying, the bat has a webbed forearm that serves as a wing. The thumb, which protrudes from the front of the wing, acts like a hook for grasping its prey. The little brown bat shown here has a wing span of ten inches.

The little brown bat is one of our most common bat species. The Myotis group to which it belongs has the widest range of any mammal in the world, with the possible exception of man. It is found everywhere, except in the arctic and antarctic regions and some of the oceanic islands.

This is the bat usually seen fluttering near houses at dusk. In the daytime it may be found hanging upside down in caves, hollow trees, or buildings. The church bell towers of old made ideal roosting spots, hence the old saying about bats in the belfry.

About three and a half- to four and a half-inches long, this bat may vary in color from dark brown to reddish brown or pale buff. It has a plain nose and tapering tragus.

Just before going into hibernation, in the late fall, this bat frequently feeds in the daytime. Insects are so scarce at this season that the bat is unable to secure enough food at night and must work longer hours. The bat is a hearty trencherman. At a single feeding it often consumes one-fourth of its weight.

On a dark, dismal day in early November I was watching a bat flying about, diving, twisting, turning, and putting on a really fine display of dexterity in flight. It seemed to me that surely no bird could fly as well. Hardly had this thought crossed my mind than a small sharp-shinned hawk dropped out of the sky, snatched the bat out of the air, and flew off with it. In that instant my speculation about the bat's superiority in flight was shattered.

In winter the little brown bats hibernate, singly or in clusters, in caves and abandoned mineshafts. These bats are true hibernators, for they go into a deep sleep, their metabolism is reduced, and their body temperature drops to about 56 degrees to match the temperature of the damp, humid, subterranean tunnel. When light strikes their moisture-soaked bodies, they glisten as though encrusted with jewels. Hibernation lasts until spring and the return of flying insects.

Raccoons and foxes regularly visit the local mines seeking to feed upon any low-hanging hibernating bats. Bats also are sought by other mammals, including other bats, snakes, and birds of prey.

The little brown bat mates in the fall and produces its young in the spring. When the time for birth nears, the female moves to a separate maternity center of the cave. This bat usually has just one offspring at a time. The helpless newborn bat is very large in relation to the mother. It is nearly naked and its eyes are closed. This youngster clings to its mother's body as she flies about gathering food. By the time it is three weeks old, the baby bat is strong enough to fly by itself.

Is there any truth to the claim that bats deliberately become entangled in hair, particularly in women's long hair? The answer is, No. Bats simply are not interested in hair, long or short. I used to demonstrate this when conducting Boy Scout nature hikes. Plucking a bat from its perch in a mine, I placed it in a boy's hair. Invariably the startled bat flew away at its first opportunity. Perhaps the association between bats and hair stems from the superstition that if a bat gets in the hair, an unhappy love affair will result.

Bats often roost up under the eaves of a house or in the attic, crawling through tiny cracks and crevices. These hideaways offer sleeping bats good protection from enemies. When a bat gets into a house, the aroused tenants usually seize broom, mop, or other handy weapon and proceed to wreak havoc on walls and furniture in frantic efforts to knock the bat down. All that is really necessary is to open a window wide, and the bat generally will fly right out.

In some quarters it is considered lucky to catch a bat in a hat, as evidenced by the old rhyme "Bat, bat, come under my hat." But the luck is canceled if the bat brings bedbugs with it, probably implying that a bat coming into the house means the tenants will be moving out. Certainly there is no truth to the association of bats and bedbugs. If a bat saw a bedbug, it would eat the insect, not carry it about. The objection to bats roosting in houses stems from the fact that they leave behind a musky odor, greasy spots on the wall where they have clung, and droppings. When collected from the floors of bat caves these droppings, called guano, are valuable as fertilizer.

Red Bat

(*Lasiurus borealis*)

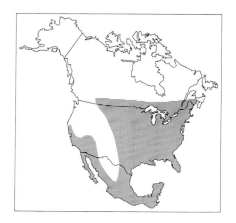

SIZE: *4 inches, including tail. Wingspan 14 inches.*
WEIGHT: *⅓-ounce.*
HABITS: *Migrates to south in winter. Female flies with young under her wing.*
HABITAT: *Forested areas.*
FOOD: *Flying insects, especially beetles.*
BREEDING: *Litter of 1–4 born April or May. Gestation 240 days.*
ENEMIES: *Owls, snakes, raccoons, opossums.*
LIFE SPAN: *8–10 years.*

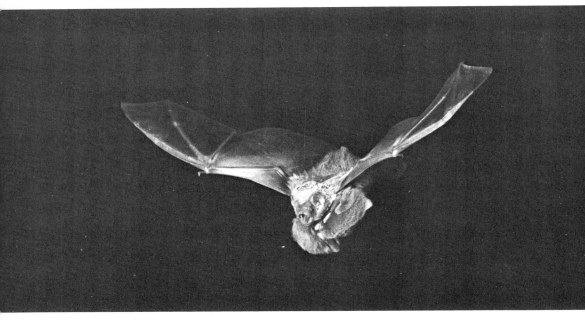

New-born red bats have good grasping reflexes for clinging to their mother, who carries her offspring with her as she searches for night-flying insects.

The red bat is easily identified by its russet-red fur, which is paler in the female than the male. Measuring over four inches in length and having an overall wingspan of twelve to fourteen inches, this bat is somewhat larger than the little brown bat. It has short, rounded ears and tragus, narrow wings, and a swooping, spiral flight.

This bat has a restricted range and is found in the eastern United States, where it prefers forested areas. The red bat does not enter caves or houses. It usually spends the daylight hours hanging upside down among the leaves of a tall tree, or huddled up against the bark of its trunk. The red bat does not hibernate in the same region it inhabits in summer, but migrates hundreds of miles to the south. Stray individuals, probably blown off course, have been found in Bermuda. Migrations usually occur at night, but occasionally this bat moves on overcast days as well. As soon as the first flying insects appear in the spring, the red bat heads north.

Although the red bat mates in August, delayed fertilization of the egg cell postpones birth of the young until the following April or May. There may be as many as four in a litter. As the time of birth approaches, the female clings fast to a branch with feet and thumb hooks. In this position, her wings and tail membrane serve as a sort of inverted umbrella to catch the babies as they are born.

Naked and blind, the new-born bats have good grasping reflexes for clinging to their mother, who enfolds them in her wings for protection while they nurse. When the mother bat sets out at dusk in search of night-flying insects, she takes her offspring with her. The combined weight of her young is less than her own at first, but the situation is reversed as the young develop. Soon the family outweighs the mother.

I was amazed to see the mother bat in the photograph carrying her four babies, whose combined weight was double hers. Bats are able to carry so much weight because their wings are larger in proportion to their bodies than a bird's. Bats take much longer, stronger strokes than a bird, and each of their wings describes almost a half-circle. There is no loss of air rushing through the membranes of a bat's wing as there is through the feather-slotted wings of a bird.

When the young bats grow large enough to hang head down by themselves, the mother parks them among the leaves, where they will not be seen, and sallies forth to search for food. At about the age of three weeks, the young bats are strong enough to fly and to search for food themselves. Then the mother bat weans them, and they are on their own.

Bats may spend as much as an hour a day grooming themselves. Every part of the body is thoroughly washed. What cannot be reached with the tongue can be reached with a saliva-moistened thumb or foot. Although bats occasionally may have fleas, they share that condition with many other creatures.

Rabies has occurred in bats, but only in isolated instances. Actually, you stand a better chance of getting rabies from your dog or cat than from a bat. As a safeguard, do not handle bats. They do not like to be picked up, and will bite. Please do not kill them. Bats feed upon many insects and are perfectly designed for the role they perform in life.

4

❧ ❧ ❧

Lagomorpha—

Hares and Rabbits

The order Lagomorpha consists of two families—the hares and rabbits (Leporidae) and the pikas (Ochotonidae), sometimes called conies or rock rabbits. The lagomorpha, vegetarians all, live in a variety of habitats almost everywhere in the world. The male and female of all species are look-alikes.

At one time the hares, rabbits, and pikas were classified as rodents. Later they were placed in the separate order Lagomorpha because they have an additional set of small incisor teeth growing behind the main upper pair of incisors. These small incisors of the lagomorphs grow continuously throughout their lifetime, as do those of the rodents.

The hare has long legs and leaps, the rabbit has short legs and runs. Both the pika and the rabbit give birth to young that are naked and blind, while the young of the hare are fully furred and have their eyes wide open. A young hare can fend for itself in a matter of hours after birth, but the young of the other two species must be nurtured and provided for.

The pika looks like a small rabbit, but has much shorter, well-rounded ears and no visible tail. The soles of its feet are entirely covered with hair, with the exception of small, naked pads at the base. These provide traction on the rock slides of western North America, where the pika makes its home.

The pika differs from the rest of the lagomorphs in a number of ways. It does not hop or sit up, and all four of its legs are about the same length. Unlike the rabbit and the hare, the pika is active chiefly during the daytime. It also is the only member of this order that collects food for the future. It gathers grasses and spreads them out to dry. The dried grasses then are stored beneath overhanging rocks, which the pika uses as a barn.

Varying Hare
(Lepus americanus)

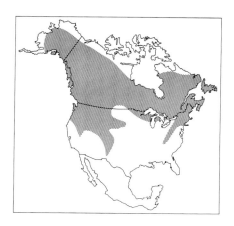

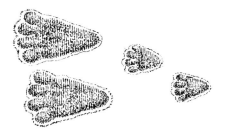

Size: 18 inches, including 2-inch tail. Hind foot 5½ inches.

Weight: 4–5 pounds.

Habits: Promiscuous mating; does not burrow. Coat changes from brown in summer to white in winter.

Habitat: In thickets and among vegetation.

Food: Grasses, herbs, and green vegetation in summer; bark in winter.

Breeding: 2–3 litters of 4–6 born each year. Gestation 30–38 days.

Enemies: Fur-bearing animals, horned owl.

Life span: Up to 3 years.

Sometimes called the snowshoe rabbit, the varying hare has long snowshoe-like feet with which it can run on the surface of the snow. When the days turn short in the fall, the varying hare's coat turns white, blending in with its winter surroundings.

For centuries the hare has played a prominent role in the world's folklore. The fable of the hare and the tortoise, popularized by Aesop, has its counterpart among many African peoples and was brought by transplanted Africans to the New World. The Indians of eastern North America prized the hare so highly that they credited it with having formed and ordered the world.

The varying hare sometimes is called the snowshoe rabbit. In the fall, long stiff hairs grow from the side of its feet, doubling their surface area when the toes are spread apart. This permits the hare to run over the soft snow without sinking in as deeply as it would ordinarily. Few creatures attempt to move while the snow is falling. Immediately afterward the varying hare will start to make trails. If the snow has crusted or been packed by the wind, the hare will run on the top and trails will not be needed. Then the hare's enlarged foot is an advantage.

This hare acquired its other name because it is a turncoat. In winter its summer coat of brown turns white. This change is not caused by snow or cold weather but by a phenomenon related to the hare's eye. Its eye is in effect a photoelectric cell that is activated by the number of daylight hours. The eye picks up less light in the short daylight hours of autumn, thus allowing the pituitary gland at the base of the animal's brain to become inactive. This gland controls the amount of pigment that goes into each hair of the hare's body. When the pituitary gland is inactive, no pigment is formed in the hair, and the new winter growth of hair is white. As the brown summer coat is

In summer, the varying hare's coat changes to brown, making it hard to spot among the brushy undergrowth. In this picture, its sensitive ears have turned forward to pick up sounds of danger.

shed, the hare gradually turns completely white, with the exception of its black ear tips.

The entire process is reversed each spring. Beginning in late December, the number of daylight hours increases. By March, patches of brown hair appear in the white coat. By the end of May, the white hair, except for the underside of the hare's short tail, has been replaced by the new summer coat of brown.

The varying hare is not alone in turning color. Some of the other creatures living in the snowy wastes—such as the Arctic fox, the weasel, and the ptarmigan share this ability. That it is controlled by daylight has been proved by scientists through various experiments. In midsummer, hares in their seasonal pelage were placed in cages from which light was excluded; immediately they began to turn white. Other hares were confined in cages in winter and exposed to electric lights for a number of hours equal to those in a summer's day. The hares' white pelage turned brown.

This adaptability is an important factor in the varying hare's survival, for it inhabits forested and brushy areas of the United States and Canada where snow remains on the ground for at least six months of the year. This hare does not use a burrow, but simply seeks out a sheltered spot in a thicket, against the bole of a tree, or under the drooping, snow-ladened branches of a spruce. In winter the hare's white pelage makes it all but invisible. In summer its brown coat gives similar protection by allowing the animal to blend in among the dark vegetation.

Varying hare populations are noticeably cyclical. They reach a peak about every ten years and then decrease. At the height of a cycle they may rise to a total of as much as 3,400 per square mile. The number of these hares is of vital importance in the North. Indians as well as fur-bearing animals count on the hare as a basic food. When hares are scarce, furbearers are hard to find, the Indians have trouble gathering furs to trade for other food, and starvation stalks the land. When hares are abundant, their fur-bearing predators are plentiful, trapping is good, and the Indians find that living is a little easier.

What causes these periodic cycles of abundance and scarcity? Nature does not allow any species to overpopulate its area. Numbers build up to a certain peak; then disease, parasites, predators, or starvation take over. Like the rabbit, the hare is susceptible to tularemia. Its chief predator is the lynx, with the bobcat, fox, weasel, mink, marten, fisher, and wolf all taking their share. Among the winged predators the great horned owl takes the greatest toll.

After a cyclic decline varying hares are reduced to a minimal population. This scarcity of hares allows their food supply to grow abundantly—grasses, herbs, and other green vegetation in summer; young pine, spruce, birch, willow, aspen whose bark would be stripped in winter. The remaining well-fed females have larger and healthier litters, and the population boom is on its way again.

Varying hares first breed when they are about one year old. They are promiscuous, and do not pair off. During the mating season the male pursues the female over forest trails at speeds that sometimes reach thirty miles per hour. Battles between contending males are bloody and vicious. The hares kick each other with their powerful hind feet and make deep, raking cuts with their long, strong claws. I once saw a male killed in one of these battles whose rival had torn most of the hide off his body. The expression mad as a March hare aptly describes these courtship antics.

To maintain its population, the varying hare has two or three litters a year. Four to six young are born at one time in a secluded site chosen by the female. The babies weigh about three ounces, and are able to run about on their first day. Their eyes are open, and their bodies are covered with gray fur that gradually changes to brown. By the time they are a month old, young hares weigh about one and one-quarter pounds, are weaned, and soon get about by themselves. A full-grown adult weighs four or five pounds and is about eighteen inches long. The female is larger than the male. Many hares do not survive the first year, but a small handful may live as long as three years.

These hares are much sought after by hunters for their meat and are widely trapped for their pelts as well as their meat by the northern Indians, who make them into blankets. Although hares kill many sapling conifers by gnawing off the bark in winter, this girdling is helpful in some ways because it gives the surviving young trees more space in which to grow. I have tried to raise varying hares as pets, but without success. Every time I opened the pen to feed them, they would try to kick or to bite my hand.

Black-Tailed Jack Rabbit
(Lepus californicus)

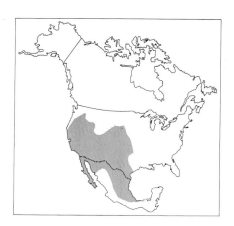

SIZE: *Head and body 2 feet; tail 3–4 inches.*

WEIGHT: *Up to 7 pounds.*

HABITS: *Runs up to 45 miles per hour. Does not burrow, but digs depressions in earth to sit in.*

HABITAT: *Open prairies and semi-arid regions.*

FOOD: *Alfalfa, grama grass, mesquite, sagebrush.*

BREEDING: *1–2 litters of 3–4 a year. Gestation 41–47 days.*

ENEMIES: *Coyotes, badgers, bobcats, foxes, hawks, owls.*

LIFE SPAN: *5–6 years.*

The jack rabbit gets its name from the jackass because of the resemblance of its long, floppy ears. With its powerful hind legs it leaps twenty feet at a time and runs up to forty-five miles per hour.

The native jack rabbit has been an important source of food for the Indians inhabiting the dry regions of the Southwest. Prehistoric Indians held rabbit drives, hunting the jack with spears and throwing sticks as well as with the bow and arrow. Archaeologists excavating ancient pueblos have uncovered the bones of countless jack rabbits, attesting to the early Indians' prowess.

The jack rabbit gets its name from the jackass, both having long, floppy ears. Despite its name, the jack is not a rabbit. It is our largest native hare; its young are born with a full coat of fur and with their eyes open.

The black-tailed jack rabbit has a distinctive black patch on its rump and on the top of its three- to four-inch tail. Its ears are black-tipped, and its grayish-brown body measures almost two feet in length; it may weigh as much as seven pounds. Both sexes look alike, but the female is the larger. Long ears and legs are vital to the survival of the jack in its native habitat, the open prairies and semi-arid region of the Southwest, where cover usually is sparse or nonexistent.

Burrow-digging is not an activity indulged in by the jack rabbit. The only digging it does is to scratch a form, or slight depression, in the earth for use as a sitting-in place. Running is the jack rabbit's forte. It is one of the fastest animals in the country. Speeds of up to 45 miles per hour have been recorded. The jack rabbit, with its heavily muscled hind legs, is capable of making 20-foot leaps. Unless it is being hotly pursued, this animal usually bounds along, making every fourth or fifth hop a little higher than the others so that it can look behind to see if potential enemies are in the vicinity. If the jack is running through high weeds or brush, or if it is frightened, some of these leaps may be exceptionally high.

Trickery is another ruse employed by the jack rabbit. It has a very limited territory (about two acres) for an animal that is capable of covering so much ground and so knows thoroughly every topographical feature of its domain. When chased by a predator, the jack twists and turns through the brush and dodges along its trails. If closely pursued, the jack rabbit may duck under a barbed wire fence in the hope that its pursuer will decapitate itself. This trick has been recorded so many times that it must be a favorite of the jacks.

The salt-and-pepper, light brown coat of this hare makes an amazingly good camouflage. When huddled in its form, with its long legs folded up beneath its body and long ears folded down over its back, the jack is extremely difficult to see. The jack remains hidden in its form until it knows it can avoid detection no longer, then off it bounds.

The coyote, whose speed matches the jack rabbit's, is its most feared enemy. The jack's only hope of escape lies in its ability to dodge and turn shorter and faster. Coyotes often hunt in pairs, one partner making a direct pursuit, while the other waits to see where the chase is going before trying to intercept the jack. Badgers, bobcats, foxes, hawks, and owls all eat young jack rabbits if they fail to catch the adults. Disease and parasites also make a drain on the jack rabbit population.

After a gestation period of a little more than a month, females in the northern part of their range produce one litter of three or four young in the spring. In the warmer southern states, two litters are not uncommon. The young may be born individually in different places rather than in a family group. Very little is known about the family life of these hares. Most naturalists believe that the female nurses her young for only two or three days at the most. After that time she is not seen with her young.

An unsociable creature, the jack rabbit has little to do with its fellows except during the breeding season. In periods of drought, driven by hunger rather than any desire for togetherness, jacks may concentrate in areas where food is available. Like most arid-land dwellers, the jack rabbit remains largely inactive throughout the hot daylight hours and does not require much water to drink. Most of the moisture it needs is derived from its food supply of succulent plants, such as alfalfa, grama grass, mesquite, and sagebrush.

Many hunters in the eastern part of the United States turn green with envy when they read about the periodic rabbit drives conducted in some of the western states to control the number of jacks. To some western farmers the jack rabbit is as much of a plague as the European rabbit in Australia, which reproduced in such staggering numbers that it defoliated the countryside and made ranching impossible.

In some sections of the United States the jack rabbit population has sky-rocketed. Faced with the disappearance of forage and crops, ranchers from time to time conduct huge drives. Encircling the infested area, they move gradually in toward the center. At first the circle is so large the jack rabbits see only a curving line and run toward the center rather than breaking through the line. As the circle of men tightens about them, the jacks are forced into wire enclosures built to confine them. There they are killed. As many as 20,000 jack rabbits have been killed on a single drive.

Eastern Cottontail Rabbit
(Sylvilagus floridanus)

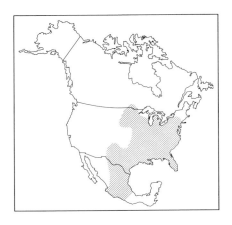

SIZE: 14–17 inches, including 2-inch tail.

WEIGHT: 2½–3 pounds.

HABITS: Promiscuous mating. Does not dig burrows of its own, but uses those abandoned by other mammals.

HABITAT: Woods and thickets.

FOOD: Herbs, grasses, vegetables, berries in summer; dried vegetation and bark in winter.

BREEDING: Usually 4–5 litters of 5–7 per year. Gestation 28 days.

ENEMIES: Birds, all meat-eating animals, snakes.

LIFE SPAN: Up to 8 years.

A typical rabbit, the cottontail has shorter legs than a hare, and runs, rather than leaps, to escape danger.

The cottontail may well be our best-known wild animal. Few have not encountered one of these little creatures in one way or another, as a pet or game animal, in folklore and myth, in comic books, or in animated cartoons. To carry a rabbit's foot is considered lucky, despite the fact that the limb's original owner obviously came to grief. This superstition may be attributed to the erroneous belief that rabbits are born with their eyes open and thus have the power of the evil eye to ward off danger and misfortune. Associated with Eostre, the sacred Anglo-Saxon goddess of spring, is the Easter rabbit with its brightly colored Easter eggs. The rabbit is the chief animal trickster in the mythology of many Indian tribes. Br'er Rabbit was the star of the famous Uncle Remus stories by Joel Chandler Harris.

Measuring between fourteen and seventeen inches in length, the cottontail is about the size of the varying hare, but has shorter ears and legs that are better suited to running than to leaping. The woods and thickets of eastern United States provide the type of escape cover required by this rabbit. A rusty patch at the nape of the neck marks its otherwise grayish-brown coat. When

Female cottontails raise an average of four to five litters a year, with five to seven in a litter. The babies are born blind and naked and weigh about one ounce. In three weeks they leave the nest and become completely independent.

it bounds away the rabbit displays the pure white, cottony underside of its tail that gives this species its name.

As the number-one small game mammal in the United States, the cottontail rabbit is the target of roughly thirty per cent of all the ammunition manufactured in the country. Over 25,000,000 cottontails are taken annually by hunters for food and sport; eighty-five per cent of all rabbits die or are killed off each year in other ways. To the surviving fifteen per cent is given the job of repopulating the countryside, and as soon as they are nine or ten months old they set to work with vigor.

The breeding season starts in February and continues until September. During this time courting couples often perform acrobatic leaps and dashes, and contending males indulge in furious battles. Although the female cottontail is capable of raising seven or eight litters a year, four to five litters is the average. Five to seven young per litter are usual, but litters of eleven and twelve have been recorded. Gestation period is twenty-eight days. The female frequently mates again within twenty-four hours of giving birth. May is the peak month of rabbit production.

About a week before giving birth, the female prepares a nest, usually a shallow, saucer-like depression about four inches deep and six inches wide. She lines this form with dry grasses, and makes a blanket of grasses and hair that she plucks from her breast. When the female leaves the nest, she pulls this blanket over the little ones, serving the dual purpose of warmth and camouflage. At birth the blind, practically hairless young weigh about one ounce, and their ears lie flat on their heads. In about three days they are fully furred. Within a week their eyes open and their ears stand upright. The rabbit depends for its survival on its three-inch ears and bulging eyes that detect sounds and sights from the rear as well as from the front and sides.

Throughout the daylight hours the mother cottontail stays away from her babies, and remains hidden in a form that she has prepared for herself nearby. At nightfall she returns to the nest. Rolling back the blanket that covers the young, she crouches over them so that they can nurse. When the babies have been fed, the mother covers them again and goes off to seek food for herself.

Between the ages of two to three weeks the young rabbits are weaned and leave the nest to become completely independent. They do not go too far from their birthplace. Usually the female spends her entire life on about two acres. The male has a much larger range that overlaps the ranges of several females.

When a new area has been selected, the cottontail loses no time in familiarizing itself with every inch of its territory. As the rabbit explores and lays out its territory, it makes a network of paths by constantly using the same passage-

Chewed bark and rabbit droppings—two sure signs of the cottontail in winter.

way and chewing away brushy obstructions. Then it builds several forms, using its body to hollow out bare spots in the high grasses. Every abandoned woodchuck burrow is memorized as an escape tunnel. The rabbit does not relish getting into an unfamiliar area, where it would be more vulnerable to danger. When pursued by a dog or other predator, the cottontail runs in a circle. If pushed too hard, it ducks into the woodchuck's burrow.

The rabbit never digs a burrow of its own. Instead, it utilizes one abandoned by another mammal. In wintertime, when the snow is deep and winds are bitter, the cottontail takes up a more or less permanent residence in an underground burrow. On bright winter days it can be observed sunning itself at the mouth of the burrow.

The rabbit eats almost every type of green, growing plant—herbs, grasses, even poison ivy. Its taste for vegetables, berries, and fruit often gets it in trouble with farmers and gardeners, for the cottontail does considerable damage to crops, shrubs, and trees. Because the rabbit feeds on dried vegetation or bark in winter, it often requires water. If there is no free-flowing water available, the rabbit eats snow and licks ice. Ordinarily, this animal does not need to drink water, as it licks off the drops of dew that cling to each blade of grass at night. All its summer food has a high water content, and this too helps to supply the necessary moisture.

Given adequate food and shelter, the cottontail is more than able to hold its own in the face of almost constant adversity. Besides hunters, automobiles and parasites take a tremendous toll. Birds, mammals, and snakes prey upon the rabbit whenever they get the chance. The rabbit is particularly prone to tularemia. This disease is important because it can be transmitted to man and to other mammals, such as the beaver and muskrat. Fortunately, antibiotics can cure the disease in man. Tularemia is spread among wildlife by the biting and blood-sucking flies, ticks, and mosquitoes. These parasites, in addition to fleas and warbles, make life miserable for the cottontail even when tularemia is not present. The rabbit needs more than good luck represented by its four feet to live out its potential life span of eight years.

5

✿ ✿ ✿

Rodentia—

Gnawing Mammals

Rodents are the most numerous of all mammals, representing more than half the living species of mammals that have been identified by man. Because they have successfully adapted themselves to a great variety of living conditions, members of the order Rodentia are found on every continent. In size they range from the tiny mouse to the giant South American capybara, the largest rodent in the world.

There are so many species and subspecies of rodents that it is not surprising that members of the order Rodentia are among our best-known mammals. Rodents are easily recognized by their two incisors (gnawing or cutting teeth) in both the upper and lower jaws, which continue to grow throughout their lifetime, give them a buck-toothed appearance, and in some species are brightly colored. The outer edge of the incisor is composed of hard enamel, while the rest of the tooth is of softer dentine. Constant gnawing and chewing by the animal wears down the dentine and keeps the incisors chisel-sharp. Rodents often sharpen their teeth by grinding them together. Incisors that are mismatched and fail to meet frequently grow so long that they curl back into the rodent's head and kill it. There is a large gap between these cutting teeth and the cheek teeth that grind and masticate food.

Rodents are plantigrade: like the bear and man, they walk on the sole of the foot or palm of the hand. The forelimb usually terminates in five digits, although the digit corresponding to the human thumb may be inconspicuous.

The hind foot commonly has five digits also, although in some species there may be as few as three.

Some rodents are specialized in their mode of living: they may spend most of their time below ground, on the ground, in the treetops, or in the water. They may be swift of movement or slow and awkward. Some rodents have valuable pelts and some make interesting pets. Many rodents are an important item of food for man, while others are so destructive that they rate among man's worst enemies. Rodents commonly have a high birthrate. Because they are the staple food of the meat-eaters, this helps to control their numbers.

Woodchuck
(*Marmota monax*)

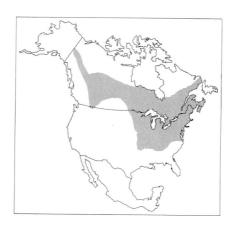

SIZE: *Head and body 24–27 inches, tail 6 inches.*

WEIGHT: *Up to 10 pounds.*

HABITS: *Hibernates October–March. Sits erect on haunches when watching for danger.*

HABITAT: *Underground burrows with entrances under rocks or tree roots.*

FOOD: *Alfalfa, clover, garden vegetables.*

BREEDING: *1 litter of about 4 a year. Gestation 28 days.*

ENEMIES: *Foxes, dogs, hawks, owls, other animals.*

LIFE SPAN: *9 years.*

Woodchucks are born naked, pink, and blind. This young chuck, nineteen days old, still has not opened his eyes. But it has grown a beautiful, golden-brown coat.

As its name implies, the woodchuck—commonly found from Hudson's Bay to Alaska, south to Louisiana and eastward to the Atlantic Ocean—was originally a forest-dweller. It is one of the few creatures that has actually benefited by man's cutting down the forest. As trees were felled in the 1700s, clearings were filled with succulent crops. The woodchuck moved out into the fields, where it acquired the name groundhog. The name is fitting because the woodchuck does live in the ground, and also eats like a little pig. In some sections of the country the woodchuck is called the whistle pig. This name comes from the woodchuck's habit of whistling loudly and shrilly when it is alarmed or senses danger. The sound carries for a long distance.

The woodchuck, or groundhog, is the only animal having its own special day on the calendar. Long acclaimed as a weather prophet, it is supposed to be able to predict an early or late spring. According to tradition, it emerges from its burrow on February 2 to see whether the sun is shining. If it is, the woodchuck's body casts a shadow, signifying six more weeks of winter's cold and snow. If the day is so overcast that no shadow can be seen, winter is over. This old wives' tale dates back to Colonial times. In Europe, the badger traditionally looked for its shadow on Candlemas Day (February 2), and its gift of prophecy was transferred to the woodchuck when Europeans settled in the New World. Actually, most woodchucks in the northern portion of their range never see their shadow on the specified day because they still are deep in hibernation.

The woodchuck is a true hibernator; all its body processes slow down during its winter's sleep. In late summer and early fall, the woodchuck gorges all day long on whatever vegetation is available. Alfalfa and clover are supplemented by garden vegetables, steadily increasing the layers of fat in and around the woodchuck's body. With the coming of cold weather in October or November, the woodchuck retires to its den and seeks out a side tunnel. Excavating and piling dirt over the entrance, the animal seals off the tunnel like a tomb. Then

The adult woodchuck has excellent eyesight and often sits erect on its haunches watching for danger. Above, it watches from a loftier perch in a tree.

the woodchuck curls up on previously arranged bedding and prepares to go to sleep.

At first sporadic, the woodchuck's sleep gradually lengthens and becomes a deep slumber. The body temperature drops from a normal average of 96 degrees Fahrenheit to 37 degrees. Once every five minutes the woodchuck takes a breath; once every minute its heart beats. All body processes and metabolism slow down until they almost stop. Contrary to popular opinion, the woodchuck can be roused from this cold, torpid condition and responds to being touched. It may not waken immediately, but it will move. If it does waken, usually it looks about, and then curls up again to resume its interrupted sleep.

Woodchucks usually stay in a torpid condition until the end of March. As the breeding season arrives, the male becomes active and goes out seeking a mate even though there still may be snow on the ground. A woodchuck emerges from hibernation in pretty good physical condition, because it has not had to use much of its body fat over the winter. Most of this stored fat is used up in early spring before the new plant growth has started.

When two males meet, they usually engage in fierce battle, inflicting considerable damage with their sharp incisors. Old woodchucks are always badly scarred. Sometimes even parts of the ears and tail are missing, bearing mute testimony to the ferocity of these battles. When a male encounters a receptive female, breeding takes place at once. The male may then seek out other females or may remain with the first female for a short while. As the time of birth approaches, the male departs to find another den so that the female will have a den to herself.

Young 'chucks, usually four to a litter, are born about twenty-eight days after breeding. Naked, pink, and wrinkled, they weigh approximately an ounce and measure about four inches long. Before their eyes open at three weeks of age, the fully furred baby woodchucks wear beautiful, golden-tinted brownish coats that resemble seal fur. By the time their eyes open, the little ones can crawl around very well by themselves, and soon emerge from the burrow to take a look at the big world outside.

At this time the young feed on all types of vegetation and soon are weaned. They stay with the mother for several months before going out to establish burrows of their own. They may either dig a new one or remodel an abandoned one. Woodchucks are always busy remodeling their burrows, and an occupied burrow usually shows signs of fresh dirt around the main entrance.

When a woodchuck starts to dig its burrow, it selects a side hill if possible. It likes to dig its burrow beneath a rock or between tree roots to prevent the entrance from being enlarged. Loosening the dirt with its powerful front feet, the woodchuck then kicks it backward with its hind feet. When it accumulates a big load of dirt, the woodchuck pushes the dirt with its head to bulldoze it from the burrow. Loosened stones also are pushed out in this manner, which explains why most woodchucks have large patches of hair worn off their heads.

A large mound of excavated dirt is piled in front of the burrow to serve as an observation post. The woodchuck often sits erect on its haunches when watching for danger. This extra height of the mound allows it to see over the surrounding vegetation. The woodchuck's sense of smell is relatively weak, but its eyesight is excellent.

A very clean animal, the woodchuck also uses this dirt heap as a toilet, burying its excrement under it. This large mound of dirt marks the obvious entrance to the woodchuck's burrow, but it is not the only entrance. Two or three other entrances are kept well hidden and are seldom used except in an emergency, as when an enemy comes between the woodchuck and its main entrance. Occasionally a woodchuck finding itself in such a predicament pops down into another woodchuck's burrow. The fugitive usually pops right back out when the rightful owner discovers that it has an uninvited guest.

The woodchuck's burrow varies widely according to the whim of each individual. Some tunnels are forty to fifty feet in length. Each tunnel, or burrow, has a sleeping chamber and perhaps two or three additional rooms. Except for a mother with her young, woodchucks live a solitary existence.

The woodchuck is widely hunted for sport, and young chucks, parboiled and seasoned with onions, parsley, and celery, make good eating. Hawks, owls, and many animals kill or feed on the woodchuck. Some farm dogs become so adept at stalking the woodchuck that they know exactly how far from its burrow the animal must be in order to overtake it before it can reach safety. The fox probably is enemy number one. It not only eats the woodchuck, but also takes over the woodchuck's burrow to enlarge into a den of its own.

The plucky woodchuck can give a good account of itself in a fight, but it usually is outclassed because it seldom weighs more than ten pounds. If cut off from its burrow, the woodchuck does not hesitate to scramble up a nearby tree.

Although the woodchuck's hearty appetite and habit of burrowing make it unpopular with farmers, this animal does a certain amount of good by providing homes for other wildlife. Most mammals do not dig a home of their own, but like the fox take over one made by a woodchuck. Wildlife, particularly rabbits, would be far more limited in the eastern states if they had no woodchuck burrows to use for homes and for escape from their enemies.

Yellow-Bellied Marmot
(Marmota flaviventris)

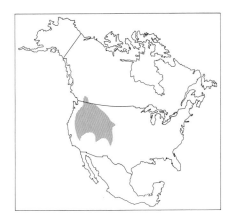

SIZE: 28 inches, including 7-inch tail.
WEIGHT: 15–17 pounds.
HABITS: Hibernates October–March. Uses sharp whistle to warn of danger.
HABITAT: Hillsides and mountains.
FOOD: All types of weed grasses, plants, and herbs.
BREEDING: 1 litter of 3–4 per year. Gestation 30 days.
ENEMIES: Eagles, coyotes, bobcats, mountain lions.
LIFE SPAN: 10 years.

The yellow-bellied marmot makes its den among the rocky debris at the base of cliffs, safe in the knowledge that larger predators will be unable to dig it out.

I saw my first yellow-bellied marmot while driving through the Absaroka Mountains in Wyoming. At first glance I mistook the heavy-bodied, short-legged creature for an extra-large woodchuck, but a closer look told me that no woodchuck was colored in that way. Although this marmot is called yellow-bellied, every one I have seen has had bright yellowish-brown underparts. In size it is midway between the woodchuck and the hoary marmot—a large specimen weighs from fifteen to seventeen pounds. It measures about twenty-eight inches in length, including a seven-inch tail.

The favored home of this marmot is among the broken rock heaps at the base of cliffs. Here among the topsy-turvy jumble of rocky debris it makes its den, safe in the knowledge that none of the larger predators will ever be able to dig it out. Usually the marmot selects a high rock dominating the surrounding area for use as a joint observation post and sun-bathing spot. The agility with which this marmot climbs over and scrambles among the rocks has given it the nickname of rockchuck. Occasionally this marmot makes its burrow beneath an abandoned mountain shack.

The yellow-bellied marmot has the smallest range of the North American marmots, and is found only in parts of Washington, Oregon, California, Idaho, Nevada, Montana, Wyoming, Utah, Colorado, and New Mexico. Its range is restricted to the hills and mountains. This marmot never appears on the level areas. Although the hoary and the yellow-bellied marmots may live in the same states, their actual ranges do not overlap.

This marmot feeds on all types of weed grasses, plants, and herbs. If the marmot can reach a cultivated field or garden plot without too great an exposure to danger, it will add crops to its food list.

The yellow-bellied marmot remains active until September or early October before going into hibernation. At last, as the cold winds and rain come whistling down from the peaks, the marmot retires into its den, where it has stored dry grasses to be used as bedding. Sealing up the entrance with earth, the marmot sits on its haunches, bends its body forward into a ball, and goes to sleep. Its temperature drops and its body processes almost stop, proving that the yellow-bellied marmot is a true hibernator.

Marmots come out of hibernation in April and breeding takes place immediately. The annual litter of three to four young are born about thirty days later. Blind and almost naked at birth, the eyes of young marmots open in about three weeks. As soon as they can see, the little ones scramble out of the den to start feeding on vegetation. The young usually leave the maternal den by midsummer to seek a den of their own.

The yellow-bellied marmot uses a sharp whistle, less powerful than the hoary marmot's, to warn other members of its colony of impending danger. Eagles, coyotes, bobcats, and mountain lions feed on this marmot when they get the rare opportunity to do so. It is the young marmot, lacking the knowledge and strength to escape, that is most apt to get caught.

Hoary Marmot
(Marmota caligata)

SIZE: 30 inches, including 3- to 4-inch tail.

WEIGHT: Up to 20 pounds.

HABITS: Hibernates up to 9 months. Sounds piercing whistle when alarmed.

HABITAT: Rocky mountains, often above timberline.

FOOD: Alpine grasses, lupine, wild lettuce, mountain phlox.

BREEDING: 1 litter of 3–4 per year. Gestation about 1 month.

ENEMIES: Golden eagles, bobcats, coyotes, bears, mountain lions.

LIFE SPAN: Up to 13 years.

Sleeping eight or nine months a year, the hoary marmot probably spends more time in hibernation than any other mammal. In warm weather it sunbathes on high mountain rocks.

French-Canadian trappers in the Rockies called the hoary marmot *le siffleur*, "the whistler," after the loud, piercing alarm call it frequently uses. To approach anywhere near the volume that this marmot produces, a human being would have to whistle with his fingers. On one occasion my peace of mind was wildly shattered by the sudden blast emitted by an unseen marmot perched atop a mountain in Glacier National Park. The marmot apparently had spied or heard me coming before I saw it and had retreated down into its den in the rock slides. When I walked past, the marmot sounded the alarm signal. The whistle, echoing among the rocks, was twice as loud as usual. The unexpectedness of the whistle startled me, even though I knew immediately what it was. I had often been whistled at by woodchucks back east. The hoary marmot, however, has a louder, more piercing whistle than either the woodchuck or the yellow-bellied marmot.

The golden eagle undoubtedly is the hoary marmot's most feared enemy. Both eagle and marmot favor wild, inaccessible high places. The bobcat, coyote, bear, and mountain lion also prey upon the hoary marmot. Before any one of these predators could catch a marmot, it would have to make sure that the marmot was far enough away from the rockpile it calls home. At the slightest hint of danger, the hoary marmot bounds off to its rocky citadel, where it sits in safety and whistles derisively at the carnivores that would relish it for a meal.

The hoary marmot owes its name to its grayish coat, which appears to have been silvered with hoarfrost. On its rump are some reddish hairs, and its belly is a dirty white. On all four feet the marmot wears black boots resembling the *caligae* (footgear) of the Roman soldiers and from which its Latin name *caligata* derives. Black markings on the cheeks, around the eyes, and over the top of the head are characteristic of this marmot. Larger than the woodchuck and yellow-bellied marmot, the hoary marmot may measure thirty inches in length, including a three- to four-inch tail, and stand seven inches high at the shoulder. A really large male may weigh as much as twenty pounds.

This marmot is found in the Rocky Mountains, from the northern states up through Canada and into Alaska. It often lives above the timberline, where it feeds on lush alpine grasses, lupine, wild lettuce, and mountain phlox. Throughout its domain it creates a network of broad paths that usually terminate at some particularly favored type of vegetation. When the marmot first comes out of hibernation, it isn't at all fussy but eats the first green sprouts it can find. The marmot does not come out at night. It rises early in the morning and feeds until midmorning. Then it climbs onto a rocky observation post to keep guard and to sun-bathe. If the weather is hot at noon, the marmot retreats to its den until late afternoon. It comes out to feed again until darkness puts an end to its activities.

The hoary marmot probably spends more time in hibernation than any other mammal. It hibernates much earlier than the yellow-bellied marmot. When drought conditions prevail in dry regions of its range, the hoary marmot may go into hibernation in late June or July. By this time the clouds have emptied their moisture on the western slopes of the high Sierras. Plants on the eastern slopes become dry and parched.

Although this marmot may sleep eight to nine months out of each year, it does not lose this much time out of its life. In hibernation its entire body processes slow down to such an extent that there is little wear on any of the parts affected. Consequently, the marmot actually lives for a longer period of time than it would if it lived a year-round active life.

The hoary marmot comes out of hibernation in April. Its mountain home still may be covered with snow, so there will be no new green food available. Under these conditions the marmot uses the store of body fat that it had accumulated the previous spring before going into hibernation.

Breeding takes place shortly after the marmots emerge from their dens. There is only one litter per year. After a gestation period of about a month, three to four young marmots are born, blind and almost naked. In about three weeks their eyes are open and they are fully furred. Soon afterward they can be seen out feeding with their mother. Young marmots stay with their mother right up to hibernation time, and many authorities believe that they spend their first winter hibernating in the same den with her. Young marmots are not considered full-grown until they are two years old.

The hoary marmot is hunted for food and for its skin. Marmot hides make a light, tough leather, which is used for bootlaces. The hide of the hoary marmot often is tanned with the hair on it, and used by Indians in Canada for robes and blankets. Because the marmot is a vegetarian, its flesh makes good eating. The young ones can be fried while the older ones are best roasted or stewed.

Black-Tailed Prairie Dog
(Cynomys ludovicianus)

SIZE: Head and body 12 inches, tail 3 inches.

WEIGHT: 3 pounds.

HABITS: Gregarious, lives in "towns." Barks and chirps when alarmed to warn others. Builds underground burrows.

HABITAT: Open prairies.

FOOD: Grasses, grasshoppers, and other insects.

BREEDING: 1 litter of 3–5 per year. Gestation 35–37 days.

ENEMIES: Hawks, eagles, foxes, coyotes, badgers, snakes.

LIFE SPAN: 8 years.

A prairie dog stands guard at the doorway to its burrow. Prairie dog communities, or "towns," post sentinels to warn of impending danger. The alarm signal is a dog-like bark, which sends the entire population scrambling to safety in their burrows.

Prairie dogs inhabit western North America from southern Canada to northern Mexico. The black-tailed species is found on the open plains, while its white-tailed cousins (*C. gunnisoni*) prefer the mesas and higher elevations. Prairie dog communities, or towns, are said to have extended for 25,000 square miles at one time. Their plump, marmot-like inhabitants were familiar sights to the pioneers streaming westward in their covered wagons. Today poison, traps, and guns have all but wiped out what was once one of our most common western mammals.

The prairie dog is a chunky, short-legged, yellowish-brown rodent, slightly smaller than a house cat. It gets its name from the rasping little bark it utters when alarmed (*Cynomys* comes from *kyneos*, dog-like, and *mys*, mouse). Sometimes it emits a chirping noise as well. Some authorities claim that the prairie dog uses a different alarm call depending upon whether the danger comes from an airborne or a ground-ranging predator.

When the alarm signal is heard, the prairie dog population reacts immediately. At top speed the animals dash for safety, each one passing on the alarm. With a flying leap, they plunge head-first down the shaft of their burrows. Legs spread wide, they slow themselves down before they crash in a heap at the bottom. Then they scramble for safety into one of the lateral passageways. For perhaps ten minutes all is silence. No prairie dogs can be seen. Suddenly the top of a head is cautiously poked out of a burrow; an apprehensive eye investigates. If nothing alarming is seen, the prairie dog creeps out a little farther, then still a little farther. At last, emboldened, it sits upright. If no danger is visible, it gives the all-clear signal. At once, the entire population comes tumbling out of burrows and confusion reigns again.

The burrow of a prairie dog is an elaborate complex of connecting passageways, bedrooms, and toilets, but seldom has more than one entrance. Some burrows go down into the earth for ten or fifteen feet before leveling off into tunnels that may extend for thirty feet or more. When it digs, the dog loosens the dirt with its front feet, then kicks it backward with its hind feet, sending showers of dirt toward the rear for a distance of perhaps eight feet.

Prairie dogs are extremely possessive about their burrows. When danger

A prairie dog digs its burrow by loosening the dirt with its front feet, then kicking it backward with its hind feet. Underground, the lateral passageways may extend for thirty feet or more.

Prairie dog communities used to extend for miles across the Western prairies. Today, poison, traps, and guns have all but wiped them out.

threatens, each dashes to the safety of its own burrow. If one dog happens to dive into a neighbor's, it is immediately evicted. Danger comes in many forms. It may be a hawk or an eagle dropping down out of the blue. It may be a fox or a coyote sneaking from behind a sagebush. Or a badger may bulldoze its way down to the nesting chamber to eat the young, even if the parents can't be caught. The black-footed ferret (*Mustela nigripes*) used to be the prairie dog's chief nemesis, but it was unable to survive the slaughter of its main food source and now is among the rarest of all American mammals. There are many stories about the prairie dog sharing its burrow with the rattlesnake. You can be sure that when this happens, it is not done willingly. Snakes are deadly enemies of prairie dogs and feed upon their young every chance they get.

The prairie dog's burrow is an ideal spot for snakes, providing a source of food as well as shelter. Here the snake can hide from its own predators, avoid the midday heat, and have a place to hibernate in the wintertime. The only protection the dog has against the snake is to carry its young to another den or to try digging enough dirt to block the tunnel before the snake can get through.

Tunnels are dug with another enemy in mind—high water. Tremendous rainstorms and flash floods are common in the western states, so the black-tailed prairie dog piles the dirt it has excavated from its tunnels into a dike around the entrance to the burrow. The rim of this dike, which resembles a miniature volcano, also serves as an observation post. The dog completes its work by chewing away any vegetation that might block its view of the surrounding countryside. The white-tailed prairie dog does not construct conspicuous mounds near the opening to its burrow.

Grasses, grasshoppers, and other insects are the mainstays of the prairie dog's diet. The peak period of activity is early morning and late afternoon to avoid the heat of midday. Although the prairie dog does not store up food, neither does it hibernate. During the bleak winter months it is nurtured by the reserve of fat stored in its body, and any pleasant winter day finds it out seeking food.

The prairie dog has only one litter per year, with an average of three to five young. The young are born in April, May, or June after a gestation period of thirty-five to thirty-seven days. The babies are about two and three-quarter inches long and weigh about half an ounce. They grow rapidly. By the time they are three weeks old, they are fully furred, have increased their birth weight about five or six times, and are able to crawl about. Soon the young are strong enough to sit upright, a position that the prairie dog uses a great deal. They learn to forage on grasses for themselves and are weaned at seven weeks. Then, in an odd turnabout, the mother leaves the family burrow to the young. She goes out to dig a new one for herself or to take over an abandoned burrow whose former owner had the misfortune to be killed.

When they are three years old and sexually mature, the young leave the home nest site on their own or are forcibly evicted by the dominant male. Prairie dogs have a strict social hierarchy, wherein a strong male controls a number of burrows, females, and their young. As the young males mature, they must leave to form their own groups, called coteries, or to challenge the dominant male and try to dispossess him. A number of coteries make up the wards or precincts into which the prairie dog towns, containing several thousand individuals, are divided.

The prairie dog's crime against man was that it ate grass. The fact that the dog was on the prairies long before man arrived counted for naught. Man wanted the grass for his cattle so he tried to exterminate the prairie dog by using guns, traps, and poison. Three of the best places to see prairie dog towns today are Devil's Tower National Monument in Crook County, Wyoming; the large protected town near Lubbock, Texas; and the Wichita Mountains Wildlife Refuge in Oklahoma.

Richardson's Ground Squirrel
(Citellus richardsoni)

SIZE: 12 inches.

WEIGHT: 11–17 ounces.

HABITS: Hibernates in burrows below frost line. Sits erect, flicks tail nervously, and whistles to sound alarm.

HABITAT: Plains and farmland.

FOOD: Vegetation, grain, seeds.

BREEDING: 1 litter of 5–8 per year. Gestation 25 days.

ENEMIES: Hawks, weasels, foxes, coyotes, bobcats, badgers, snakes.

LIFE SPAN: 4–5 years.

The Richardson's ground squirrel increased in number after the coming of agriculture to the plains. Losses to forage and grain became so great that they finally had to be controlled by poisoning.

Nineteenth-century settlers crossing into Wyoming, Idaho, Oregon, and parts of California found a small, gray-backed, buff-bellied ground squirrel that sat erect as it watched their wagons roll past. So straight did the little creature sit that it reminded the settlers of one of the eighteen- to twenty-four-inch hardwood picket pins they carried with them for tethering their horses on the treeless plains at night. Picket pin was the nickname they gave this squirrel. Another nickname is flickertail, because it has a habit of constantly flicking its tail in a nervous little gesture. It also flicks its tail each time it gives its alarm whistle. The early plainsmen used to say that its voice was fastened to its tail—every time it whistled, its tail flicked.

The Richardson's ground squirrel was plentiful right from the start, but its colonies greatly increased in numbers with the coming of agriculture to the plains. In 1900 there were probably 600,000,000 of these animals. Records show that on one square mile 4,000 could be killed, and still they would not be wiped out. Losses to both forage and grain crops became so great that the U.S. Biological Survey finally worked out a method of poisoning the squirrels to control them.

A true hibernator, the Richardson's ground squirrel spends most of the winter sleeping in its snug burrow beneath the frost line. Occasionally it awakens and feeds upon some of the store of grains and seeds gathered so industriously the previous summer. After eating its fill, and perhaps stretching its muscles a bit, the ground squirrel again curls up into a ball and goes back to sleep.

Richardson's ground squirrels awaken in April, and the males soon set out to find a mate. Even a late season snowstorm fails to dampen their ardor. Snow that is too soft and deep to hold them up is not permitted to hamper their search—the squirrels simply tunnel beneath it.

Like all ground squirrels the Richardson's is promiscuous, and the males seek out as many females as possible. After a gestation period of about twenty-five days, the female gives birth to five to eight blind and naked young. Usually there is only one litter per year. The young grow rapidly. By the end of June they are one-third grown, sufficiently developed to crawl out of the dens and start to run about. At this time they begin to feed upon vegetation, and soon are ready to be weaned. By September they are full-grown, measuring about twelve inches in length and weighing from eleven to seventeen ounces, and it is almost impossible to tell them from the adults.

Hawks probably take the greatest toll of this ground squirrel. Night-flying owls seldom get a chance at the Richardson's, because it appears only during the daylight hours. The lone exception is the burrowing owl, which hunts in the daytime. Four-footed predators—weasels, foxes, coyotes, bobcats, badgers— eat every ground squirrel they can catch. Snakes also prey upon this squirrel.

Squirrels nimble enough to survive busy themselves gathering food to store in underground burrows for the winter. With cheek pouches bulging, the squirrel is a study in constant motion. Its granary, often six feet beneath the surface of the earth, may hold two to three quarts of grain and seeds. Like other rodents inhabiting semi-arid and arid regions, the Richardson's ground squirrel can get along without drinking water, because it gets all the water it needs from the vegetation it eats. Through an internal metabolic process, its body actually manufactures water from the dried starch of seeds.

This ground squirrel does not like too much heat. Instead of frolicking about all day long, it seeks the cool depths of its burrow whenever the temperature begins to creep above 90 degrees.

Columbian Ground Squirrel
(Citellus columbianus)

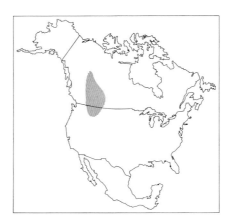

SIZE: *15 inches, including a 3–4-inch tail.*

WEIGHT: *Up to 1¾ pounds.*

HABITS: *Not gregarious, has own burrow, but lives in colonies with sentries to warn of danger.*

HABITAT: *Mountainous areas.*

FOOD: *Wild vegetation, bulbs, seeds, berries.*

BREEDING: *1 litter of 6–12 per year. Gestation 24 days.*

ENEMIES: *Hawks, eagles, meat-eating animals.*

LIFE SPAN: *4–5 years.*

One of the largest and most colorful ground squirrels, the Columbian ground squirrel is about fifteen inches long. White spots fleck its gray back, and its buff-colored sides fade into the tawny underparts. The Columbian's tawny legs and feet distinguish it from other ground squirrels.

The Columbian is one of the largest and most colorfully marked of the ground squirrels belonging to the genus *Citellus* (the little quick ones). About fifteen inches long, including a bushy three- to four-inch tail, it is three and a half inches high at the shoulder, and may weigh up to one and three-quarter pounds. White spots fleck this squirrel's gray back, while its buff-colored sides shade into tawny underparts. This color, deepest on the feet, legs, and throat, extends up over the muzzle. The Columbian's tawny legs and feet distinguish it from all other ground squirrels. Above and beneath the eyes is a heavy white bar.

This squirrel is not gregarious, preferring to have its own burrow. However, it lives in large colonies that may extend for miles. This colonization helps in the survival of the species, for it assures that some members of the group are always on the alert for danger while the rest are feeding. Unlike prairie dogs, ground squirrels do not construct mounds at the burrow entrance.

This squirrel probably spends as much time sitting up on its haunches as it does down on all fours. While sitting erect, the forepaws may hang down over its belly or be used to hold whatever food is being eaten.

The slightest speck in the sky is carefully scrutinized as a potential danger. Long before a hawk or an eagle comes close enough to be a threat, the entire squirrel colony has been warned by the air raid system of shrill whistles that echo up and down the mountainside. Each squirrel passes on the warning as it scampers to the safety of its den or burrow. The entire colony remains out of sight and silent until one of the braver members pokes its head out to reconnoiter. If no danger is visible, the all-clear whistle or chirp is given, and the colony resumes its activity.

In addition to hawks and eagles, all the four-footed flesh-eaters of the western mountain regions prey on the Columbian ground squirrel. Disease and parasites also take a heavy toll, for these two killers always spread more easily through concentrated colonies of wildlife than they do where animals live a more solitary existence.

The Columbian does little harm in its home territory, the mountainous sections of Montana, Idaho, Washington, Oregon, Alberta, and British Columbia, because it feeds on wild vegetation, bulbs, seeds, and berries. In a farming district it may be a different story, for the squirrel consumes a lot of the forage and grain that is needed by the farmer for his livestock. Where food is plentiful, the squirrel also is more numerous. Lots of good food allows the squirrel to grow larger and heavier and also to produce larger litters.

Toward the end of February, the Columbian ground squirrel wakes from its long hibernation. If there is too much snow on the ground, the squirrel remains in its burrow, feeding on its cached food. As soon as it is able to travel about, breeding takes place. Before giving birth, the female prepares a new den lined with soft plant material. There is only one litter per year, which usually is quite large, containing six to twelve young. The blind, toothless, and hairless babies are born after a twenty-four-day gestation period.

The young grow rapidly, increasing their weight every day. Long before their eyes open, the little ones crawl about in the den and through the tunnel passageways. At three weeks of age their eyes open. By the time they are six weeks old, they are large enough to start digging dens of their own, and soon they leave the maternal nest.

The Columbian does not emerge from its den unless the weather is good. Inclement, rainy or windy weather keeps this squirrel indoors. The little creature also has an aversion to heat. Bright sun is all very well if the weather is cool. Once the hot, sultry days of deep summer arrive, the Columbian prepares to retire.

Having raised its family and gorged itself on all available food, the Columbian ground squirrel now is as fat as it can get. Heat has dried out the succulent vegetation and made the world dry and dusty. As early as July, under drought conditions, the Columbian gets ready to go into its winter hibernation by constructing a special den. This chamber, about nine inches wide, is located about five feet underground, safely below the frost line. Several deeper shafts are constructed to serve as drains in case moisture seeps into the bedroom. At last all is in readiness. The Columbian ground squirrel leaves the parched outside world and enters the cool depths of its chamber. After carefully sealing up the den's entrance, the squirrel sits on its haunches and curls itself forward into a ball. Gradually its heartbeat and breathing rate slow down, and the Columbian sinks into the deep sleep of hibernation.

Thirteen-Lined Ground Squirrel
(Citellus tridecemlineatus)

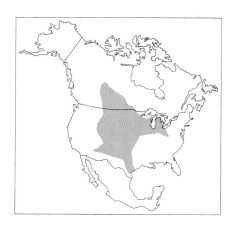

SIZE: *11 inches, including 4½-inch tail.*

WEIGHT: *5 ounces in summer, 8 in autumn.*

HABITS: *Digs underground burrows, does not live in colonies. Hibernates September–March.*

HABITAT: *Prairies.*

FOOD: *Birds' eggs and small carcasses of birds, mice, other squirrels, insects, forage, grain.*

BREEDING: *1 litter of 8–10 per year. Gestation 30 days.*

ENEMIES: *Foxes, bobcats, coyotes, badgers, weasels, dogs, house cats, snakes, hawks, bears.*

LIFE SPAN: *4–5 years.*

Often called the striped gopher, the thirteen-lined ground squirrel is appropriately named. Thirteen alternating light and dark stripes run the full length of its buff-colored back.

This little prairie dweller is found from Ohio west to the Rocky Mountains and north to Texas. Everyone who has driven in the prairie states should be familiar with this ground squirrel, often called the striped gopher. It is the species most commonly seen, and killed, on the highway.

March marks the arrival of spring and the debut of the thirteen-lined ground squirrel. Following a winter spent in hibernation, the squirrel's weight is about half what it was the preceding fall. The male usually comes out of hibernation first, and soon sets about finding a mate. Breeding most often takes place in April. Because both sexes are promiscuous, there is no actual pairing up among the adult squirrels.

There is only one litter a year. After a gestation period of thirty days, the eight to ten young are born in a snug underground nursery prepared by the mother in a side room of her den. The little ones, measuring a little over two inches in length, are blind, hairless, and toothless at birth. By the end of their

When it senses danger, the squirrel often sits straight up on its haunches to get a better look. Its alarm signal is a loud, quavering whistle.

first month, they are fully furred and have their eyes open. In just a few more days the baby squirrels are ready to leave the den and sally forth on their own.

When full-grown, the thirteen-lined squirrel measures about eleven inches long, including a four-and-a-half-inch tail, stands about three inches high at the shoulder, and has a summer weight of five ounces. One look at this squirrel tells you that it is well-named. Thirteen alternating light and dark stripes run down the buff-colored back from head to tail. Not all the stripes are solid, but are rows of squarish gray spots or splotches.

This squirrel eats more meat and has a higher protein intake (fully fifty per cent) than any other ground squirrel. The eggs and young of ground-nesting birds—and even the adult birds themselves—are taken. Mice and their nests are hunted down regularly. Cannibalism, or perhaps we should say scavenging, is common; much of this squirrel's meat intake comes from the carcasses of less fortunate relatives that failed to elude automobiles. Often the squirrel's greed for this meat is its undoing, and yet another highway fatality is chalked up.

Insects of all types are hunted eagerly; in this capacity, the squirrel actually is beneficial to the farmer. On the other hand, the squirrel also eats a lot of forage and some grains. It starts feeding early in the day, remaining active throughout the wilting, enervating prairie heat. While other creatures seek a cool, shady spot in which to pass the midday hours, this ground squirrel continues to scamper about. Now and then it pauses long enough to sit erect, looking around to see if danger is present—and usually it is.

When danger is sighted, the squirrel gives a loud, quavering whistle or shorter chirping sound. Foxes, bobcats, coyotes, badgers, weasels, dogs, house cats, snakes, hawks, and other meat-eaters feed on this squirrel whenever they can catch it. Even the big bears rake out its tunnels to get at the inhabitants. Most relentless of the predators is the badger, which serves as a control on the population of ground squirrels. While the squirrel can escape from some enemies by seeking shelter in its tunnels, the badger can dig out the tunnels faster than the squirrel can make them.

Some of these tunnels may extend for twenty feet or more. The entrance is small and well hidden, perhaps no more than one inch in diameter, so it is not likely to be noticed by the casual observer. Like other ground squirrels, but unlike most of the burrowing animals, the thirteen-lined squirrel does not pile up the excess dirt from its tunnel at the mouth of its burrow. The loosened dirt is stuffed into its cheek pouches, carried outside, and scattered at a distance from the den. While some rodents have external folds of skin to make up their cheek pouches, the ground squirrel's cheek pouches consist of loose skin over the jaws. These pouches are filled by stuffing the food inside the mouth and into the cheek areas.

Unlike the prairie dog, the thirteen-lined ground squirrel does not live in organized colonies, although many of its burrows may be located in the same area. The size of the burrow depends upon the hardness of the soil. There is usually a straight plunge hole, like an open elevator shaft, going straight down for two to four feet. A horizontal shaft runs off the entrance shaft. There may be a number of side tunnels and chambers. The master bedroom usually is quite cozy, containing a goodly amount of dry grasses. There are several storerooms that the squirrel tries to fill with dried weed seeds and grains to feed on in the winter if it wakes up during hibernation.

In the autumn, before hibernating, the squirrel is butter-fat and weighs perhaps eight ounces. With the coming of cold weather, the squirrel plugs up the entrance to its den and retires to its bedroom to sleep. This squirrel is a true hibernator, whose body temperature drops to about 37 degrees, and whose heartbeat, usually 250 to 350 strokes per minute, slows down to five strokes per minute. Its breathing actually seems to stop, because the breaths are so shallow that they are not likely to be noticed. Here, safe from the ravages of cold and frost, the ground squirrel sleeps away the winter.

Golden-Mantled Ground Squirrel
(Callospermophilus lateralis)

SIZE: *11–13 inches, including 3-inch tail.*
WEIGHT: *7–10 ounces.*
HABITS: *Hibernates September–March.*
HABITAT: *Mountain ranges; in burrows under bushes, stumps, rocks.*
FOOD: *Weed seeds, fruits, berries, insects.*
BREEDING: *1 litter of 5–8 per year. Gestation 30 days.*
ENEMIES: *Weasels, martens, bobcats, coyotes, hawks, eagles, snakes.*
LIFE SPAN: *5–6 years.*

Often confused with the chipmunk which it resembles, the golden-mantled ground squirrel also has a white stripe down its back. But this squirrel is larger, and unlike the chipmunk, has no stripes on its face. It is named for the bright golden fur on its shoulders and neck.

I saw my first golden-mantled ground squirrel high in the mountains of Glacier National Park. I was delighted to see this wildlife after a fruitless, two-day search for mountain goats. When I first detected movement among the rocks, I took it to be just another chipmunk, for that is what this squirrel resembles. In fact, its Latin name, *lateralis*, designates the white stripe that runs lengthwise along its back. This stripe is bordered with black stripes, giving the squirrel a most striking chipmunk-like appearance. Sometimes called the golden chipmunk, it is chipmunk-like in its actions and has the same type of cheek pouches. The bright fur up over the squirrel's shoulders and neck give it the golden mantle that accounts for its common name. It has light-colored sides and whitish underparts. Its black eyes are bright, shiny, and alert. Unlike the chipmunk, it has no facial stripes. This squirrel is larger than the common chipmunk, measuring from eleven to thirteen inches, including a three-inch tail. Its weight varies from seven to ten ounces, or a little more in the fall before it goes into hibernation.

The golden-mantled squirrel feeds primarily on weed seeds, fruits, berries, and whatever insects it happens upon in the Rocky and Cascade mountain ranges where it makes its home. The squirrel I saw lived on such a barren, forbidding rock heap that I marveled that it could find enough seeds to sustain life. Of course, we humans often tend to base our judgments on human consumption, and fail to realize that a quart or two of food represents enough nourishment for some of these smaller creatures for an entire year. Although the one I saw had to feed on weed seeds, some of these squirrels occasionally live at lower elevations where some farming is done. Under such circumstances they eat grain. Occasionally the golden-mantled squirrel frequents camp grounds, where it readily accepts handouts of food.

This squirrel lives in a burrow that it excavates. The burrow usually is under a bush, stump, or rock, which gives added protection from the weasels, martens, bobcats, coyotes, hawks, eagles, and snakes that are the squirrel's main enemies. Bears also find it a toothsome morsel, and dig it out whenever they get the chance.

In September, as the first snow begins to fall, the golden-mantled squirrel retires underground to hibernate in a den lined with soft, dry grasses. After plugging up the entrance, the squirrel curls into a ball and goes to sleep. A true hibernator, the golden-mantled squirrel sleeps deeply, its body temperature drops, and its heart and breathing slow down. Occasionally, it wakes, eats some of its stored food, then sinks back into slumber. Hibernation ends during the last part of March.

The males come out of their burrows first and scamper about searching for mates. Encounters between contending males lead to brief, scuffling fights. Gestation is about a month and the blind, nearly hairless little ones are born early in May. There is only one litter of five to eight young per year. By the time the squirrels are three months old, they are almost as large as the parents, and off they scatter to make burrows of their own.

Eastern Chipmunk
(*Tamias striatus*)

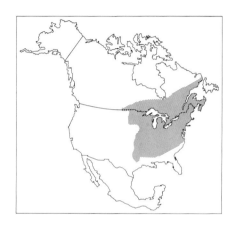

SIZE: *Body and head 5–6 inches, tail 3–4 inches.*

WEIGHT: *5 ounces.*

HABITS: *Digs underground tunnels with storage rooms for food. Climbs trees to escape enemies. Carries food in cheek pouches.*

HABITAT: *Wooded areas or among bushes or tall grasses.*

FOOD: *Seeds, berries, nuts, dried vegetable matter.*

BREEDING: *1 litter of 4–5 per year. Gestation 32 days.*

ENEMIES: *Cats, dogs, foxes, bobcats, mink, weasels, snakes, hawks, owls.*

LIFE SPAN: *2–4 years.*

The chipmunk's facial stripes and smaller size distinguish it from the ground squirrel.

Inhabitants of the eastern United States often feel slighted when they compare the handful of small mammals in that region with the multitudes found in the west. The only small mammal commonly seen in large numbers in the east is the chipmunk. The Eastern chipmunk is found in every state east of and bordering on the Mississippi River, with the exception of Florida. Fourteen species of western chipmunks range over almost all of the region west of the Mississippi.

This endearing little creature numbers into the millions, yet it rarely is so plentiful that it becomes a menace to crops. The fact that the chipmunk is a trusting little sprite and is easily tamed probably accounts for its popularity. An offering of peanut butter or sunflower seeds will win for you the chipmunk's friendship.

The chipmunk's scientific name, meaning striped one who cuts up and distributes, is related to its appearance and habits. Smaller than the ground squirrels, the chipmunk is five to six inches long, with a bushy three- to four-inch tail. Five black stripes alternate with white ones along the reddish-brown back and sides, which shade into whitish underparts. Facial stripes distinguish this little fellow from the other mammals over most of its range.

The industrious chipmunk spends most of its time gathering food, which consists largely of seeds, berries, nuts, and dried vegetable matter. Nature has provided the chipmunk with shopping bags, in the form of cheek pouches, so that it may carry home more easily large stores of food without having to make so many trips. The amount of food this little creature can put into its cheek pouches is almost beyond belief. In order to bribe a chipmunk to sit in the area where I wanted to photograph it, I fed it prune pits. The chipmunk could actually stuff nine prune pits in its mouth at one time. To get those pits, unfortunately, I had to eat all the prunes.

Another time I found a chipmunk that had been killed on a back road when attempting to return to its den with a mouthful of seeds. The scattered seeds caught my attention—I counted 413. Some seeds were so tiny I marveled how the chipmunk managed to pick them up. Each chipmunk tries to store away at least half a bushel of food to tide itself over the winter.

In summer the chipmunk gathers nuts and carries them away in its cheek pouches to underground storerooms. Above, with cheeks well stuffed, a chipmunk holds a prune pit in its forepaws.

When cold weather comes, the chipmunk curls up into a little ball and goes to sleep. During the winter it wakes up periodically to eat some of its cached food.

Unlike mice, rats, and some of the other rodents, the chipmunk does not want to invade your home. It prefers one of its own construction, usually in wooded areas. The chipmunk makes one of the most cleverly concealed burrows I have ever tried to locate. This burrow is dug in reverse fashion from most other mammals' burrows, and lacks the telltale heap of dirt at the main entrance. When digging a burrow, the chipmunk carries off the excess earth and scatters it about. The main entrance is dug upward from below, and opens out beneath a root, rock, or other obstruction. Dead leaves usually are placed over the hole to make it invisible. The underground tunnels may be fifteen to twenty feet in length, are comparatively shallow, and have little siderooms that are used as granaries or for storage. Special rooms include a nursery, bedroom, and on a lower level, a toilet.

Cats, dogs, foxes, bobcats, mink, weasels, snakes, hawks, owls, and other meat-eaters take a chipmunk whenever they are able to catch one. The chipmunk, a ground-dwelling tree squirrel, can escape a ground-dwelling enemy by climbing a tree. (Most ground squirrels do not climb trees, because there seldom are trees in the areas they inhabit. They also have long toenails, which are advantageous for digging but detrimental for climbing.) In the springtime especially, the chipmunk is likely to be seen climbing around in the trees. If pursued on the ground, it tries to escape by squeezing through an underground hole too small to permit the attacker to follow. If pursued into its burrow, the chipmunk attempts to close up the entrance by digging up earth to pack against the opening from the inside.

In the early spring, before the summer birds return north, the little bird-like chirp of the chipmunk can be heard, as the males call and search for a mate. An unreceptive female will drive the male from her burrow. There usually is one litter per year. The naked, blind, and helpless young, commonly four or five, are born thirty-two days after a successful breeding. The black-and-white stripes begin to show when the babies are about a week old. Their eyes open at the age of one month, by which time the young are fully furred and begin to crawl out of the den. At about six weeks of age, they are weaned, and in another month or so they leave the mother's den to seek or construct one of their own. Like most of the smaller ground squirrels, the chipmunk has a life span of from two to four years.

With the arrival of August, the chipmunk retires to its burrow and sleeps away the hot, energy-draining days. This sleep, known as estivation, may last a month. Early autumn brings cooler days, and the chipmunk again is seen dashing about. It never seems satisfied with its supply of stored food, and the frenzied activity continues right up to cold weather.

With the advent of cold weather, the chipmunk retires underground. First, it blocks off its tunnels with dead leaves and dirt to prevent unwanted visitors from dropping in unannounced, then it descends to its master bedroom and seals it off. At last, satisfied that it can do no more, the chipmunk curls up and goes to sleep.

The chipmunk is a hibernator that suffers from a touch of insomnia. Even in its underground chambers, it seems to be responsive to temperatures in the world outside. When the temperature drops, the chipmunk sinks into a deeper sleep; when the temperature rises, the chipmunk bestirs itself, even though it may remain underground. After several weeks of sleep, the chipmunk wakes and eats part of its cached food. Then it goes back to sleep for another two weeks, again wakes up for a while, and again has a snack. Thus the entire winter is spent in alternate periods of wakefulness and deep sleep.

I once kept a pet chipmunk in a cage in the kitchen. Evidently, because of the constant warmth, my chipmunk did not go into a deep sleep in the winter. It was usually active for a part of each day, although not nearly as active as it would be in the summertime. My chipmunk also worked out on its exercise wheel at all hours of the night, even though the kitchen was totally dark. I've often wondered if this was just because my chipmunk was different or because chipmunks in the wild customarily forage at night. This question still baffles me, for I have never been able to observe wild chipmunks in the dark.

Red Squirrel
(Tamiasciurus hudsonicus)

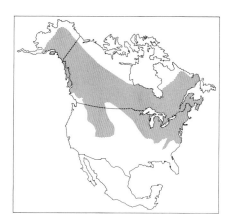

SIZE: *Up to 14 inches, including 6-inch tail.*

WEIGHT: *7–9 ounces.*

HABITS: *Gives warning chirp when frightened. Active all year, does not hibernate. Fights other squirrels that infringe on territory.*

HABITAT: *Evergreen forests.*

FOOD: *Pine cones, acorns, mushrooms, hickory nuts, beechnuts, walnuts, maple seeds.*

BREEDING: *1 litter of 3–5 per year. Gestation 40 days.*

ENEMIES: *Hawks, owls, snakes, foxes, bobcats, lynxes, martens, fishers.*

LIFE SPAN: *10 years.*

The red squirrel builds a leaf nest or underground den only when it has to. It prefers to occupy a hollow tree or empty woodpecker hole. Above, it perches on a shelf bracket fungus on a dead tree.

The red squirrel always reminds me of a fellow in a story I read many years ago. Every time something went wrong, this fellow gave the supposed culprit a piece of his mind. Finally, he had no mind left for himself. The red squirrel hasn't reached this unhappy condition but it, too, notices and comments upon everything that happens in its vicinity.

Just about everyone who has walked in the forest has heard the red squirrel's scolding chatter, whether he realized its source or not. The squirrel's excited scoldings, whistles, and shrieks are punctuated by accompanying jerks and twitches of its upright tail. *Adjidaumo*, tail-in-the-air, was the name appropriately given to this smallest of the tree squirrels by the Ojibway Indians. When undisturbed, the red squirrel produces a rolling, high-pitched chirp or cluck that often is mistaken for that of a bird. The related western Douglas squirrel (*T. douglasi*) derives its popular name, chickaree, from its musical call.

Although this racket serves to alert other creatures in the forest to the possibility of danger, one is inclined to wonder whether predators that feed on the red squirrel do not recognize it and are attracted to its source. It would seem to be most foolhardy to be constantly calling attention and danger to oneself, yet the red squirrel population does not appear to decline.

The red squirrel inhabits evergreen forests from Alaska to Newfoundland and southward to the Appalachian Mountains. Less extensive in their range are two western species, the Douglas squirrel of the Northwest, and pine squirrel (*T. fremonti*) of the Rocky Mountains.

This squirrel prefers to occupy a hollow tree or empty woodpecker hole, but builds a leaf nest or dens underground when it has to. The young, usually three to five in number, are born in April or May. Blind and naked, they measure about four inches in length, including the tail. In six to eight weeks the youngsters are weaned and, when about one-third grown, begin to venture from the nest. By late summer the young squirrels are large enough to go out foraging for food on their own.

Summer and fall are periods of intensive food-gathering activity. Not content to let the evergreen cones fall of their own accord, the red squirrel dashes up the tree and clips off the cones with its teeth. Spruce cones are taken first,

The Indians appropriately named the red squirrel "tail-in-the-air." A noisy commentator on forest activities, it produces a high-pitched chirp, often mistaken for that of a bird.

Unlike ground squirrels, tree squirrels do not hibernate and will build underground nests only if they have no choice. They prefer to live in hollow trees or empty woodpecker holes.

green and sticky with gum. Soon the squirrel is matted with the gooey substance. Then the pine cones, some six to eight inches in length, cascade down. The size and weight of the cones makes walking under a pine tree hazardous when the squirrel is at work. I have also seen the red squirrel gather deadly *Amanita muscaria* mushrooms and store them high in the tree branches until the sun and rain had leached out the poison and they could be eaten safely. Acorns, hickory nuts, beechnuts, walnuts, as well as maple seeds also are used for food.

The red squirrel usually has several preferred spots, chosen at random, where it likes to sit while eating. These spots are easy to locate, because the squirrel simply drops all the unwanted parts of its dinner on the ground to form large refuse or midden heaps. When composed of discarded pine and spruce cones, the heaps may be three to four feet in diameter and as many feet high.

This squirrel remains active all the year round, for the tree squirrel, unlike the ground squirrel, does not hibernate. With the coming of cold weather, however, the red squirrel changes color. The bright rusty red coat it wears all summer is replaced by a more somber coat of brown that usually retains a red streak down the back. On the ears small tufts of hair appear.

Hawks, owls, snakes, foxes, bobcats, and lynxes prey upon this squirrel. Its most relentless enemies are the pine marten and the fisher. These two large weasels are so fast that they can outclimb even the squirrel with ease. The red squirrel is the marten's chief item of diet; its only chance of escaping this certain death is to squeeze into a tree hole or opening in the ground too small for the marten to penetrate. The red squirrel doesn't hesitate to swim if it must. I have often seen this little fellow swimming from island to island in the Canadian lakes.

Woods hawks, such as the Cooper's and goshawk, take a great many red squirrels. They also miss many of them. When under attack, the red squirrel freezes to the branch as the hawk hurtles through the air. Just before the hawk's flashing talons fasten onto its prey, the squirrel drops to the underside of the branch or around the other side of the tree trunk. If the hawk misses its target on the first attempt, it often pursues the squirrel, spiraling around after it down the tree trunk. Nine times out of ten, the squirrel is able to out-maneuver its foe.

Battles between the red squirrel and the larger gray squirrel take place but, in all my years of observation, I have never actually seen a fight. I have seen many chases, some where the red squirrel was the pursuer and some where the gray one did the chasing. I have also seen both of these squirrels feed side by side at a bird feeder without molesting each other.

Most disagreements between squirrels occur over contested territorial rights. Almost every animal has a piece of land or territory that it considers its own. This prevents any given area from being overpopulated; it also limits competition for food. When a gray squirrel or another red squirrel invades a red squirrel's territory, a chase ensues that sometimes culminates in a fight. If the red squirrel were a larger animal, it probably would try to drive human beings, as well, out of its territory. Under the circumstances, the best it can do is cling to a tree and hurl insults.

On one occasion, when packing food to take on a canoe trip into the Canadian wilderness, I set the pack on a crude split log table. Peering down into the pack, I detected a red squirrel busily digging away at the food inside. "Hey! What are you doing there?" I demanded. The squirrel stopped chewing long enough to look up into my face, then resumed its work. Suddenly, it did a double-take. Realizing how close it was to danger, it shot out of the pack, whizzed off the table, and dashed up a nearby tree, forgetting for once to make a derogatory remark.

In general, the red squirrel is distrustful of man and not easily tamed. Nevertheless, I am always glad to encounter this garrulous little creature in the woods, especially in winter when many of the other animals seem to have forsaken the woodlands.

Eastern Gray Squirrel
(*Sciurus carolinensis*)

SIZE: 18 inches, including 8–9 inch tail.

WEIGHT: ¾–1¾ pounds.

HABITS: Makes nest in hollow tree, buries food for winter. Sounds chattering buzz
when alarmed.

HABITAT: Hardwood and evergreen forests.

FOOD: Acorns, hickory nuts, chestnuts, walnuts, fruits, buds, baby birds.

BREEDING: 1–2 litters of 4–5 per year. Gestation 44 days.

ENEMIES: Foxes, bobcats, house cats, dogs, martens, fishers, owls, hawks, snakes.

LIFE SPAN: 15 years.

A gray squirrel sits in the doorway of its den in a hollow tree. The squirrel helps forest conservationists by burying nuts which grow into trees.

The Eastern gray squirrel is one of our best-known mammals, equally at home in forest, suburb, or city park. Less excitable and more easily tamed than the smaller red squirrel, the gray is also more tolerant of man and his foibles.

The hardwood and evergreen forests stretching from Maine to the Dakotas and from the St. Lawrence River to the Gulf of Mexico comprise this squirrel's normal range. Part of this range is shared with the red squirrel. A larger cousin, the western gray squirrel (*S. griseus*), inhabits the coastal areas of the Pacific states. All-white and all-black specimens are fairly common among the eastern grays. Along the St. Lawrence River, for instance, black squirrels outnumber the gray ones.

Although we still have plenty of Eastern gray squirrels, their numbers cannot compare with the former gray squirrel populations. These grew to such fantastic proportions that squirrels migrated en masse to forested areas in other states. Some of these huge moving blankets of squirrels contained hundreds of thousands of animals. Rivers presented no obstacle to the squirrel hordes, even though vast numbers drowned in the crossing. Within a year or two the greatly reduced squirrel population in the abandoned areas again increased to astronomical proportions.

The most effective control of this explosive squirrel population was the destruction of most of the eastern hardwood forests to satisfy the demands of human habitation. The felling of the oak, hickory, chestnut, walnut, and other large forest trees deprived the squirrel of the nut crop it used, and destroyed most of its den sites. A tree usually has to be both big and old before its cavities start to rot. These hollowed tree dens are particularly favored by the squirrel because they provide the maximum protection for its family.

Often when a tree limb rots off, a continuous yearly growth of bark closes the opening. The squirrel must keep on stripping back this encroaching bark with its teeth so that it can continue using the den.

The eastern gray may also make leaf nests in the uppermost branches of trees. These warm-weather nests are used for raising a family only if no tree den can be found. Occasionally a tree den becomes so infested with mites, lice, and other parasites that the gray squirrel uses the leaf nests to escape from them. On the whole, tree dens and nests are notoriously insecure, which probably accounts for the gray squirrel's nervousness during windstorms. I once came across a tree nest in which two gray squirrels had been crushed to death by a windblown limb.

This industrious panhandler is active all year long. It is especially busy in the fall, gathering nuts to be used for winter food. A supply of nuts is stored in the den, while the surplus is buried beneath the leaf mold. The gray squirrel is a great help to forest conservation, because every nut it forgets to dig up is a tree planted. Some people claim that the squirrel's ability to find the nuts it has buried is sheer luck. This is not the case, for I have seen the squirrel dig down through a foot of snow and locate a nut it had buried in the ground. This squirrel also eats fall fruits, spring buds, an occasional bird's egg, and in rare instances, baby birds.

The greatest activity occurs between the hours of 6 and 9 in the morning and 3 and 6 in the afternoon. The squirrel is especially busy on drizzly days. Then, holding its beautifully plumed, white-tipped tail umbrella-fashion over its head, it sits and feeds. When the tail becomes saturated, a few nervous twitches send the water droplets flying off and it again is ready for use. According to legend, the squirrel had a rat-like tail during its residence in the Garden of Eden. When Adam and Eve partook of the forbidden apple, the squirrel hid the shameful sight from view by covering its eyes with its tail and was rewarded with a lovely, new feathery tail.

The gray squirrel usually breeds during December in the southern part of its range, where it produces two litters, and a month later in the northern part, where it may produce one or two litters. The male is polygamous and takes no part in raising the young, born about forty-four days after mating.

Four or five young per litter is the average. Blind, naked, and helpless at birth, the young squirrels need all the loving care the mother customarily lavishes upon them. She spends every possible moment with them, leaving just long enough to feed.

When baby squirrels are threatened, the mother attempts to move them away from the danger zone if possible. She picks up the little ones by the fur of their bellies and they wrap themselves around her head. As soon as one baby is deposited safely, the mother dashes back for another. Of all the chirps and growls a squirrel emits, the prolonged chattering buzz is perhaps the best known. This is the call to which the young ones pay the most attention, because it is given to warn of danger or something strange in the vicinity.

The young squirrels' eyes open when they are about six weeks old. They are fully furred by then and ready to climb about in the treetops. The young squirrels commonly remain with the mother all through the summer, fall, and even their first winter. A large tree den may contain a dozen or more squirrels, for the sociable gray squirrel is fond of company.

Because the gray squirrel spends much of its time feeding on the ground, it is vulnerable to predation by the fox, bobcat, house cat, dog, and, in some sections, the marten and fisher. Owls, goshawks, Cooper's and red-tailed hawks attack from the air. Hawks do more damage than the owls because the squirrel is not active at night. I have seen a red-tailed hawk dive straight into a leaf nest and catch a fugitive squirrel hidden there.

Snakes often prey on young squirrels. Most destructive is the tree-climbing black rat snake (known also as the pilot black snake), which persistently investigates every crevice and hole searching for them. An adult squirrel usually is too tough an opponent to tackle and may even attack the snake in defense of its young. A seven-foot black rat snake, which in my neighborhood took up residence in a large, hollowed maple tree, succeeded in wiping out the entire squirrel colony that was living in the area.

Man is the greatest threat to the squirrel. Wherever it is hunted for sport, food, or fur, the squirrel tries to keep a tree between itself and the hunter. As the hunter circles the tree, the squirrel darts around to the opposite side. If there are two hunters, the squirrel stretches out along the top of a branch, where its gray coat makes it practically invisible.

The early American frontiersman was famed for his skill in using a rifle; most of this skill was acquired hunting the gray squirrel. This squirrel was small enough to be a difficult target and a real test of skill, yet large enough to be an important food for the hunter. The smaller caliber rifles, those of .32 to .38 caliber, generally were considered to be squirrel guns as compared with the larger caliber guns used for deer and bigger game. Today the gray squirrel still is an important game animal in the United States. Although small, squirrel pelts in the millions are sold annually.

Eastern Fox Squirrel

(Sciurus niger)

SIZE: 28 inches, including tail.

WEIGHT: 2–3 pounds.

HABITS: Builds leaf nests; not a good tree climber. Buries each nut individually.

HABITAT: Oak groves; prefers open land to heavy forests.

FOOD: Nuts, seeds, buds, berries.

BREEDING: 1–2 litters of 3–4 per year. Gestation 6–7 weeks.

ENEMIES: Hawks, foxes, owls, bobcats, raccoons, snakes.

LIFE SPAN: 10 years.

Weighing two to three pounds, the eastern fox squirrel is the largest member of the squirrel family in the United States. Its coat varies from rusty red to black.

The acorn-loving fox squirrel is found wherever oak trees are plentiful, although its range is shrinking and it has disappeared completely from some of its former haunts in New England, New York, New Jersey, and Pennsylvania. Owing to its size and flavor, this squirrel has been sought by generations of eager hunters. In New Jersey about 1850 the fox squirrel was hunted to extinction. Today conditions in that state are more to the squirrel's liking, now that heavy forests have given way to more open land, but all attempts to re-establish the squirrel have failed.

This squirrel displays a variety of colors, depending upon its locality. In the northern part of its range its coat is a rusty red, resembling that of a red fox; in the south it shades into black; while in the east it is gray. In all color phases the top of the head is dark and the ears are light. There is considerable intermingling of these color phases, so that any of the variations or shadings can be found in all the different areas.

The fox squirrel also has the distinction of being the largest member of the squirrel family in the United States. It measures up to twenty-eight inches in length, including its long, bushy tail, and stands about five inches high at the shoulder. The average weight is two to three pounds.

Owing to its larger size and its habit of spending a good deal of its time on the ground, the fox squirrel is not a good tree climber compared with other members of the squirrel family. It is also less nervous than some of its cousins and so takes more readily to captivity. While other squirrels, particularly the gray, is up and about early, the fox squirrel is a sluggard. It makes up for lost time by working late into the evening, foraging for nuts after the other squirrels have retired. The fox squirrel's keen sense of smell helps it to recover the nuts it stores away. Moisture always aids scent; buried nuts are easier to locate when the ground is wet than when it is dried out by drought. Unlike the red squirrel, which makes a large food cache, the fox and gray squirrels bury each nut individually.

Like the rest of the squirrel family, the fox squirrel builds leaf nests. Some of the warm-weather nests are sloppy affairs, built in a hurry and usable only for a short time before they disintegrate. More carefully constructed is the winter leaf nest, whose material is impacted so that it can withstand the rigors of the winter winds and cold. Although the fox squirrel remains active all winter, it prefers to come home to a snug den.

The fox squirrel commonly leads a solitary life, although a number of these squirrels may inhabit the same woodland. About the only time of the year that this squirrel has anything to do with its fellows is during the breeding season, which begins in January. Occasionally, in the South, the squirrel may breed twice. Three to four young are born about six or seven weeks after mating. Blind, hairless, and helpless, the newborn squirrels are about four inches long and weigh less than one ounce. The babies begin to fur out nicely about ten days after birth. At three weeks of age they start to crawl about inside the nest; in three more weeks their eyes open and they venture outside.

Here danger lurks, for the young that have not been devoured while still in their nests by tree-climbing snakes now are preyed upon by hawks, owls, foxes, bobcats, and raccoons. When one of the babies gets into trouble, the mother carries it back to the nest by grasping the loose skin of its belly between her teeth, as the baby curls its body doughnut-fashion around her head.

At two months of age young fox squirrels are able to feed on nut meats, but two more weeks must elapse before they are strong enough to gnaw open the shells by themselves. Soon afterward they scatter to seek dens of their own.

Southern Flying Squirrel
(Glaucomys volans)

SIZE: *10 inches, including 4-inch tail.*

WEIGHT: *2–3 ounces.*

HABITS: *Climbs trees and glides downward to objectives, at distances up to 100 feet. Awkward on ground; unable to swim.*

HABITAT: *Woodlands.*

FOOD: *All nuts except walnuts, wild cherries, insects.*

BREEDING: *1–2 litters of 3–5 per year. Gestation 40 days.*

ENEMIES: *Owls, cats, foxes, bobcats, snakes.*

LIFE SPAN: *5 years.*

The "flying" squirrel actually does not fly. Instead, it glides downward by spreading its limbs and stretching the loose folds of skin that extend between the ankles of its front and hind legs.

With its silky, reddish-brown coat and creamy white underparts, the flying squirrel is one of our most beautiful native squirrels. The Southern flying squirrel inhabits the eastern United States from the Atlantic Ocean to the prairies west of the Mississippi River, while its larger northern cousin (*G. sabrinus*) is found in forested sections of Canada and Alaska. Although the flying squirrel is fairly common in its range, most people have never seen one. Chances are they never will, for this squirrel comes out only at night.

The term flying squirrel actually is a misnomer. This little creature does not fly, it glides. It does so by spreading its limbs and stretching the loose folds of skin, or membranes, that extend between wrists and ankles. Because the squirrel cannot soar upward, it must climb to the top of a tree and glide down to its objective. Once it has attained the necessary height, the squirrel determines the distance from there to the tree it wishes to reach by means of triangulation, bending its body first to the left and then to the right. This provides the squirrel with two different sightings and works on the same principle as a camera's range-finder.

Once the distance has been determined, the squirrel gathers its body into a small ball and then uncoils, giving a tremendous kick with its hind feet and launching itself into space. Quickly, it extends its arms and legs, tightening the gliding membranes into a flat plane. Small, protruding pieces of cartilage on the wrists give added length to the arms. Although this squirrel weighs a mere two to three ounces, its more than fifty square inches of soaring surface enable it to glide more than 100 feet.

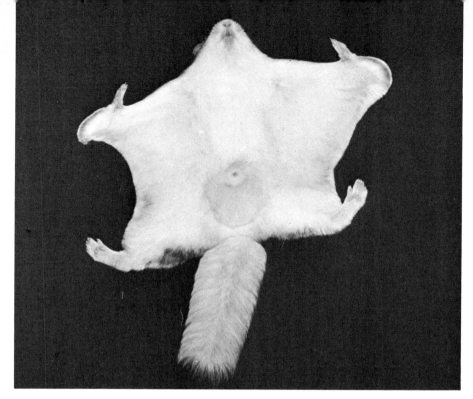

The "flying" squirrel viewed from below. When soaring, the squirrel can glide about 175 feet.

In flight, the squirrel controls its direction by steering with its tail and by varying the tension of the gliding membranes. Bending one of the forelegs backward slackens the tension on the membrane on that side, allowing the membrane to cup air and pull the squirrel around in the new direction. In landing, the squirrel first lowers its horizontally flattened tail, then jerks it up. This action is similar to that of ailerons or stabilizers on an airplane; by dropping the rear part of the body, the squirrel approaches its objective in an almost vertical position. Instead of being used as wings, the gliding membranes now act as brakes, enabling the animal to make a feather-soft landing. On the ground the membranes hamper the squirrel's movements and make it extremely awkward. They also make it impossible for the squirrel to swim.

The flying squirrel gets along well with its fellows and tends to live in groups. It prefers to take up residence in a tree cavity or leaf nest, but in an emergency does not shun an abandoned bird's or squirrel's nest or even an empty mailbox or attic. On several occasions one of these squirrels has entered my home by way of the chimney. Each time the torn curtains, scattered bric-a-brac, and general havoc testified mutely to the squirrel's frantic efforts to escape.

This squirrel feeds on all nuts except the walnut, whose hard shell seems to be too tough for it to open. It has a special fondness for hickory nuts, wild

The squirrel comes in for a landing by lowering its tail and the rear part of its body, approaching its objective in an almost vertical position.

cherries, and insects. Because the flying squirrel does not hibernate, it feeds during the winter on caches of nuts and pits. Large amounts of water at frequent intervals also are a necessity.

The breeding season starts in February. The flying squirrel produces one or two litters per year. About forty days after breeding three to five young are born. They are blind for almost twenty-eight days. By the time their eyes open, they are fully furred and have started to scamper about. At eight weeks of age young flying squirrels make their first short gliding flights. The flights lengthen as the youngsters develop skill and confidence. In about two more months the young acquire their adult coat of fur, which is changed every September. Not until they are about eighteen months old are they fully grown.

A flying squirrel fortunate enough to elude its predators has a life expectancy of about five years in the wild state. Owls constitute the chief threat at night, while cats, foxes, and bobcats catch the squirrel when it feeds on the ground. Tree-climbing snakes often invade a squirrel's den and eat the helpless young.

A soft churring is the only sound I have ever heard this squirrel make. It is shy and gentle, with the nicest disposition of any wild mammal. The flying squirrel seldom tries to bite when picked up, nevertheless I always advise caution. Every animal is an individual, and it is impossible to predict precisely what it will do. This squirrel makes a most interesting pet, particularly if you don't mind having one whose periods of wakefulness are exactly the opposite of your own.

On the ground the loose membranes hamper the squirrel's movement. Still, with its silky, reddish-brown coat and creamy white underparts, it is one of the most beautiful squirrels in America.

Beaver
(Castor canadensis)

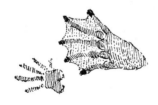

SIZE: 42 inches, including 12-inch tail.

WEIGHT: 50–65 pounds.

HABITS: Mates for life. Builds dams and lodges of mud, rock, and wood. Excellent swimmer, able to stay underwater 15 minutes.

HABITAT: Rivers or streams in wooded country.

FOOD: Inner bark of aspen, birch, willow, maple; water lilies; fungi; algae; aquatic plants.

BREEDING: 1 litter of 4 (average) per year. Gestation 4 months.

ENEMIES: Otters, wolves, coyotes, bobcats, bears, wolverines.

LIFE SPAN: 15 years.

Famed for its industriousness, the beaver gathers twigs along the water's edge for building dams and lodges.

No other animal has played a more important or historic role in the development of North America than the diligent beaver. Its dam-building activities resulted in the creation of much of our most fertile land, and some strategic landmarks as well. The Indian name for Montreal was *Hochelaga*, beaver dam. The beaver also prompted much of the early exploration and settlement of the continent. The first settlers soon learned that fortunes could be made trading in furs. Beaver were everywhere, and the search for them lured trappers ever deeper into the wilderness. In the early 1800s the European beaver was almost exterminated after Beau Brummel in England established the vogue for beaver hats. What seemed to be an inexhaustible supply of beaver on this continent was trapped with relentless vigor to fill the demand for hats, coats, and robes. Early in the nineteenth century the winds of fashion shifted. Silk replaced beaver fur in the making of men's hats, prices declined, and the beaver boom was over. By then beaver were practically extinct east of the Mississippi River.

The beaver is the largest rodent in North America; when full-grown it may weigh as much as fifty to sixty-five pounds. Actually, it never stops growing; if its life span could be increased beyond the fifteen-year average it enjoys, the beaver conceivably might rival the 400-pound prehistoric beaver, *castoroides* (the Latin name for the beaver, *castor*).

Both male and female have scent glands, or castors, and exude a strong, oily musk. The beaver uses this sweet-smelling musk to mark trails, to attract potential mates, and to waterproof its chocolate-brown fur. After emerging from the water and combing its fur with the cleft second toes of its hind feet, the beaver applies the oil with its dextrous front paws. The hind toes have webs of skin.

In the water the beaver's broad, paddle-shaped tail is used for steering and propulsion; on land it serves as a prop when the beaver sits upright. When

The beaver piles up mud, rock, and wood to build its cone-shaped lodge in the middle of a stream. When the water freezes in winter, the inhabitants move about freely beneath the ice.

danger threatens, the beaver gives a warning signal by slapping its tail on the surface of the water with a resounding crack. There is no basis to the claim that the beaver employs its tail as a trowel in its building activities.

This busy vegetarian cuts down trees with its chisel-shaped incisor teeth, stripping off the juicy inner bark of the aspen, birch, willow, and maple that constitute its chief food supply. Ferns, water lilies, fungi, vitamin-rich algae, and other aquatic plants bordering the ponds and streams inhabited by beaver also provide good fare.

Thanks to special physiological adaptations, the air-breathing beaver can remain underwater for as long as fifteen minutes. Valves in its nose and ears close automatically when the beaver submerges and open when it surfaces. The eyes are equipped with built-in underwater goggles—thin membranes that can be drawn over the eyeballs. The beaver also has an oversized liver that filters out impurities in the blood, an enlarged lung capacity, and a high tolerance to carbon dioxide. When the beaver submerges, a cardiovascular reaction slows the flow of blood to its feet and paws, allowing the oxygen in the blood to be diverted to the brain. At the same time the beaver's internal body functions slow down to reduce the drain on the heart and the oxygen supply.

Because the beaver needs water to live safely, it makes its home near the banks of ponds and streams. If the water is not deep enough to suit its requirements, the beaver constructs a dam to remedy the situation. More than any other mammal, with the exception of man, the beaver alters its habitat to suit its needs. Sometimes its activities clash with man's interests, as when beaver dams cause flooding of roads and farmland. On other occasions, beaver dams have benefited man and wildlife by helping to conserve water and to prevent floods.

In the water, the beaver's only enemy is the otter, which kills young beavers but hesitates to tackle a full-grown animal. When forced to seek food on land, the beaver is vulnerable to attacks by the wolf, wolverine, coyote, bobcat, bear—and man.

Industriousness is a fabled attribute of the beaver, as evidenced in such expressions as eager beaver, busy as a beaver, and work like a beaver. The truth of the matter is that this industriousness is seasonal. In the fall, the beaver works like one possessed as it prepares for winter. Trees are cut to strengthen dams, branches and limbs for winter food are anchored in the mud underwater to prevent their floating away, and lodges are readied for occupancy.

Some beaver lodges are mere burrows in the stream bank, having an underwater entrance and a living area above water. Others are built on the bank. The ultimate in lodge construction is the cone-shaped structure built in the stream, surrounded on all sides by a protective water barrier. To build such a lodge, the beaver piles up mud, rock, and wood until the mass reaches a height of some six feet above water level and a width at the base of eight to ten feet. Then the beaver submerges to chew and dig its way up through the center of the mass. Reaching a space above the surface of the water, it excavates a den or room with a feeding platform, raised sleeping platform, and escape tunnels leading from the floor into the water. With its paws the beaver gives the outside of the lodge a protective coating of mud dredged up from the stream bottom.

When winter seals the pond with a layer of ice and freezes the lodge's mud

Although it breathes air, the beaver can remain underwater for fifteen minutes at a time. When it submerges, the beaver's internal body functions slow down to reduce the drain on the heart and oxygen supply.

The mainstay of the beaver's diet is the juicy inner bark of the aspen, willow, birch, and maple.

covering to the consistency of concrete, the beaver relaxes in comfort and safety. Predators can walk out on the ice to the lodge but cannot break through its roof, while the beaver travels about freely beneath the ice, selecting a succulent branch from its submerged store when hunger strikes and carrying it back to the lodge.

In the wintertime a beaver household usually consists of the parents, who mate for life, their recent offspring, and those born the previous year. The family stays together until the ice thaws in the spring, when the female, ready to give birth to a new litter of young, drives the other members from the lodge. The male and the yearlings take up residence in a nearby lodge or burrow before eventually returning home; the two-year-olds leave the colony for good to make their own way in the world.

In April, about four months after mating, the female gives birth to her young. Usually about four in number, newborn beaver are fully furred and open-eyed, measure about fifteen inches long and tip the scales at around one pound. The whimpering cry of a baby beaver sounds like a puppy's, while older beaver growl and hiss. The babies can swim when only a few hours old. At about one month of age young beaver are weaned; they begin to feed on vegetation as soon as they venture forth from the lodge.

The beaver devotes the rest of the spring and summer to eating and loafing. Although most of its activities take place under cover of darkness, the beaver comes out in the daytime to sun itself when it is not molested.

The beaver pictured on Canadian postage and currency and the beaver-pelt values marked on Hudson's Bay Company blankets are vivid reminders of the era when the beaver was king in North America. Beaver pelts are still important in the manufacture of fur coats, although prices sometimes drop as low as $15 per pelt, and beaver musk is used as a base for perfumes as well as for scents used to trap meat-eating animals. But today the United States and Canada have protective laws to protect the beaver from indiscriminate trapping and the threat of virtual extermination.

White-Footed Mouse
(Peromyscus leucopus)

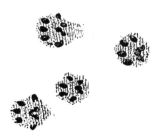

SIZE: 7½ inches, including tail.

WEIGHT: 1 ounce.

HABITS: Prefers country to cities, but will enter houses. Grooms itself carefully.

HABITAT: Woods or brushlands.

FOOD: Insects, grubs, snails, caterpillars, carcasses.

BREEDING: 5–8 litters of 5–8 per year. Gestation 21–24 days.

ENEMIES: Shrews, foxes, owls, snakes.

LIFE SPAN: 5½ years.

Shunning large cities, the white-footed mouse favors brushlands, where it nests underneath logs, in tree hollows, or in rock crevices.

The handsome adult white-footed mouse wears a golden-brown coat of fur on its back and, as its name implies, its feet and underparts are pure white. The young whitefoot has a gray coat, which gradually turns brownish as the mouse grows older. Because the shading usually starts where the white ends, a whitefoot at this stage may have all three colors: gray back, brownish sides, and white belly. When full-grown, the white-footed mouse is about seven and a half inches long and weighs approximately one ounce.

Personal cleanliness is so important to this mouse that it spends many hours a day washing, combing, and grooming itself. I have never seen a white-footed mouse whose appearance was not immaculate. It is not only cleaner than the smaller house mouse, but also is far less destructive.

A native of North America, the white-footed mouse is found almost everywhere in the United States east of the Rockies and into southern Canada and northern Mexico. It shuns large cities in favor of woods or brushlands, where it nests in burrows underneath logs, in tree hollows, or in rock crevices. This mouse is perfectly willing to partake of man's food and shelter, especially when cold weather arrives.

One summer our camp in Canada was overrun by white-footed mice. To circumvent their pilfering, we put out table scraps for them to eat and were able to observe their eating habits. Because the mice move about with freedom only under the cover of darkness, it was about 10 P.M. before the first visitor arrived. If there was any activity in the kitchen tent, the mice did not come out to feed, although we would see them dashing up a tent shear pole or climbing a rope.

As soon as things quieted down, the mice would appear. Seldom would more than one mouse feed at a time. A head cautiously poked out from behind a box, its large ears twitching, protruding black eyes searching about for danger, and long whiskers sweeping back and forth like radar antennae. At last, satisfied that all was clear, the mouse began to feed. Each bit of food was held daintily between its forepaws. When the meal ended, the mouse washed its paws, combed its whiskers, then scampered away to make room for another. The mice are not actively aggressive toward each other, although they most probably have some sort of caste system or pecking order. We noticed that the younger mice came in to feed after all the adults had finished.

The diet of the white-footed mouse is varied; probably it eats as much animal matter as plant food. Insects, grubs, snails, slugs, and caterpillars are eaten whenever they are found. Animals that have been killed or have died also provide food, and the whitefoot occasionally may devour its own kind.

This mouse, in turn, is a staple item for all the meat-eaters of the forest, from the tiny shrew to the giant bear. Winged predators, notably the great horned and barred owls, take a tremendous toll. The white-footed mouse can swim if necessary, but is reluctant to enter the water, where it is preyed upon by fish. Snakes not only kill adult mice, but also slither into their burrows or climb up into their tree nests to feed on the young.

The female gives birth to five to eight young after a gestation period of twenty-one to twenty-four days. Helpless, hairless, and sightless, the young measure about one and a half inches in length. Soon they are fully furred and on the eighteenth day their eyes open. They may be weaned at three weeks of age, or the mother may continue to care for them another week or more. If she is disturbed while nursing them and scampers off, the young, having firmly attached themselves to their mother's teats, are dragged along. Not infrequently, one of the babies is jounced off along the way. The length of time the mother provides care for her babies depends upon when she mates again. The white-footed mouse is polygamous, and the female has five to eight litters per year.

When the female is ready to give birth again, she abandons her first litter to construct a new nest. In this way, the first litter retains its home nest in familiar territory. The new nest is fashioned from any available plant material, paper, or grasses. In hunting camps, the stuffing from old mattresses is often utilized.

The white-footed mouse is sometimes referred to as the singing mouse, because of the high-pitched buzzing sound it emits. This sound can be heard at a distance of forty to fifty feet, although it frequently is mistaken for the buzzing song of an insect.

Meadow Mouse
(Microtus pennsylvanicus)

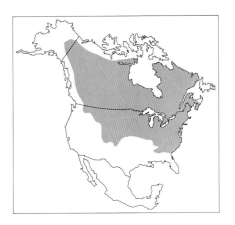

SIZE: 6–8 inches, including 1½-inch tail.

WEIGHT: 4 ounces.

HABITS: Consumes own weight in food daily. Lays out complex network of trails above and below ground.

HABITAT: Grassy meadows and bogs.

FOOD: Grain, grass, bulbs, bark, flowers, seeds.

BREEDING: Up to 17 litters of 4–8 per year. Gestation 21 days.

ENEMIES: Owls, hawks, crows, gulls, foxes.

LIFE SPAN: 18 months.

One of our most destructive native rodents, the meadow mouse is also one of the most prolific. The female produces up to seventeen litters a year.

The meadow mouse, also called the meadow vole or field mouse, is the most common and prolific of our native rodents. It is also one of the most destructive. This mouse must consume its own weight in food every day to satisfy its voracious appetite. A female has been known to produce seventeen litters in one year. Impelled by its drive for food and for reproduction, the meadow mouse enjoys few idle moments and usually has burned itself out by the end of its first year.

This mouse is found in Canada and the northern half of the United States from the Atlantic Ocean to the Rocky Mountains. Grassy meadows and bogs are its favored haunts, even though the bog often is filled with water. The meadow mouse is a good swimmer and its fur is water repellent.

One of the largest members of the mouse family, a meadow mouse measures six to eight inches long, including a short tail of a little over one and a half inches. It is about one and a half inches high at the shoulder, weighs four ounces or more, and has tiny, beady black eyes. The dark brown or dark gray coat with a few black guard hairs shades into lighter underparts. Always wear gloves before attempting to pick up this stocky, tough little mouse; it readily sinks its sharp incisors into your hand and draws blood. Even against its predators, this mouse goes down fighting.

The meadow mouse is the staple of all meat-eating animals. It is preyed upon by more species than any other creature because its activity exposes it to around-the-clock predation. In the hours of darkness, owls take their toll; in the daytime, hawks, crows, and even gulls dispatch their share. Disease and parasites help the predators reduce the meadow mouse population during the peak year of its four-year cycle. The average density is 30 mice per acre, but there is one instance on record of 12,000 meadow mice per acre. Clearly, numbers such as these must decimate every bit of plant life in the area. It has been estimated that these mice consume at least 3,000,000 tons of hay yearly and so constitute domestic livestock's most serious competitor for green plant food.

The meadow mouse subsists almost entirely on plant food. It eats grain, grass, bulbs, bark, flowers, seeds, and almost anything else that grows. It is also a hoarder, storing food in underground caches for the winter months because it does not hibernate. Often this mouse causes the damage in gardens for which other mammals are blamed. It is not the common mole that eats the bulbs of plants, but the meadow mouse. Yet the mole is blamed because its tunnel is visible and people generally assume that all tunnels are made by moles. In winter, when green vegetation is scarce, the meadow mouse frequently chews the bark from trees and bushes as high up as it can reach. When the mouse does a complete girdling job, the tree dies. When this damage occurs in an orchard, the cottontail rabbit is denounced. A close examination of the tree and tooth marks will reveal the true culprit. The mouse has much smaller teeth than the cottontail, and the grooves left by its teeth will be narrower.

The female mates for the first time when she is one month old and produces successive litters every twenty-one days. Four to eight young per litter are born in a roofed-over nest that is usually concealed in a clump of grass. In summer the nest may be hidden below ground; but in winter it may be above ground, where the protective layer of snow conceals it from predators.

The young mice remain helpless for a brief period only. In four days they are fully furred; in a week they can see and hear and are beginning to eat solid food. By the time they are two weeks old, they are weaned and ready to be out on their own.

The most conspicuous sign of meadow mouse activities is its network of pathways and trails. The pathways of the mouse often are just as complex and confusing as man's road-building efforts. The trails are laid out on top of the earth and beneath it. Although there is no joint community activity in their construction and each mouse makes its paths to suit itself, the paths may join up with its neighbors' and be used by any mice of the area. Even when the snow blankets the earth, the meadow mouse never interrupts its activity; it simply tunnels its pathways through the snow. When the snow melts away, the location of the paths on top of the grass is revealed. A careful examination shows where the mouse stored its food, where it cut additional vegetation, and where its above-ground winter nest was situated.

For the meadow mouse winter is the time of greatest security and freedom. Its mantle of snow provides warmth and protection, enabling the mouse to forage safely out of sight of its predators.

Muskrat
(Ondatra zibethica)

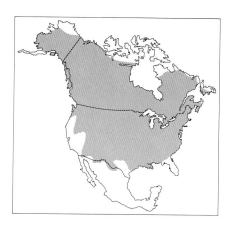

SIZE: *25 inches, including 10-inch tail.*
WEIGHT: *Up to 3 pounds.*
HABITS: *Emits strong, sweet-smelling musk. Builds lodges on riverbanks.*
HABITAT: *Marshes or riverbanks. Always lives near water.*
FOOD: *Aquatic plants, garden vegetables, fresh water mussels, fish.*
BREEDING: *Average of 3 litters of 4–8 per year. Gestation about 1 month.*
ENEMIES: *Mink, raccoons, foxes, otters, bobcats, hawks, owls, large snakes, alligators, northern pikes.*
LIFE SPAN: *5–6 years.*

Two baby muskrats perch on a log at the water's edge. They propel themselves through the water with their strong feet and by sculling with their scaly, flattened tails.

The muskrat is not a rat, but a relative of the vole and the beaver. Like the beaver, it has scent glands that emit a strong, sweet-smelling musk. The muskrat uses this musk for identification and trail-marking; man uses it in making a scent to attract furbearers into his traps.

Water is so essential for the muskrat that this rodent never roams far from its aquatic habitat. Wherever there is enough water to support it, the muskrat thrives. It is found all over North America, with the exception of Florida and Mexico.

The muskrat, like all mammals air-breathing, is adapted to life in the water in much the same way as the beaver. Flaps of skin that fold in behind the front incisors and seal the mouth allow the muskrat to use its teeth for digging and carrying roots and food without swallowing water. This rodent swims with its hind feet, which are equipped with a stiff webbing of hair between the toes; it holds its forepaws folded against its chest. Its distinctive black, scaly, vertically flattened tail serves as a rudder and for a sculling type of propulsion.

A full-grown muskrat measures about twenty-five inches, including a ten-inch tail, and rarely weighs more than three pounds. It has a coat of dense brown fur covered with coarse guard hairs and lighter-colored underparts.

The male muskrat is polygamous and the female produces an average of three litters a year. About one month after mating she gives birth to four to eight young; blind and almost hairless, each weighs about three-quarters of an ounce and measures four inches long. Baby muskrats can swim by the time they are a week old, even though they cannot see where they are going; not until a week later do their eyes open. At three weeks of age, the young muskrats begin to feed on vegetation by themselves, and soon therafter they leave the family lodge to find homes of their own.

The spot selected may be a farm pond, beaver-made lake, or any other body of clean water where food can be found. Sometimes a muskrat home is a bank lodge, which is nothing more than a burrow in the bank of a pond or stream equipped with an underwater entrance and above-water living chamber. Frequently the earthen banks of farm ponds are weakened by the burrowing activities of muskrats. Whenever possible, the muskrat builds a lodge of reeds, weeds, flags, cattails, and other aquatic plants that also will come in handy for winter food. This vegetation is piled up into a rounded mound that may reach a height of five or six feet and resemble a farmer's haycock. This lodge, too, has an underwater entrance and living chamber.

Muskrats living in the banks of a river or brook often try again and again to build regular lodges in the most untenable locations. I have watched them start such construction on mud bars, gravel bars, and partially submerged logs. The mound would reach a height of two to three feet, then the river would rise and wash everything away. Still the muskrats would persist in their attempt to build a lodge, usually starting in the same place where they failed before.

High water and floods wreak havoc on a muskrat population. The adults usually can swim to safety, but many of the young are drowned. A hard flood in a river may scour the river bottom and wash away the plants on which this rodent depends for food.

Over 13,000,000 muskrat pelts are harvested every year in the United States.

A muskrat dives head first into the water. The hind feet are equipped with a stiff webbing of hair between the toes.

Whenever possible, the muskrat builds a beaver-like lodge of weeds, cattails, and other aquatic plants that will also provide winter food. Inside, the lodge has living quarters and an underground entrance.

The fur is durable and can be dyed easily to imitate more costly furs. Yet at the present time the muskrat population is increasing. Although the professionals continue their trapping operations, declining prices for pelts have discouraged many rural, part-time trappers from trying for muskrats. The displacement of natural furs by man-made fur-like fabrics and the muskrat's high birthrate are other contributing factors.

In addition to being trapped for its fur, the muskrat also is used for food. In some areas it is sold in meat markets under the name of marsh rabbit. The meat is dark in color; its flavor is said to resemble that of the terrapin or wild duck. The muskrat is a clean animal and feeds mainly on vegetation. Cattails, bullrushes, water lilies, bur reeds, pickerelweeds, corn, apples, and parsnips are favored; occasionally fresh water mussels or fish are taken.

Many predators, in turn, feed on the muskrat, although it is not about much in the daytime. The mink heads the list of enemies, which also includes the otter, raccoon, fox, and bobcat. Hawks by day and owls by night pounce upon unsuspecting muskrats. To escape these aerial attacks, it prefers to locate its feeding platforms beneath the protective canopy of streamside tree roots or brush. Some of the big snakes, as well as alligators, take muskrats. I have also

The muskrat feeds mainly on bullrushes, cattails, and other aquatic plants. But occasionally a pile of mussel shells is left at the water's edge.

found young muskrats in the bellies of big northern pike. This fish has such a voracious appetite that it would attack an adult muskrat if the adult were not such a fierce battler.

The muskrat certainly gives a good account of itself when cornered. Once I was livetrapping some muskrats to stock a new pond, when one escaped and dove into an opening in the stream bank. To force the muskrat out so that I could net it, I shoved the toe of my rubber boot into the opening. The muskrat came out all right, with its teeth piercing a gaping hole in my boot. As the icy water rushed in through this hole, the muskrat swam away to safety.

Norway Rat
(Rattus norvegicus)

SIZE: Head and body 8–9 inches, tail about same.

WEIGHT: 14 ounces.

HABITS: Highly adaptable to varied climates and conditions. Digs tunnels under buildings or garbage piles.

HABITAT: Cities and farmyards.

FOOD: Almost anything, including chickens, soap, leather, cloth.

BREEDING: 8–10 litters of 4–12 per year. Gestation 20–26 days.

ENEMIES: Hawks, owls, foxes, dogs, cats, snakes.

LIFE SPAN: 4 years.

One of man's greatest enemies, the Norway rat does an annual damage of more than $200,000,000 in the United States alone. Because it carries disease and gnaws through everything from water pipes to concrete, intensive control measures against it have been taken on farms and in cities.

In spite of its name, the Norway rat did not originate in Norway. During the sixteenth century it was taken by ship from Asia to the Mediterranean area and from there about 1727 it infested western Europe. Stowing away aboard ships bound for the New World, the Norway rat entered North America in 1775. By the early 1900s it was firmly established all over the United States, and today it is found in most parts of Canada and coastal Alaska.

An adult rat measures between fifteen and eighteen inches in total length and weighs about one pound. It has coarse gray or brown fur, grayish underparts, and a long, scaly, almost naked tail.

Next to man, the Norway rat is the most adaptable of all living creatures. Whenever man transported grain or other foodstuffs from one place to another, he unwittingly took along the Norway rat. This intelligent rodent has demonstrated such a remarkable ability to exist under varied conditions and climates that it has become the most abundant of the house rats. It has also proved to be man's greatest enemy among the mammals.

Rat-borne diseases probably have taken a greater toll of human lives than all the wars and revolutions in history. Typhus, bubonic (black) plague, rabies, trichinosis, and *Salmonella* food poisoning are some of the diseases transmitted by rats. They also do damage of over $200,000,000 yearly in the United States alone.

Primarily a denizen of cities and farmyards, the rat eats just about anything, from chickens to soap, leather, and cloth. Like all rodents, the rat's incisor teeth are constantly in need of being ground down, and this rodent can gnaw through a variety of materials, even lead water pipes and concrete. I remember when I was a boy on the farm that mixing broken glass in the concrete worked most effectively in repairing rat holes. The rat also causes a great deal of destruction through spoilage and waste.

Although widely used in scientific research, the Norway rat is so prolific that intensive control measures against it must be taken. In large cities hundreds of exterminators are involved in the large-scale business of rat control. They use poisons and deadly gases; in the country rats are also shot or trapped. Poisons had a more limited use on the farms, because of their danger to domestic livestock and pets, until the development of a control poison that kills only rats.

A good swimmer and active the year round, the Norway rat is primarily an underground dweller, preferring to live in the labyrinth of tunnels it excavates in the earth. Although this burrowing is a communal effort, there is little evidence of any organized social order among these rodents. If possible, the tunnels are dug beneath a building or garbage or anything else that will conceal them from exposure. Often the tunnels have undermined an area so thoroughly that they have caused the ground to cave in, or even small buildings to settle. Such an occurrence may explain the superstition that the presence of rats in a building signifies that the structure is unsound or that there will be a death in the family. It doesn't help to explain why sailors believe that a ship is doomed to sink if rats desert her just before she sails.

A female Norway rat may have as many as eight to ten litters a year. In the southern United States, this rat breeds the year around; in the north, the reproductive process usually ceases during the bitterest winter months when access to food is more difficult. A litter may contain four to twelve young, although eight is the average. Baby Norway rats are blind and naked at birth, but they grow rapidly; by the time they are two weeks old, their eyes open. When they are about three weeks old, they are weaned and are ready to go out on their own. Within a few days the mother is ready to give birth to her next litter. The young start to breed when they are three months old and continue until old age overtakes them in two years' time.

Tremendous numbers of this rodent are killed by such winged predators as the marsh, red-tailed, and broad-winged hawks, and the barred, great horned, and barn owls, the latter being its number one enemy. The fox is the chief four-footed predator. Dogs, particularly terriers, and weasels are effective rat killers. Cats often take young rats, but generally hesitate to attack adults. The rat is extremely courageous and, when cornered, makes a formidable enemy. Large snakes, such as the black, fox, corn, pine, king, and rattlesnake also feed on rats.

It is fortunate for the human race that this rat has such a high mortality rate. On the basis of its breeding potential, a leading mammalogist has figured that a single rat family and its young could produce 350,000,000 offspring in three years' time.

House Mouse
(Mus musculus)

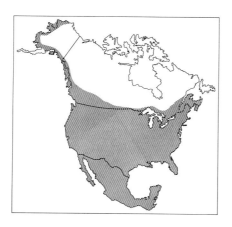

SIZE: 7–8 inches, including 3–4-inch tail.

WEIGHT: Up to 1 ounce.

HABITS: Builds labyrinth of underground tunnels. Nocturnal; destructive to cloth and fabrics; carries disease.

HABITAT: Houses, storehouses, fields, farms.

FOOD: Everything, including soap, glue, paste.

BREEDING: 6–8 litters of 4–8 per year. Gestation 13–21 days.

ENEMIES: Cats, dogs, hawks, owls, snakes, weasels, foxes.

LIFE SPAN: 3–4 years.

The house mouse eats everything man eats, as well as many things man does not—including soap, glue, and paste. It is destructive in homes because it gnaws the woodwork and shreds all types of fabric for nesting materials. Furthermore, it carries such human diseases as typhus and spotted fever.

One day, a robber carrying a small box entered an exclusive furrier's establishment staffed entirely by women. Selecting several valuable fur coats, he opened the box and released four house mice. While the shrieking women panicked, the robber calmly picked up the coats and departed.

Just why this tiny creature has the power to reduce womankind to a state of helplessness is not easy to explain. In other times and places, for instance, the standard remedy for coughs, colds, fits, and fevers consisted of a tasty portion of baked, roasted, stewed, or fried mice prepared by mother's own hand. But on the whole, the mouse, as its name implies, has been held in low esteem. The Latin *mus* derives from the Sanskrit *musha*, meaning thief. The mouse shares all the vices of its much larger cousin, the rat, as well as its single virtue—usefulness (in its albino form) to scientific research.

The house mouse is not native to the United States. It originated in Asia, spread to Europe, and from there was brought to North America. The southern subspecies (*M. m. brevirostris*) accompanied the Spaniards to Florida and Latin America in the early 1500s, while the northern form (*M. m. domesticus*) turned up with the French and English a century or more later. Everywhere the settlers went, the mouse was sure to go, transported by flatboat, prairie schooner, and farm wagon. Then as now, this mouse lived with man, sharing his house and food. It is not often that the house mouse sets up housekeeping by constructing a home of its own outdoors. In fact, I have only seen this happen in the southern part of the United States.

This mouse eats everything a man eats, as well as many things he does not, including soap, glue, and paste. What makes the house mouse so destructive and wasteful is that it spoils and soils much more than it actually consumes. Its ability to survive on very little is described by the familiar expression, poor as a church mouse. Continual gnawing causes further damage, and the fact that the mouse shreds all types of fabric, including clothing, for nesting material does nothing to enhance its popularity. The mouse, furthermore, is a carrier of such human diseases as typhus and spotted fever.

Traps, cats, and poisoned bait are employed to keep this rodent under control. Any slackening of vigilance results in an immediate upswing in its numbers. On the other hand, it is impossible to eradicate this pest, because it lives in such numbers in so many places. If there are too many mice in one area, they simply spill over into an area where the population is low.

House mice are promiscuous, and their breeding potential is extremely high. Where they live in warm buildings, mice are capable of breeding all year long. In unheated buildings, the cold prevents their breeding during the winter months. One female may have six to eight litters a year, with four to eight young per litter. Prior to giving birth, she constructs a snug, soft nest. The newborn babies are pink, blind, and hairless. They are well cared for and grow rapidly. Within three weeks the young are weaned and go off on their own. Females are capable of breeding when less than two months old. A mouse has a life span of about three to four years.

A full-grown house mouse measures a mere seven to eight inches in length, one-half of which is its long, naked, scaly tail. The mouse stands about one inch high at the shoulder and may weigh as much as an ounce. Its short, grayish-brown fur is just a shade lighter on the underparts.

Being so small in a world so fraught with danger, the house mouse is extremely timid, emerging only at night. It realizes that to step out into the open is to invite death, so the mouse scurries along the walls of a building, taking advantage of every bit of cover it can find. In climbing, the mouse uses its long tail for balance and support so that it will not lose its footing. Although it can swim, it prefers not to. The singing and waltzing talents attributed to some mice are in reality nothing more than barely audible twitterings in the one instance and defective balance in the other.

Cats, dogs, hawks, owls, snakes, weasels, and foxes are all efficient mouse killers. Frequently the European ferret is used against the mouse. Because they can penetrate the mouse's labyrinth of underground tunnels, weasels and snakes are the most effective exterminators. The mouse-hunting proclivity of the milk snake often has been its undoing. Although this snake does not and cannot drink milk from a cow, many a farmer has accused it of doing so and has proceeded to eradicate every milk snake found around the barn. What had attracted the snake to the barn in the first place was the presence of mice. Thus, the farmer unwittingly killed the best mouser he was ever likely to get.

Woodland Jumping Mouse
(Napaeozapus insignis)

SIZE: *10 inches, including 6–7-inch tail.*

WEIGHT: *Less than 1 ounce.*

HABITS: *Jumps as far as 10 feet, without leaving trail. Hibernates in winter. Seldom bothers man.*

HABITAT: *Abandoned fields, brush, woodlands.*

FOOD: *Grass seeds, berries, fruits, insects, meat, dead fish.*

BREEDING: *2 litters of 3–5 per year. Gestation 30 days.*

ENEMIES: *Owls, foxes, weasels, bobcats, snakes.*

LIFE SPAN: *1–2 years.*

With its enlarged hind feet, the woodland jumping mouse jumps as far as ten feet in one leap, enabling it to escape its enemies without leaving a trail. The long tail acts as a counterbalance. Without it the mouse would merely turn somersaults. Here we see a young mouse.

The woodland jumping mouse is one creature that evidently doesn't believe in the maxim look before you leap, because frequently it jumps smack into trouble. Its jumping ability far exceeds its seeing ability, with the result that the mouse often launches itself into the air before it can see where it is going.

While digging foundations for a new scout camp building one summer, I regularly caught several jumping mice in a single night. The mice just bounced along without realizing that the pits were there until they suddenly dropped five or six feet down to the bottom. Once in the pits, they were unable to crawl back up the sheer side walls. It was a simple matter then to corner the mice, pick them up, and release them above ground. They never tried to bite, oddly enough, for mice generally are quick to use their sharp incisors.

The woodland jumping mouse is the greatest jumper for its size in the mammal world. When alarmed or pursued by an enemy, this mouse has been seen making jumps of over ten feet. This may not seem remarkable until you realize that for a man to jump as far for his weight, he would have to cover four miles in a single jump. This mouse also has a distinctive manner of jumping. While other mice travel on all four feet, the various species of jumping mouse—woodland, meadow (*Zapus hudsonius*), and western (*Z. princeps*)—hop only on the hind feet, which are greatly enlarged. The long tail acts as a counterbalance, enabling the mouse to jump and turn sharply. When the jumping mouse travels, it resembles a miniature kangaroo or a wood sprite on a pogo stick. Not only is its leaping ability a good defense against predators, but it also eliminates the making of trails and runways that might be helpful to them. When startled, the mouse bounds away over the grass, leaf litter, and debris. Because there is no trail to follow, the predator is much more likely to lose track of its prey. If the mouse ever loses its tail, it is reduced to turning somersaults instead of being able to jump in a straight line. With its principal defense gone, the mouse is an easy prey for such meat-eaters as the owl, fox, weasel, bobcat, and snake.

The jumping mouse feeds primarily on grass seeds of all types, cutting the grass stalk to make it drop its seeds on the ground within reach or crawling up the stalk until it bends down to the ground. Berries, fruits, insects, any meat it can find, and even dead fish, all are part of this rodent's diet.

Few people have seen a jumping mouse, for its numbers are few, it leads a solitary existence, and is too highly strung to make a good pet. The jumping mouse moves only under the protective cover of darkness and does not invade human habitations. There is little conflict between this mouse and man.

The woodland jumping mouse is found in eastern Canada, along the Great Lakes, in New England, and southward along the Appalachian Mountains to Georgia. It prefers to live in abandoned fields that have grown up into brush or in the woodlands. When possible it lives near water and frequently is found around bogs. Even in favored territory its numbers vary sharply from year to year. This mouse usually constructs a house of grass and dried vegetation packed into a ball about eight inches in diameter. The nest may be on the ground or elevated, either in a tangle of heavy weeds or in a bush. In addition to its jumping and climbing abilities, this mouse also swims well.

An adult of this species is about ten inches long, of which six to seven inches constitute its long tail. It weighs less than one ounce. The coat is a beautiful golden brown, the underparts are white, and the tail is marked with a conspicuous white tip. Unlike most other mice, the jumping mouse hibernates in winter. In September or October the mouse becomes dormant. Retiring to its snug den underground, where it has packed the bedchamber full of dried grasses to make it warm and comfortable, the little creature prepares to sleep until the arrival of spring.

Breeding occurs in late March or early April, shortly after the jumping mouse emerges from its den, and again in midsummer. The male is promiscuous and leaves the female after mating. After a gestation period of about thirty days, three to five young are born. The babies measure about one and three-quarters inches, are blind, naked, and helpless. At two weeks of age, almost fully furred, they begin to crawl about; a week later their eyes open. By the time the young mice are six weeks old they are full-grown and almost indistinguishable from the adults. The young now are capable of taking care of themselves and leave to establish dens of their own.

Nutria
(*Myocastor coypus*)

SIZE: *3 feet, including 14-inch tail.*

WEIGHT: *12–15 pounds average.*

HABITS: *Aquatic, similar to beaver and muskrat; eats constantly.*

HABITAT: *Woodlands, near streams or ponds.*

FOOD: *Cattails, arrowheads, water lilies, water weeds.*

BREEDING: *2–3 litters of 5–10 per year. Gestation 100–132 days.*

ENEMIES: *Otters, alligators.*

LIFE SPAN: *4 years in wild to 12 years in captivity.*

Imported from South America, the nutria has flourished on this continent and extended its range as far north as Canada. Although similar to the muskrat and beaver, the nutria has distinctive, bristly white whiskers and a round tail.

This large aquatic rodent is a native of South America, where the conquistadors, mistaking it for an otter, gave it the Spanish name for that animal, *nutria*. The nutria is found in Chile, Argentina, Uruguay, Paraguay, and Bolivia, where it is considered an important furbearer. During a visit to Argentina, I saw beautiful, high-priced coats made from nutria fur displayed in exclusive fur shops in Buenos Aires. I also purchased a felt hat made of nutria hair. Because of the nutria's potential market value, the nutria was introduced into the United States.

The first nutria were imported into this country in 1899 by Will Frakes of Elizabeth Lake, California, but his efforts at raising the animals failed. In 1932 a fur rancher on the Green River Farm in the state of Washington tried another importation of nutria and had no better luck. The first successful importation was made by E. A. McIlhenny in 1937 on his estate in Louisiana. However, the breeding of nutria in captivity was beset with problems. The ranchers experimented with raising nutria in individual wire pens as well as in large concrete tanks. The animal's appetite was the biggest drawback, for it ate constantly. In 1940 the Mississippi River flooded, smashing the pens of some ranchers and enabling hundreds of nutria to escape into the wild.

The nutria quickly adapted to the wild state and flourished, reproducing in numbers and extending their range. In some of the southern states along the Gulf of Mexico trappers take thousands of pelts each season. Today nutria have been reported from Wisconsin, Ohio, Pennsylvania, and western Canada.

Nutria were imported into Texas to serve as an economical method of controlling cattails, arrowheads, water lilies, and other noxious water weeds in some of the lakes. Turned loose, they immediately went to work. The trouble was that they didn't know when to stop eating. In a short time all the water weeds were gone, but so was every vestige of other vegetation. The completely denuded lakes became muddy potholes in which even the nutria found it impossible to live, while ducks and muskrats, deprived of the vegetation needed for food and shelter, were forced out of their favorite habitat. This is another example of man's interference with the balance of nature without first ascertaining the consequences.

One of the difficulties in importing any exotic species is that it may compete with the native stock. In this country the nutria competes with the muskrat, which has a staple cash value. Because it consumes more food than the muskrat, the nutria may replace the muskrat completely in some areas, thus causing a great loss to professional trappers.

Nutria fur has never been popular in this country and it has remained low in price. Although there is very little commercial raising of nutria in the United States today, breeding stock is still offered at inflated prices. These sellers of breeding stock are the only people who can make money from nutria, whose furs bring less than $10 apiece on the market today and often as little as two dollars.

The nutria is larger than a muskrat and smaller than a beaver. When its body is in the water and the tail is hidden, it is sometimes difficult to tell the three rodents apart. Out of the water the nutria reveals its distinctive, bristly, walrus-like white whiskers and its round tail. Like the beaver, it slaps its tail on the surface of the water to give an alarm signal, and it also has skin webs between the toes of its hind feet.

A full-grown adult is about three feet long, of which about fourteen inches is tail. Its weight averages between twelve and fifteen pounds, but may go as high as twenty pounds. On its back the nutria has a coat of yellowish or reddish brown fur. The blue-gray fur of the belly is the only part used by furriers because the female has nipples along her sides rather than on her belly. This arrangement allows the female to nurse her young as she swims about, with the little ones clinging to her hair or riding on her back.

The nutria is capable of breeding when it is six months old. It is polygamous and extremely prolific. Because a female's average litter contains five to ten young, and she may have two or three litters a year, her life span of about four years is roughly half that of the male. The nutria's den usually is a burrow in a stream bank and has an underwater entrance.

The mink, fox, some snakes, and other predators are capable of taking a young nutria, but a full-grown adult is another matter. The otter and the alligator are the sole natural controls on its numbers in this country, because they are the only predators both aquatic and large enough to take on a twenty-pound nutria.

Porcupine
(Erethizon dorsatum)

SIZE: *Head and body 30 inches, tail 6 inches.*
WEIGHT: *15–20 pounds average, but may reach 40 pounds.*
HABITS: *Arboreal; strong swimmer. Bristles quills when alarmed.*
HABITAT: *Woods.*
FOOD: *Leaves, twigs, bark.*
BREEDING: *Single offspring born in March. Gestation 4 months.*
ENEMIES: *Fishers, wolverines, wolves, coyotes, lynxes, mountain lions.*
LIFE SPAN: *7–8 years.*

In defense position, the porcupine lowers its head between its forelegs and turns its back and tail to the enemy. It raises its quills through muscle contractions, then lashes out with its tail. The quills are barbed and sink deeper with every movement of the victim's body.

The porcupine is a mighty peaceful creature as long as it is left alone. It doesn't look for trouble, but prefers to sit quietly in the treetops where it can get a firm grip with its claws and fill its ample belly with succulent leaves, twigs, and bark. This squat, heavy-bodied rodent is sluggish mentally and physically, but armed as it is, it has no real need to be either bright or speedy. Otherwise known as porky or quill pig, its common name comes from the Latin *porcus*, swine, and *spina*, spine. The generic name, *Erethizon*, means one who rises in anger.

The porcupine is covered with a coat of dense, heavy underfur overlaid with long guard hairs. Set in the fur are almost 32,000 needle-shaped quills. These sheath the animal's entire body, with the exception of the face, belly, and underside of the tail. Each quill is barbed at the business end, like an arrow, and tapered at the base where it enters the skin, permitting it to be easily detached. As quills molt or are lost, new ones grow in to replace them.

A strict vegetarian, the porcupine will not attack other animals as long as it is left alone. It prefers to sit quietly in the treetops where it munches on leaves, twigs, and bark.

Contrary to common belief, a porcupine does not throw its quills. When threatened, the animal first lowers its head between its forelegs to defend its unprotected underparts and grunts a warning to the aggressor. If the latter persists in the attack, the porcupine pivots around to present its back and tail to the enemy, raises its quills through muscle contractions, then lashes out with its tail. The results can be disastrous. I have had a porcupine sink quills a half inch deep into the gum rubber heel of my boot; in flesh, of course, they would penetrate much deeper.

When a porcupine quill enters flesh, the heat and moisture of the victim's body cause the quill to swell. Every movement of the victim's muscles pulls against the barbs, forcing the quill in deeper. Quills fairly imbedded cannot be pulled out by hand; they must be removed with pliers. Occasionally, an

A relative called the Western porcupine makes its home in the caves, crevices, or tree hollows of Canada and western United States, including Alaska.

animal is able to pull out some of the quills with its teeth. I have also seen quills work out of a dog a month after it had been attacked. Generally speaking, an animal struck by a large number of quills is doomed to death, because eventually the quills pierce vital body organs. Similarly, an animal with a face full of quills is unable to open or close its mouth and starves to death.

Because the quills are hollow, they give the porcupine great buoyancy in the water. This animal is a strong swimmer, if not a very fast one. When I was leading a group of teenage boys on a summertime wilderness canoe trip down Canada's Ottawa River, we spotted one of these spiny creatures swimming across the river. Two boys maneuvered their canoe alongside the porcupine and one of the boys extended his paddle to it. With its long, strong claws, the porky clung fast to the blade, and the boy lifted it aboard. As the porcupine charged toward the back of the canoe, the stern man, in a panic, jumped overboard. Then the animal swiveled around and headed for the bow. That was all the warning the bow paddler needed, and he too abandoned ship, leaving the porky in sole command of the canoe. The rest of us were laughing so hard we had trouble pushing the captured canoe to shore so that the porcupine could continue on its way.

The porcupine is found in forested areas of Canada and northern and western United States, including Alaska. It makes its home in rock caves, crevices, hollow logs, or trees. There is no particular mate selection among porcupines, which breed in November. Four months later the single offspring is born. This youngster is about eleven inches long and weighs over one pound. It is open-eyed and fully furred and quilled. The quills, at first soft and covered with a membrane, harden within a half hour after birth. The baby porky can climb by itself when only two days old; in about a week's time it starts to feed itself. At the age of three years the porcupine is mature, although it continues to grow. A full-grown porky measures about thirty inches long and has a six-inch tail. Its usual weight is about fifteen to twenty pounds, but a really big one may tip the scales at over forty pounds. Next to the beaver, the porcupine is the largest rodent in North America. Its principal distinction is that it is the only North American mammal with quills.

A strict vegetarian, the porky in some regions prefers to feed on the bark of evergreens such as hemlock and white pine; in other sections its taste runs to the sugar- and starch-rich inner bark stripped from sugar maple, birch, beech, and other hardwoods. Trees encircled, or girdled, in this way by the porcupine's sharp incisors often die. This animal's craving for salt often makes it a nuisance around a camp or farm. It considers as fair game anything on which the human touch or body has left a residue of salt. Many a saddle, paddle, ax, shovel, or saw handle has been gnawed to shreds by a greedy porky.

Throughout most of its range the porcupine does little damage. Where valuable timber and fruit trees are girdled and killed, however, this can be a very expensive creature to have around. Some states have placed a bounty on the porcupine in an all-out effort to eliminate it from the forests. Other states have laws to protect it, because even a man weakened by exposure and hunger can kill a slow-witted porcupine with the sharp blow of a club on its nose.

Natural controls are provided by the fisher, wolverine, wolf, coyote, bobcat, lynx, and mountain lion. Deadliest of the predators is the fisher, which kills the porcupine by tossing it over on its back and tearing open the unprotected belly, all without undue damage to itself from the quills. Tularemia and other diseases also take their toll of porcupines.

The porky makes an interesting pet, in spite of its owner's having to observe a hands-off policy, and in captivity may live as long as eight years. Its flesh can be eaten and is said to be tender, albeit with a strong flavor of pine bark. The Indians of northern North America used the porcupine's guard hairs in making headdresses and its quills for basket and costume decoration. Otherwise, the porcupine has had little usefulness or economic value to man.

6

❦ ❦ ❦

Carnivora—

Meat-Eaters

Carnivores (*carnis*, meat, *vorare*, to eat) are descended from
the low-slung, long-tailed Creodonts, which appeared during the early Paleocene
epoch and made their final departure during the Pliocene. They inhabit every
land area in the world, with the exception of Antarctica, New Zealand, and
various oceanic islands. In North America, the order Carnivora is represented
by six families: bears (Ursidae), raccoons and coatis (Procyonidae), ringtails
(Bassariscidae), weasels, skunks, and their relatives (Mustelidae), dogs, foxes,
and wolves (Canidae), and cats (Felidae).

These mammals have small incisor teeth, but strong canines and molars for
biting and tearing flesh. They have powerful claws, keen eyesight and sense
of smell, and a great deal of animal intelligence. Although most are ground-
dwellers, some climb well, and others are excellent swimmers. Many carnivores
are strong, swift, and vicious. Almost all are densely furred, and some, such
as the mink, are among the most highly prized furbearers on the market.

Just as some insectivores, bats, and marsupials also feed on meat, certain
species of carnivores supplement their diets with insects and vegetable material.
To obtain a supply of their staple food, the meat-eaters hunt or pursue their
prey. Some travel in packs, but the cats usually prefer to hunt alone. The
predatory, or hunting, mammals benefit man by keeping their prey animals,
principally rodents, under control.

The young of all predatory mammals learn by imitation, as they accompany their parents on nightly forays for food. They observe how the parents hunt, starting their education by catching the easier types of prey, then moving up to more difficult and elusive prey. Predatory mammals raised in captivity have a hard time learning how to hunt if they should escape or be released. Many times, they fail to recognize the prey animal as a potential meal. They have no idea how to stalk it, to capture it, or to kill it. They would have learned all these things naturally by accompanying the parents.

Black Bear
(Ursus euarctos americanus)

SIZE: 6½ feet nose to tail.

WEIGHT: 300–600 pounds.

HABITS: Excellent climber and fast runner. Does not hibernate, but sleeps in den during winter. Cubs stay with mother 2 years, with each other 3 years.

HABITAT: Wooded areas.

FOOD: Fresh meat, carrion, grains, grasses, berries, nuts, fruits, insects.

BREEDING: 1–3 (usually 2) born every other winter. Gestation 7 months.

ENEMIES: Occasionally other bears.

LIFE SPAN: 12–15 years.

In spite of its clumsy appearance, the black bear can run up to twenty-five miles an hour for short distances. The adult bear may weigh as much as 600 pounds.

The most popular bear in the United States today is Smokey, whose picture on National Park Service posters is a reminder that forest fires cost this country about $70,000,000 annually. Rescued as a cub from a New Mexican forest fire in 1950, this black bear responded to treatment and soon became a great pet. Smokey is now housed in the National Zoological Park, Washington, D.C. Such is his fame that he receives over 2,000 pieces of mail every week from school children and even has his own zip code.

In 1902 another black bear cub catapulted to fame when it was adopted as a pet by President Theodore Roosevelt, who refused to shoot it despite the urging of members of his hunting party. Using this cub as the model for a toy, a Brooklyn doll manufacturer obtained White House permission to call it Teddy. This was the first of some 30,000,000 Teddy bears sold in the United States alone.

Modern man is not the first to choose the bear as a symbol. Many American Indian tribes looked upon the black bear as a deity and refused to kill one. Some tribes thought that the bear was kin to man. With its shuffling gait, clumsy appearance, and fondness for getting into mischief, the black bear sometimes is referred to as the clown of the woods. Far from being clumsy, however, this bear can run at a speed of twenty-five miles per hour over short distances and is an excellent climber. Its odd, flat-footed shuffle derives from the fact that the bear walks on the sole of its foot the way humans do. Its generic name sometimes is given as *Eu*, true, *arctos*, bear.

Originally, this smallest, commonest, and most widely dispersed of our bears was found in wooded areas all over North America and throughout Mexico and Central America as well. The black bear is still found in almost every state having heavily wooded areas in which it can hide. Even little New Jersey, with a human population of about 900 people per square mile, has a bear-hunting season. Not many bears are reared in New Jersey; most swim across the Delaware River from Pennsylvania. The black bear has a high degree of natural intelligence and, if given the slightest opportunity to hide, will survive practically on man's doorstep.

Not all black bears are black, although that is the predominant color in the east. Some are brown or cinnamon, shading into bleached blonde. Glacier bears, found near Yakatut Bay, Alaska, are blue. One thing all black bears have in common is a brown face and, usually, a splash of white on the chest. They have short tails, longish muzzles, and small, rounded ears. Their claws are non-retractable, that is, they cannot be drawn back into the toes. Toes and claws show in the bear's tracks, which resemble human footprints.

During most of the year the male is solitary. In the summer he mates with one or more females. Seven months later, while the female is sleeping in winter quarters, the furred, blind, mice-sized cubs are born. Three-year-old females giving birth for the first time usually have a single offspring; thereafter, twins are usual and there are occasionally triplets.

Young bear cubs play almost continually, fighting, biting, and wrestling with each other and with their mother. They remain with her for two years until she is ready to mate again.

The black bear will climb almost any tree that will support its weight.
Here, a bear has left its claw marks on the bark of an aspen tree.

The bear is not a true hibernator, because its body temperature and breathing rate remain unchanged, and it is easily roused from its deep sleep. The den may be a cave, a protected spot beneath the roots of an uprooted tree, or located in a mass of leaves behind a pile of fallen timber that acts as a windbreak. By the time the mother is ready to leave the winter den, the cubs are large enough to follow after her. The family group has no regular den, but roams over a territory encompassing approximately ten square miles.

The black bear mother takes good care of her young, teaching them how to get along when they are on their own and especially how to satisfy their healthy appetites. The cubs play almost continually, fighting, biting, and wrestling with each other and with their mother. While tolerant of most of their actions, she never hesitates to discipline them when necessary. This is accomplished by cuffing hard enough with her paw to send the offender tumbling head over heels. The mother keeps the cubs with her through their first year, as she mates only every other year. When ready to mate again, she either deserts the cubs or sends them away. The cubs stay together until they are about three years old.

Although classified as a carnivore, the bear eats everything from fresh meat, carrion, grasses, berries, and nuts to fruits, grains, and insects. Blueberries are consumed in vast quantities. I have seen acres of blueberry patches torn apart and stripped of their fruit by bears. Acorns are especially favored, and the ease with which they are gathered helps to layer fat on the bear's body. The bear also is partial to pork and somtimes raids backyard pigpens. Beehives always are prime targets for pilfering, for the bear is notorious for its sweet tooth and will eat adult bees and larvae as well as the honey and comb. It is easy to pick out an apple tree that has been worked over by a bear to reach the fruit, as most of the outer limbs will be broken off and pulled in toward the trunk of the tree.

Eating so much of anything and everything, the bear grows rapidly and puts on a lot of fat. From a birth weight of eight ounces, the black bear grows to an average weight of 300 to 400 pounds and to a total length of over six feet from nose to tail. A really big boar (male) may weigh up to 600 pounds. The female usually is smaller in size and lighter in weight. Owing to its size and strength, the bear has to contend with few enemies, with the exception of man, during the twelve to fifteen years of its existence in the wild. Occasionally, the male poses a threat to the cubs, as many bears are cannibalistic, so the female loses no time in attacking him. Aware that the boar would not hesitate to devour one of his own offspring, she charges him with a roar of anger and drives him away.

In its search for food, the bear now and then raids the camps of hunters and fishermen and even breaks into a cabin. The black bear also is quick to take advantage of free handouts. In Yellowstone, Glacier, Yosemite, and Great Smoky National Parks, it loses its native caution and intelligence and becomes a professional panhandler. Remember that it is dangerous to feed a bear. All too frequently it becomes angry when you run out of food to give away. Many persons who have attempted to feed bears have been clawed or bitten by them, so it is best to obey the park rules and "don't feed the bears."

The black bear is hunted for sport, for the oil derived from its fat, and for its pelt. In 1953, 3,000 pelts were fashioned into guardsmen's busbies for the coronation of Great Britain's Queen Elizabeth II. Bear meat is dark and, with the fat trimmed off, edible. Bear grease is used for softening boot leather.

Raccoon
(Procyon lotor)

SIZE: 26–38 inches, including 10-inch tail.

WEIGHT: 15–20 pounds; occasionally up to 60 pounds.

HABITS: Plays with or "washes" food before eating. Nocturnal; retreats to den during cold weather but does not hibernate.

HABITAT: Partially cleared land with trees.

FOOD: Birds, mammals, carrion, poultry, fish, frogs, shellfish, fruits, nuts, vegetables, grains, berries.

BREEDING: Annual litter of 2–6. Gestation 64 days.

ENEMIES: Foxes, bobcats, owls, dogs.

LIFE SPAN: 14 years.

Young raccoons have such an inquisitive nature that they try to handle everything within reach. Frequently they appear to "wash" their food before eating.

The word that best describes the raccoon is adaptability. In the face of an ever-increasing human population, the raccoon not only is holding its own, but also is adding to its numbers and its range. This familiar, sharp-nosed, black-masked, ring-tailed, mischievous mammal is widely dispersed. Except for sections of the Rocky Mountains, the raccoon is found throughout the United States, in southern Canada, and into Central America, wherever there is water.

If any American mammal can be said to have hands, that mammal is the raccoon, which the Algonquin Indians called *arakunem*, "he who scratches with his hands." The raccoon has such an inquisitive nature that it tries to handle everything within reach. Its Latin name *lotor*, washer, refers to the animal's habit of handling food that might have been trapped in mud or sand. Water accentuates the sense of touch in the many sensitive nerve endings of the five, long, flexible toes of the raccoon's black forepaws. As much of the raccoon's food is secured in or near water, this "washing" action is frequently seen. It is also seen when food is eaten far from water, and sometimes it is not seen at all. The raccoon's salivary glands are well developed, so that this washing or softening up of the food is not needed. The answer may be that the raccoon, or coon, simply enjoys feeling and playing with its food.

The raccoon likes partially cleared land that still retains stands of maple, beech, and oak. Although preferring to den in hollow trees, it frequently is

Two baby raccoons stand at the entrance of their den in the hollow of a tree. Even the young have well-defined black masks.

found in caves, mines, woodchuck burrows, drain tiles, rock ledges, and even in barns and under buildings. Curled up in a ball or stretched out flat on its back with forepaws over its eyes, the coon sleeps the day away, emerging at dusk to search for food. Although the raccoon does not hibernate, it becomes inactive and dens up when the temperature drops below 26 degrees.

Like its big cousin the bear, the raccoon is omnivorous. Its diet consists of young birds, small mammals, carrion, poultry, fish, frogs, and shellfish. Crayfish are eaten avidly. All types of fruits, nuts, berries, vegetables, and grains are enjoyed. Whenever sweet or field corn is in the milk stage, the coon goes into a frenzied orgy of gluttony. It consumes all the corn it can hold and wantonly destroys perhaps two or three times that amount. The coon never completely finishes eating the corn on one ear before hurrying to climb up the next stalk to pull down a fresh one.

From late January until March, the promiscuous male seeks a mate. Although its home range usually covers about two to four square miles, the male may travel as much as fifteen miles a night in the breeding season, taking shelter wherever it happens to be when daylight breaks. Gestation requires sixty-four days, and the annual litter may contain two to six young, although three or four is most common. The young have coats of fuzzy fur and well-defined black masks. Long before their eyes open, in about nineteen days,

A young raccoon climbing on a dead tree. The babies often find climbing up easier than climbing down and squeal for mother from the top of the tree.

the young coons are able to move about spider-fashion on outstretched legs. This is a climbing reflex; little raccoons can climb, or at least cling to the rough bark of a tree, even before they can see.

In six weeks the young venture forth and immediately become involved in all kinds of predicaments. Like most young animals, baby raccoons find climbing up easier than climbing down. On reaching the topmost branches of a tree, they hang on and squeal for mother. Up she goes to fetch them by the scruff of the neck and bring them back to the den. A raccoon usually descends from its perch tail first, but it is almost as accomplished an acrobat as the gray squirrel. When contented, young raccoons make a churring sound. Adults churr, growl, hiss, and make a sound like a screech owl.

As soon as the young coons are strong enough to follow her, the mother takes them to the ponds and streamsides to hunt for food. At the first sign of danger, she hustles her brood up the nearest tree. Many of the larger mammals, such as the fox and bobcat, kill a young coon when possible, and the great horned owl also takes its toll. The bobcat could kill an adult raccoon, but is unlikely to tackle this ferocious battler.

The raccoon's dense, durable fur was highly valued by the Indians. Powhatan supposedly presented to Captain John Smith a coonskin robe in the early 1600s. In Colonial times coonskin caps were worn with the black-and-white ringed tail hanging down on one side, and coonskins were used for currency in the Mississippi Valley states. In the 1920s, when every college boy had to have a raccoon coat and the pelts were high in price, the coon was hunted almost to extinction. The fur has now dropped in value, after a short-lived boom in Davy Crockett caps in the early 1960s, and the number of raccoons has sky-rocketed until in most areas they are considered a nuisance. Hunters rugged enough to stay out all night chasing raccoons with their hounds seem to be in short supply these days.

The raccoon is a superior game animal. Its large size, compact body build, sharp teeth and claws, plus its determination, make it a formidable quarry. The average adult raccoon weighs between fifteen and twenty pounds, although some big males have tipped the scales at from fifty-five to sixty pounds. Pound for pound, a big old boar coon can beat any dog his size. But because most coon dogs are much heavier and fight in packs, the raccoon usually comes out the loser. If the raccoon can reach water, the tables usually are turned, for the coon is likely to climb right up on the swimming dog's head and drown it. Many a coon becomes adept at escaping from pursuing dogs, employing various ruses and utilizing different escape routes. The practice of all family members to seek refuge in the same tree is disastrous, for a careless hunter there may wipe out the entire family. The raccoon that seeks safety underground has the greatest chance of survival.

The raccoon conflicts very little with man's interests. Even the damage done to crops frequently is the work of squirrels. In the southern part of its range, where its coat often is of poor quality, the coon commonly is killed for its meat, which is said to taste like a combination of chicken and lamb.

More persons try to make pets out of raccoons than of any other wild creature. Attractive, appealing, and intelligent, the coon may live to an age of perhaps fourteen years in captivity. It cannot be allowed to run loose in the house, owing to its penchant for getting into mischief. The damage it can do is almost beyond belief. With its dextrous paws, the coon opens doors, bottles, and latches. It is almost impossible to restrict a raccoon, however, unless you confine it to a cage. After a year's time, most pet raccoons have a tendency to become nasty and to bite—as I have the scars to prove.

Coatimundi
(Nasua narica)

SIZE: 50 inches total, about half of which is tail. Male about twice as large as female.

WEIGHT: Up to 20 pounds.

HABITS: It may twine its tail around limbs when climbing. Male travels alone; females and young in bands of 50 or more.

HABITAT: Forests, desert canyons, rimrock.

FOOD: Small mammals, birds, eggs, fruits, berries, nuts, grains, iguanas, grubs, insects, vegetables.

BREEDING: Litter of 3–5 born any time of year. Gestation 71–77 days.

ENEMIES: Jaguars, ocelots, mountain lions, bobcats, coyotes, wolves, dogs.

LIFE SPAN: Captives live to 14 years.

A cousin of the raccoon, the coatimundi is equally at home in tree tops or on the forest floor. The coati twines its long tail around branches when it climbs and uses its snout to root out grubs, insects, and vegetables from the ground.

This long-tailed cousin of the raccoon comes in two distinct color phases, one predominantly reddish, the other grayish. Across its eyes the coati wears a dark mask; above and below each eye is a white spot. The chin, breast, and underparts are a yellowish-white. The partly ringed tail is the coati's most noticeable feature. Long, tapering, and sparsely furred, it is carried almost perfectly erect, with just the tip bent over. The tail is not prehensile, yet the coati twines it around a limb when it climbs. When the coati wants to turn around, it rises on its hind legs and pivots around on its hind feet, using the tail as a balancing pole to maintain its upright posture.

This action comes naturally to an animal accustomed to turning around on a narrow tree limb high in the air, for the coati is equally at home in the tree-tops or running about on the forest floor. Rare in the United States, the coati-mundi is found only in southern Arizona and New Mexico, in hot desert canyons and rimrock. Most naturalists agree that this animal is enlarging its range, so that they should be encountered in larger numbers. This northward migration of coatis undoubtedly is being brought about by the gradual warming trend of temperatures over the country.

The male is about twice as large as the female, and at one time it was believed to represent a different species. A large male may have a total length of fifty inches or more, half of which will be its tail. It measures about ten or eleven inches high at the shoulder and weighs up to twenty pounds. Living in a warm climate, the coati may breed at any time of year. The male is polyg-amous, and young have been found in both spring and fall. Three to five blind, furred young coatis are born at one time. In about eighteen days the eyes open, and in another three to four months the young are capable of caring for themselves.

The den may be a hollow tree, a nest in the treetops, or a fissure or cave in the rocks. At any time of the day or night the coati may be active. It sleeps whenever it chooses to, even through the intense heat of the tropical midday in some parts of its range. The rest of the time it is busily searching for something to eat. While the male prefers to travel alone, the females and their young tend to travel in bands of perhaps fifty or more.

Described by its generic name *Nasua* as the nosey one, and often called hog-nosed coon, the coati has a long, rubbery, flexible nose, which it uses in the same way a pig uses its snout to root out from the ground grubs, insects, tubers, and other vegetables. Like its raccoon cousin, the coati will eat almost anything. Small mammals, birds, eggs, fruits, berries, nuts, and grains are utilized for food, but only rarely does the coati feed on domestic fowl. A partic-ular delicacy is the large tree lizard, or iguana. Although the iguana looks sluggish, it is a rare coati that can catch one by itself. The iguana remains motionless as the coati climbs up the tree. When the coati approaches and is a few feet away, the iguana drops to the ground and scampers up another tree. When a band of coatis feed together, the story has a different ending. One member of the band flushes the iguana from its hiding place in the tree, while the others wait on the ground for the lizard to drop. Then the iguana is torn to pieces and eaten. Cooperation of this kind in hunting denotes more than average intelligence, yet it is quite common in the mammal world.

Jaguars, ocelots, mountain lions, bobcats, coyotes, and wolves feed on the coati. Many dogs are trained to hunt this animal because the natives of Mexico and Central America use it for food. It takes a big dog to kill a full-grown coati, which will try to escape by climbing into the treetops and leaping from one tree to another. If cornered on the ground, the coati is capable of putting up a good fight, making deep slashes with its long canine teeth and using its claws to rake its aggressor into ribbons.

Coati pelts have no commercial value, because the hair is sparse and stiff. When taken young, the coati may be tamed as a pet and is as endearing and affectionate as the raccoon. As it grows older it may turn nasty, but this is to be expected with almost any wild animal in captivity. Like the raccoon, the coati cannot be given its freedom in the house; driven by its curiosity, it soon has the place turned into a shambles.

Ringtail

(Bassariscus astutus)

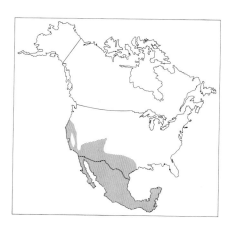

SIZE: 32 inches, including 17-inch tail.

WEIGHT: 2½ pounds.

HABITS: Nocturnal. Adults remain together after young are grown. Emits sweet odor when frightened.

HABITAT: Wooded, rocky country.

FOOD: Rats, mice, squirrels, chipmunks, bats, gophers, birds, eggs, reptiles, insects, fruits, nuts.

BREEDING: Litter of 3–4 born May or June.

ENEMIES: Owls, snakes, large mammals.

LIFE SPAN: Up to 8 years.

The ringtail's most prominent feature is an abundant black and white tail measuring seventeen inches long. The large black eyes help it see during the nighttime hours when it is most active.

The Aztec Indians of Mexico called this cousin of the raccoon *cacomixtle*, rush cat, but it has a bewildering number of popular names as well—ring-tailed cat, coon cat, band-tailed cat, mountain cat, American civet cat, squirrel cat, and raccoon fox are some of them. Its Latin name means clever (*astutus*) fox, which is about as appropriate a description as you could find.

Topping its sharply pointed, fox-like features are large, erect ears and extra-large black eyes that enable the little creature to see in the darkness during its nocturnal activities. Its coat is golden tan with lighter underparts. The ringtail's most prominent feature is its black-and-white ringed tail, larger and more luxuriant than that of the raccoon. When full grown, it is about thirty-two inches long, including its seventeen-inch tail. The five toes on each foot have partly retractible claws. This feature helps to protect the claw tips when the ringtail clambers among the rocks, caves, or old, abandoned Indian dwellings in the wooded or desert areas of the Far West and Southwest where it makes its home.

Sometimes called miner's cat, the ringtail soon rids a mine shaft of every mouse and rat foolhardy enough to seek refuge there. Thus, it is seldom driven away if it attempts to make its home in a cabin or farm barn. In addition to rats and mice, its diet includes ground squirrels, gophers, chipmunks, bats, small reptiles, birds and their eggs, insects of many kinds, and all types of fruits and nuts.

In turn, the ringtail is fair game for any large mammal that can catch it. Because it is quick and alert, it is able to elude most of its enemies. The great horned owl probably takes the greatest toll among adults, while the snake is about the only predator that can squeeze through the narrow rock crevasses and into the small hollows in trees to get at the young in the nest.

In May or June the female gives birth to a normal litter of three or four young. The male leaves the den to seek shelter elsewhere, returning within a few weeks to help provide food for the young. The babies' almost hairless tails clearly show dark rings, and their eyes are sealed for about a month. They are nursed until about six or seven weeks old, then receive basic instruction in hunting from their parents and learn how to forage for themselves. At four months of age, young ringtails leave the parental den and strike out on their own. The adults remain together after the young are grown.

The ringtail has musk glands that give off an unoffensive, sweetish odor. The scent cannot be thrown or ejected like that of the skunk, but just oozes out when the animal is frightened. This musk probably is used to communicate by means of scent posts. Very rarely, the ringtail is seen out in the daytime, taking a sun bath. Even then it is seldom more than a jump or two from the den into which it quickly retires if disturbed. If disturbed during the daytime it wears a look of perpetual confusion or puzzlement and occasionally makes a rasping barking noise as if unable to figure out why anyone would want to disturb it.

Curiosity often overcomes this extremely shy creature, which cannot refrain from investigating everything it comes upon. Trappers take advantage of this trait, and the pelts of thousands of these little animals are sold commercially, in spite of the low price they command. The fur is used for trimming inexpensive coats, while the tails are sometimes seen flying from automobile antennas or motorcycle handlebars.

Gentle-natured and easily tamed, the ringtail makes a fairly good pet. Owing to its nocturnal habits, however, it prefers to sleep throughout the day. If you want to play with your pet, you will have to reschedule your period of activity to conform with the ringtail's.

Fisher
(Martes pennanti)

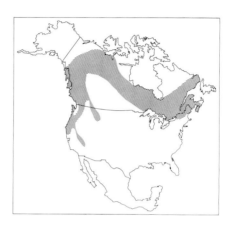

SIZE: *38 inches, including 12-inch tail. Female about ⅓ size of male.*
WEIGHT: *15 pounds.*
HABITS: *Excellent climber and runner. Stores uneaten food.*
HABITAT: *Coniferous forests.*
FOOD: *Fish, chipmunks, squirrels, weasels, mink, marten, muskrats, porcupines, birds, eggs, frogs, insects, nuts.*
BREEDING: *1 litter of 3 (average) per year. Gestation 350 days.*
ENEMIES: *No natural predators can catch it when full-grown.*
LIFE SPAN: *8–10 years.*

One of the fastest tree-climbing mammals in the world, the fisher can outclimb even a squirrel or a marten. It is so fast on the ground that it frequently will attack a porcupine—an animal most other predators avoid.

The name fisher may have been given to this large American weasel because of its fondness for fish. Trappers found fish to be excellent bait for catching this animal. The fisher also avidly consumes dead fish that wash up on shore, regularly following along stream and river banks within its territory in search of this delicacy. Although a swimmer, the fisher does not enter the water to catch fish.

Other names given the fisher include black cat, black fox, and Pennant's cat (after Thomas Pennant, an early authority on North American furbearers). Most appropriate of all was the Chipewyan Indian name *tha-cho*, big marten. About twice the size of the marten, an adult male fisher may weigh up to fifteen pounds, have an overall length of thirty-eight inches (including a bushy, twelve-inch tail), and stand about ten inches high at the shoulder. It has the short legs and sharply pointed head of the weasel clan, and the ears are short and rounded. The silky, dark brown underfur, protected by white-tipped guard hairs, shades to jet black over its rump. The female is about one-third the size of the male. Both sexes have a distinct odor, but it is not so strong as that of most weasels.

Although never really plentiful, the fisher originally had a much more extensive range than the one it now enjoys. In the time of the early settlers, the fisher was found as far south as the Appalachian Mountains in North Carolina. Through excessive trapping, the fisher was almost wiped out in the United States. Today, thanks to rigid protective laws and importation, the fisher is making a strong comeback in the Adirondack Mountains of New York and in New Hampshire and Vermont. It is still found in the Sierras and in some sections of the Rocky Mountains. Ontario, Quebec, and British Columbia are fisher strongholds in Canada.

The regions inhabited by the fisher today are those possessing the deep coniferous forests that it prefers. Although more of a ground dweller than its close relative, the marten, the fisher is one of the fastest tree-climbing mammals in the world. Most of you probably have seen a gray squirrel or the even swifter red squirrel climb about on a tree. A pine marten is so fast that it can outclimb a red squirrel. The fisher is faster still, so fast that it can outclimb the marten. Anything faster would have to be flying.

On the ground the fisher is almost as fast, and so strong and persistent that it can run down a varying hare. Chipmunks, squirrels, mink, weasels, marten, muskrats, young birds, eggs, everything that can be caught is consumed by the fisher. It also likes frogs, insects, and nuts, and even kills a deer bogged in deep snow. Although the fisher often kills in excess of its immediate needs, it is extremely frugal, storing or caching every bit of uneaten food to be used at a later date. This creature of the northern wilds has no need to be reminded of the harsh winters, when food of any kind is exceedingly scarce.

One odd item of diet the fisher thrives on is the porcupine. Whereas most other animals go out of their way to avoid a porcupine, the fisher actively seeks it out. If the porcupine is on the ground, the fisher uses its blinding speed to dart around the porcupine until it can reach a forepaw under the creature's unprotected belly and flip the porky over on its back. Before the porky can right itself, the fisher has torn out its stomach. If, on the other hand, the porcupine is up in a tree, the agile fisher streaks up the tree and underneath the branch where the porky has sought refuge and quickly knocks it over. Even where the fisher eats the porcupine quills, they seem to have little ill effect on its digestive system. The fisher doesn't always win; several of these animals, with their faces full of quills, have been found dead of starvation. Authorities are trying to re-establish the fisher in New England in the hope that it will help to control the number of porcupines that have done so much damage by girdling valuable forest trees.

Because of its speed and its nocturnal habits, the fisher has little to fear from any predator except man. The fisher likes to roam alone over its territory and resents any interference. Intruders are warned off with hisses and growls. If the fisher is aloft in the trees, it descends headfirst and taps out a warning against the tree trunk, alternating with one forepaw, then the other.

The fisher leads a solitary existence, except for the two or three days of the mating season in late spring. The female seeks a hollow tree, log, or rock cavity having an entrance hole no wider than four or five inches. The small hole is needed to give protection to the young while the female is out searching for food. Almost a year (350 days) after mating, the female gives birth to an average litter of three blind, helpless young. The gestation period of the fisher, along with some other carnivores such as the bear and the marten, is unusually long due to delayed implantation. These animals breed at various times of the year, but the fertilized egg does not become attached to the wall of the uterus until the proper number of months remain for the embryo to develop and be born in the spring—when chances are best for survival of the babies. The mother fisher, one week after giving birth, leaves her young temporarily to seek a new mate. She does not allow the male to come near the babies, for he may kill and eat them. After mating, the female hurries back to her domestic duties.

At seven weeks of age, the little ones' eyes open. As soon as they are three months old and can follow her, the mother takes them hunting. The group explores its hunting territory, seeking a different den site every night. By the middle of summer, the young leave the mother. They are ready to mate at two years of age.

This rarely seen animal is hunted and trapped for its valuable, silky fur. The female's is of finer quality than the male's and so commands a higher price. Because the fisher does not breed readily in captivity, it is not raised commercially on a large scale.

Long-Tailed Weasel
(Mustela frenata)

Size: *12–20 inches, including 4–6-inch tail. Female much smaller.*

Weight: *12 ounces.*

Habits: *Fur turns white in winter. Often kills in excess of needs. Emits strong-smelling musk when frightened.*

Habitat: *Woods or fields.*

Food: *Mice, rats, chipmunks, poultry.*

Breeding: *1 litter of 3–6 per year. Gestation 220–337 days.*

Enemies: *Lynxes, mink, martens, fishers, house cats, birds of prey.*

Life span: *5 years.*

The weasel's long, low-slung body is well adapted to pursuing its prey into underground burrows. It hunts by scent, with its nose held close to the ground.

The various species of weasel are found all across North America from the Arctic down through Central and South America. Most common and most widely distributed of the true weasels is this long-tailed member, whose generic name *Mustela* means "those who carry off mice." It frequents almost every type of habitat throughout its vast range.

The weasel looks like a snake with legs. An adult male measures from twelve to twenty inches in length, including a four- to six-inch tail. The female is much smaller. Its back and sides are dark brown. The underparts are creamy white, and the long tail has a black tip. In the Southwest, this weasel has a white band, or bridle, across its face. During the winter in northern regions the fur turns white, with the exception of the black tail tip. This winter pelage is known as ermine. As in the varying hare, the color change is the result of reduced light passing through the animal's eye to stimulate activity of the pituitary gland, which controls the amount of pigment going into its hair. Sometimes the change is only partial, so that the winter pelage has a piebald or spotted coloration.

In the spring following a late summer or fall mating, three to six blind, pink-skinned young are born. One litter per year is normal. An underground den, rocky crevasse, or mole burrow is chosen for the den. The parents provide well for the young, and the nest, lined with feathers, bones, and fur of their prey, is warm and soft. Although their eyes do not open until the fifth week, the baby weasels are weaned and able to crawl about in the den long before then. The male usually helps provide food for the young. At seven or eight weeks of age, the youngsters are old enough to hunt. They stay with the female until late summer, when they go off on their own.

Day or night, even in the coldest weather, the weasel is out hunting. Occasionally it may hole up for a day or so, but it is such a high-strung bundle of energy that it cannot stay long in one spot. In the soft snow, weasel tracks can be seen leading from one bit of cover to another. Every hole, nook, and cranny is explored. The weasel climbs and swims, but is essentially a ground hunter.

As a major predator of small rodents, the weasel's long, low-slung body is well adapted to pursuing its prey deep into underground burrows, where it is then killed. This is one of the few mammals that seems to kill out of sheer pleasure; often it kills far in excess of its needs. Wild prey often is cached, to be eaten at a later date. So long as this devastation is directed against mice and rats, man is the beneficiary. The weasel becomes the enemy of man when it preys on his livestock and poultry. Once inside a chicken coop, a weasel may indulge in such an orgy of bloodletting that it may kill sixty to seventy chickens in a single night.

On the farm where I was raised we once had to get a weasel out of the barn in a hurry. It had been attracted to the barn by the presence of mice around the feed box. As our chicken coop was only about 100 feet away from the barn, we couldn't take a chance on having a weasel around. Four or five of us set about getting rid of it. That weasel was so fast and so agile that it made all of us look like clumsy clowns. When we moved the feed box away from the wall to flush out the weasel, the animal shot around the other side of the box, scampered underneath it, and up over the top. It appeared wherever we least expected it. Try as we could, we could not catch the beast. Once the weasel sprang off the lid of the feed box, ran up my sister's arm, and leaped off her shoulder. This happened so fast that she did not have a chance to be frightened, and the weasel obviously did not realize that she was one of the enemies. The weasel finally ended the chase by dashing out the barn door. It had had enough, apparently, because it did not come back to molest our chickens.

A fierce little creature, the weasel never hesitates to tackle animals much larger than itself. An adult male weighs about twelve ounces, yet weasels often feed on rabbits that weigh four or five times as much. On one occasion I discovered a weasel dragging a young rabbit that it had killed across an open field. When I approached, the weasel dropped its victim, ran off a short distance, then stopped to watch me. I took a few steps back, and immediately the weasel returned to its kill. Again I approached, and again the weasel ran off. Once more, I stepped backward. The weasel returned to its prey and started to drag it off. When I approached this time the weasel refused to relinquish the rabbit, and a tug-of-war ensued. At one juncture, as I lifted the rabbit clear of the ground, the weasel, too, was swung aloft, loudly squealing its protests. I finally put the rabbit down, and the weasel lost no time in dragging it under a nearby woodpile.

Although it hunts by scent, with its nose held close to the ground, the weasel's senses of sight and hearing are well developed. It bounds along until it starts its prey or locates a hot track. Stopping to investigate, the weasel swings its small head atop its long, sinuous neck from side to side. Even though most of its prey can run faster, the weasel is persistent and usually overtakes its exhausted victim or corners it in a hole. The weasel kills its prey by biting through the back of the neck at the base or by cutting through the jugular vein. Most rabbits hesitate to den up in holes if weasels live in the vicinity.

In turn, the weasel is preyed upon by larger animals, such as the lynx, mink, marten, fisher, fox, bobcat, house cat, and by the raptatorial birds of prey. The great horned owl is the weasel's chief enemy, because both are night hunters seeking the same prey in the same area. The larger, stronger owl usually is the victor, yet there are several instances where the bodies of both protagonists have been found locked together in death. The weasel's speed and agility make it a difficult prey to catch, and the strong-smelling musk secreted by glands under its tail is enough to discourage all but the most determined predator.

The weasel's lack of fear makes it easy to trap, because it doesn't associate danger with a trap. Its fur is soft and durable, the best North American pelts coming from Alaska. Although weasel or ermine pelts are worth only about $1.50 each, they are traditionally associated with royalty and are used in trimming royal robes. Over 50,000 ermine pelts were used on the occasion of the coronation of King George VI of Great Britain in 1937.

When taken young, the weasel can be tamed, but makes a somewhat noisy pet. The young squeak and the adults bark and hiss. In captivity, a weasel may live for about five years.

Mink
(Mustela vison)

SIZE: 20–30 inches, including 8-inch tail. Female about half size of male.

WEIGHT: 3½ pounds.

HABITS: Emits offensive, acrid scent when frightened; usually active day and night, but becomes nocturnal where hunted.

HABITAT: Woodlands, near lakes, ponds, or streams.

FOOD: Fish, frogs, salamanders, snakes, waterfowl, eggs, small mammals, including rodents, rabbits, muskrats, chickens.

BREEDING: 1 litter of 5–8 per year. Gestation 45 days or longer.

ENEMIES: Bobcats, lynxes, owls, foxes.

LIFE SPAN: Up to 10 years.

The wild mink's fur is uniformly dark brown to black. Because of the high prices paid for pelts, this little animal is becoming increasingly scarce.

Today, mink is one of the most sought-after furs in the world. But it is not only a status symbol. Mink fur is also luxurious—with a high sheen that traps and reflects light—and durable. With the demand keeping the prices of their pelts high, wild mink are becoming increasingly scarce, at least in the eastern United States.

The wild mink's fur is uniformly dark brown to black overall. Usually, there is a white spot under the chin and sometimes one on the chest. Occasionally, a mink has light underfur and is known as a cotton mink. Such pelts are practically worthless. Larger than its long-tailed weasel relative, and possessing a bushier tail, the mink has a weasel-like long neck and body, small, sharply pointed face, small ears, and short legs. It varies in length from twenty to thirty inches, of which about eight inches is tail, and stands about four to five inches high at the shoulder. A big male weighs about three and a half pounds. The female is about half the size of the male.

All members of the weasel family have scent glands. Although the skunk has better control and can direct the spraying of its scent, the mink's actually is the more offensive of the two. The mink, furthermore, is not as reluctant to use its acrid scent as the skunk is. The mink also appears to use its scent more as a courting display to attract members of the opposite sex than as a defensive mechanism.

The mink mates in February or March, when it is about one year old. Both male and female are promiscuous. After impregnating every available female the male moves in with one of the females to help her raise the family. The den selected may be located under a stone pile or under the roots of a large tree growing near the water. Sometimes the mink takes over a deserted wood-chuck hole or the house of a muskrat that it has killed. Gestation is usually about forty-five days, but may be longer.

At birth, the five to eight young in the litter are blind, but their bodies are covered with fine hair. The mother nurses the young until they are about five weeks old and their eyes have opened. They are fed solid food and soon are allowed to go outside the den. Both parents share the task of caring for the young. When necessary, the adults pick up the young and carry them by the scruff of the neck. In the water they allow the little ones to ride piggyback.

The mink lives near lakes, ponds, streams, and other water courses throughout the greater part of North America from the Arctic Circle to Mexico. Aided by the webbing of stiff hairs between the toes of its hind feet, a mink can outswim a fish. Out of the water, a mink is as playful as the otter and shares its fond-ness for sliding down muddy stream banks.

Much of the mink's food is taken in or near water. In addition to fish, the mink eats frogs, salamanders, snakes, waterfowl and their eggs. Small mammals, such as mice, rats, chipmunks, rabbits, and muskrats, are preyed upon. Some-times a family of mink may wipe out an entire muskrat colony. Often a mink takes over a muskrat's house for its own. Like the weasel, the mink commonly kills in excess of its needs. Around a barn it soon wipes out all the rats and mice—and the farmer's chickens as well. Usually, the mink carries back its surplus food to a den where it can move in with its supplies.

The mink may be active day or night, although in areas where it is hunted and trapped, it becomes exclusively nocturnal. Yet I have seen mink running along the edge of the Delaware River just a few feet from the thundering noise of truck traffic on New Jersey's Highway 46. Mink are a common sight in the daytime along Canadian lakes and rivers. In the summer, the entire family hunts over a large territory and covers every body of water in the area. By fall the family splits up, each member going its separate way. The female has a small area that can be hunted over every two or three nights, while the male has an extensive range that may require ten days to circle.

When traveling on land the mink bounds along. This tireless gait can be kept up for hours. Although the mink can climb, it seems reluctant to do so. In all but the bitterest weather, the mink is out hunting every night. During cold spells it may curl up and sleep for several days.

The mink is an unsociable creature and gets into frequent fights, squealing,

A mink emerges from a hollow log. In areas where it is hunted or trapped, this little animal comes out only at night.

hissing, and making a terrific racket. Many mink pelts are badly scarred from these battles. But a mink coat, especially when worn by a mink, can take a lot of punishment. When caught in a trap, a mink is a real fury. Woe to the careless trapper who lets a hand or leg get near the captured animal. Aside from man, the mink is preyed upon by the bobcat, lynx, fox, and the great horned and snowy owls. As a general rule, this swift, ferocious little mammal can kill anything smaller than itself and can escape from anything larger.

About two-fifths of the marketable pelts come from mink ranches, where the animals are raised in separate wire pens. Mink were first raised commercially by H. Ressegue of Oneida, New York, in 1866. Today most of the mink ranches are located in the northern tier of states and in Canada. The mink should be raised where the climate is cold enough to require the animal to produce a good coat of fur for warmth. This is why the fur of mammals caught in the southern states is less valuable than the same type of fur taken in the north. The preferred breeding stock is a cross between the dark Labrador and large Alaskan specimens. A ranch mink may live for about ten years.

So many different color variations have been developed that a wild mink would have trouble recognizing its captive cousin by sight. The pure white mink is known as the jasmine. The hope, tourmaline, and autumn haze are various shades of pastel brown, while the silverblu and cerulean are pastel shades of gray or blue. About seventy pelts are needed for a full-length mink coat. Prices paid for wild mink usually run about $15 to $25 per pelt, while the various types of ranch mink bring from $30 for the regular brown mink to $400 per pelt for some of the mutations.

Wolverine
(Gulo luscus)

SIZE: 44 inches, including 6-inch tail. Female slightly smaller.

WEIGHT: 25–35 pounds.

HABITS: Solitary, strong, hunts by stealth. Destructive to hunters' traps, eating kill. Gluttonous appetite.

HABITAT: Forests, bushland, tundra.

FOOD: Rabbits, mice, gophers, rats, birds, eggs, carrion, trapped animals.

BREEDING: Litter of 2–3 born per year. Gestation 120 days.

ENEMIES: No natural predators.

LIFE SPAN: Up to 16 years.

One of the strongest animals in the world for its size, the wolverine has sharp teeth, powerful claws, and a gluttonous appetite. It often causes trouble to trappers by springing their traps or devouring their kill.

The wolverine is a powerhouse, one of the strongest mammals in the world for its size, with rippling muscles, sharp teeth, strong claws, and a surly disposition. A fearless fighter, it readily attacks animals twice its size and has no natural predators. Numerous instances have been recorded of wolverines driving bears away from their kills. Once a wolverine was seen forcing a pack of wolves to abandon their supper so that it might take over.

The wolverine's attitude is that if anything can be eaten, it should be. In some areas it has been appropriately nicknamed the glutton. Its generic name *Gulo* refers to the gullet, or esophagus, the tube that conveys swallowed food into the stomach. The wolverine's powerful, efficient, and fast-acting digestive juices enable it to eat large amounts of food in a very short period of time. Although it feeds on carrion and any trapped animal or food that it can steal, the wolverine catches most of its food by itself. This commonly consists of rabbits, mice, gophers, marmots, rats, birds, and birds' eggs and young.

This largest member of the weasel family is an animal of forests, brushland, and tundra. Once found throughout the northern United States, the wolverine is rarely seen outside of Canada. From time to time, a stray wolverine is reported from one of the far western states, but this a rare occurrence.

An adult male measures about forty-four inches in length, of which six inches is its stubby tail, stands about fifteen inches high at the shoulder, and weighs around twenty-five to thirty-five pounds. The female is slightly smaller. The wolverine's long, fine, dark brown fur is marked with a light tan streak on either side of its body. It is a plantigrade mammal, meaning that it walks on the soles of its feet, like the bear and man. The wolverine can keep up its awkward, shuffling lope for hours without tiring. An inveterate traveler, it may wander over a home range covering hundreds of square miles, sleeping in any available shelter. In spite of its awkwardness, the wolverine climbs trees well and doesn't hesitate to swim if the need arises.

Like other weasels, the wolverine has scent glands from which it ejects a strong musk when angered. The musk also is sprayed on food, despoiling it to discourage other animals from taking it. This habit prompted the Indians in Canada to give the wolverine yet another nickname—skunk-bear.

Inside a trapper's lodge, a wolverine quickly devours everything in sight.

The wolverine does not attack man, but can cause him a great deal of trouble. While some of the trappers' stories and Indian legends extolling this animal's superior cunning are exaggerated, others are not. It is the wolverine's voracious appetite that gets it into trouble with man and makes it thoroughly hated and despised. Many trappers have been forced to expend long hours and vast amounts of energy in catching a wolverine that was plaguing their traplines. The choice was between catching the animal or going out of business.

Upon discovering a trapline, the wolverine follows the packed trail made by the trapper's snowshoes. When the trap is reached, the animal either devours the bait or kills and eats any furbearer that may have been caught in the trap. It is extremely difficult to catch a wolverine in a trap. When the wolverine finds one, it may spring the trap by turning it upside down or by dropping a stick into it. This canny mammal has even been known to carry the trap away and bury it in deep snow. Because this animal is so strong, large traps must be used. Trappers sometimes fasten the trap to a small, movable log, so that the ensnared wolverine cannot get a solid pull on the trap and release itself. There have been instances when the wolverine pulled both trap and log for miles before being tracked down and killed. Some Indians quit trapping and move away when a wolverine enters their area, for the animal will continue to raid their traps daily until it is caught and killed.

When a wolverine breaks into a trapper's cabin, it makes a shambles of the place in short order. Everything edible is devoured; the rest is ripped apart and sprayed with musk. Using its strong canines, the wolverine punctures and tears open all the canned goods. Literally nothing is safe from this rapacious mammal. The trapper whose isolated cabin may be hundreds of miles from a store may get very hungry himself before he can replace the food spoiled by the wolverine. The glutton has also been known to carry off food it cannot eat immediately and cache it for a later repast.

Probably it is just as well that wolverines are scarce and solitary by nature. The only time several are seen together is during the brief mating season in late summer or early fall. As is usual with many solitary mammals, the two or three young are not born until the following spring. They are nursed by the mother until late summer, remaining with her for a year or two. At four years of age, the young are sexually mature. Wolverines have a life span of about sixteen years.

Wolverine fur is in demand for trimming the hoods of parkas and brings a good price. The fur is valued by travelers in the far north because it remains frost-free and does not mat or ice up when the parka wearer's hot breath is exhaled into the frigid air.

River Otter
(Lutra canadensis)

SIZE: 54 inches, including 12-inch tail. Female much smaller than male.

WEIGHT: Up to 25 pounds.

HABITS: Fast swimmer, outswims trout. Breeds in water. Vulnerable and clumsy on land, safe in water.

HABITAT: Wherever there are freshwater fish.

FOOD: Carp, suckers, squawfish, game fish, frogs, crayfish, turtles, snakes, birds, eggs.

BREEDING: 1 litter of 2–3 per year. Gestation about 2 months.

ENEMIES: Dogs, wolves, bobcats, lynxes, bears.

LIFE SPAN: 15 years.

A river otter feeds on a frog at the water's edge. On land the otter waddles awkwardly on its short legs. But in the water it can swim half a mile on a single breath of air.

Otters are found throughout the United States and Canada wherever there is sufficient water to support the fish that constitute their staple food. Other animals may be bigger, stronger, and swifter than the otter, but I know of none that rivals its combination of strength, agility, and intelligence, or that shares its ability to get so much sheer pleasure out of life. Most animals have to take life seriously to survive. The river otter, also known as the land or common otter, is the acknowledged playboy of the mammal world.

Bellywhopping down steep mudbanks is a favorite otter diversion. Scrambling up to the top of the bank, the otter folds its legs backward and shoots down on its chest and belly into the water. Its wet fur moistens the slide until it becomes as slippery as grease. All members of an otter family join in the fun, the adults chirping, chattering, and grunting, and the pups chuckling with delight. They play for hours, until hunger forces them to seek food. Having established a slide, the otter uses it every time it passes through the area. In winter, snowbanks are utilized in the same manner. This tobogganing technique also is used for traveling over the snow, even on level land. The otter bounds along for a few paces, flops down on its belly, slides as far as it can, then repeats the process.

On land, however, this playful member of the weasel family looks awkward, with its long body, short legs, and tapering, twelve-inch tail. A full-grown male may have an over-all length of fifty-four inches, but stands only nine inches high at the shoulder. Larger and much heavier than the mink, a large male may weigh as much as twenty-five pounds. The female is much smaller and lighter in weight. Otter fur is rich brown above, with paler underparts and whitish lower jaw and throat. The flattened, weasel-like head has small ears and a broad snout. All four feet have webbed toes.

Undoubtedly, the otter is the fastest swimmer among North American land mammals, capable of outswimming such game fish as trout or salmon. But the otter eats less game fish than carp, suckers, and squawfish because these trash fish swim slower and are more easily caught. In eating fish, the otter usually starts at the head, clipping off the fins and tail. The otter also feeds on frogs, crayfish, turtles, snakes, birds and their eggs.

In the water, the otter moves about continually, rolling, tumbling, diving, and floating on its back. On trips through Canada's wilderness lakes, I have had pairs and families of otters swim ahead of my canoe for miles. On first observing the approach of a canoe, the otter raises its long, sinuous neck and head above water like a periscope. The head swings from side to side and the forepaws hang motionless, while the otter treads water with the hind legs. Suddenly, as though someone has shouted the command "Down periscope," the otter sinks from view, leaving scarcely a ripple to mark the spot. Off the otter swims underwater, only to reappear hundreds of yards away. The otter is protected from the cold by a thick layer of fat under the skin. Its small ears and nostrils close when in the water, enabling the otter to swim half a mile underwater on a single breath of air, and to remain submerged for as long as four minutes.

During the late winter or early spring breeding season, the male may mate with several females, but spends most of its time with one. Breeding takes place in the water, and the female may be bred shortly after giving birth. The den may be an abandoned muskrat house or beaver lodge, a cavity in a bank, or a hollow tree. Sometimes a simple nest beneath a tangle of heavy vegetation is used.

The young, usually two or three, are born in mid-April in the north, somewhat earlier in the south. Covered with silky black fur, the pups are blind for about five weeks. The mother keeps the male from them until they are four months old, weaned, and ready to swim. Odd as it may seem, young otters are reluctant to enter the water at first and must be taught to swim. The adults sometimes swim with a pup on their backs, then dive, leaving the pup to fend for itself. Confidence builds rapidly, and the young soon are at home in this new element. Mother and pups remain together for about eight months, when they part company.

The otter has a wide range that may take as long as ten days to two weeks to cover. The animal may go up a river, branch off to a lake, follow a tributary to the headwaters, cross a height of land, follow another brook back down to the river, and then repeat the entire circle, perhaps fifty to seventy-five miles in circumference. Most meat-eaters instinctively know that to remain and hunt in the same spot depletes the food supply, thus forcing an inevitable migration into another area.

While aware that it is at a disadvantage, the otter does not hesitate to cross land. It runs with a clumsy, rolling gait and can be overtaken easily by a dog, wolf, bobcat, lynx, or bear. When that happens, the otter is a formidable fighter, capable of giving as much as it takes. When frightened or angered, it emits a strong musk. In the water, the otter is supreme; nothing can catch it.

Although the otter has never been really plentiful, its numbers today are being reduced. This is happening principally because man is restricting the otter's range by the development of waterways and coastal regions. The otter is able to exist in the same area with man, often without being discovered, but it much prefers to remain unmolested. In wilderness areas, the otter is active at any time of the day or night. Human proximity is forcing it to become exclusively nocturnal.

An otter may take an occasional muskrat or game fish, but other food is more readily available, so it seldom interferes with man's interests. Man, on the other hand, values the otter's beautiful, durable fur for trimming women's coats and jackets. A limited number of otters are trapped according to state and federal regulations. The best eastern pelts come from Labrador, the best western ones from Alaska.

If captured young and properly cared for, the otter makes a delightful pet in spite of its doggy odor and fondness for tearing through a house like a small cyclone. It can even be trained to act as a retriever.

Spotted Skunk
(Spilogale putorius)

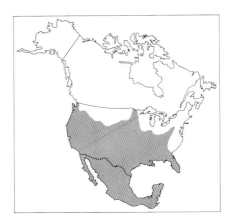

SIZE: 20–22 inches, including 9-inch tail. Female smaller than male.

WEIGHT: 2 pounds.

HABITS: Good climber. Warns off enemies by raising tail and stamping forefeet and by emitting strong musk.

HABITAT: Dry, desert regions.

FOOD: Chickens, eggs, rats, mice, snakes, lizards, fruits, berries, grain, insects.

BREEDING: 1–2 litters of 5–8 per year.

ENEMIES: Owls, dogs, foxes, bobcats, badgers.

LIFE SPAN: 6 years.

Although smaller than the striped skunk, the spotted skunk, above, emits a stronger and more penetrating odor when alarmed. This small skunk is named for the three white stripes across its face—one in the center of the forehead and one under each ear.

This smallest, most agile, and most beautifully marked of the skunks boasts a color pattern that is unique among mammals. The narrow, broken white stripes on its black coat give it the spotted appearance described in its generic name (from the Greek *spilo*, spotted, *gale*, polecat). In the middle of its forehead and under each ear is a white spot. The silkiness of the spotted skunk's hair distinguishes it from the other skunks, and its tail usually is white tipped. A full-grown male is about half the size of an ordinary house cat, weighing about two pounds, measuring twenty to twenty-two inches in length, a good part of which is tail, and standing perhaps six inches high at the shoulder.

A good climber, the spotted skunk dens up in hollow trees on occasion. It clambers up fence posts and squeezes into farm buildings from which its striped cousin is barred because of its size. Not infrequently it enters chicken coops and eats the eggs or the chickens. On the whole, however, this skunk is beneficial to the farmer, for it is an excellent ratter and mouser. In the winter and spring, the skunk feeds on other small mammals in addition to rats and mice. In summer, when the male has a home range of about one-half to two miles, the skunk adds snakes, lizards, birds' eggs, fruits, berries, grain, and insects to its diet.

This little animal has a curious way of warning off enemies. When threatened or alarmed, the spotted skunk hoists its tail, stamps its forefeet, and rakes at the grass with its claws. If this fails to deter the enemy, the skunk then performs a handstand by upending on its forepaws with hind feet in the air and tail waving aloft. The skunk may advance and even discharge its musk from this position, although it more commonly does so with all four feet firmly planted on the ground. In spite of its smaller size, the spotted skunk emits a musk that is much stronger and more penetrating than that of the striped skunk.

More nocturnal and retiring than its larger cousins, the spotted skunk is not so familiar a sight, although it is found throughout most of the United States, with the exception of the northeast. It is the skunk most commonly found in dry, desert regions, yet it can and will swim if it has to. Playful, energetic, and active in winter, it puts on less weight than does its striped relative.

The male is polygamous and mates with many females during the late winter breeding season. The so-called mad behavior of the male at this time is sometimes attributable to rabies, to which disease this skunk is thought to be peculiarly susceptible. What has actually happened is that the male has lost his natural fear and feels big enough to challenge the world. Any secluded cavity or hollow is used as a den and is lined with dried vegetation. The five to eight young that make up the average litter are born in early spring. In the southern part of the skunk's range, there may be two litters per year. At birth, the four-and-a-half-inch-long babies weigh about a third of an ounce and their eyes are closed. Their hair, so fine as to seem nonexsitent, reveals an already-discernible spotted pattern.

In about a month's time the young have their eyes open and soon follow the mother. As she turns over rocks and digs out beetles, the squealing, chirping little ones quickly run in and catch them. On such a high protein diet, the young grow swiftly. In another month they are weaned, and by the time they are five months old, they are almost as big as their mother, with whom they may stay all winter. For a period of perhaps three and a half months, a single den may contain a random population of eight to ten gregarious spotted skunks at one time.

When food is short, the bobcat, fox, badger, or other large mammal may feed on this skunk. The great horned owl probably is its chief natural predator. Dogs and automobiles take their toll.

Farmers often kill the spotted skunk to protect their chickens. Even if they don't have any chickens, they kill the skunk, unaware of its value as a mouser, ratter, and devourer of insects. Thousands of spotted skunks are trapped and killed for their soft fur, although pelts bring an average price of only 25 to 50 cents apiece. The fur is used to trim inexpensive cloth coats. In the fur trade, this skunk often is called a civet cat, although it is not related to either the civets of Europe or to the cat family.

Striped Skunk
(*Mephitis mephitis*)

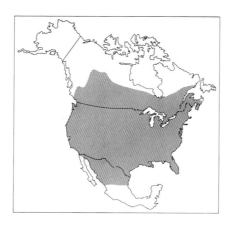

SIZE: *30 inches, including 7½-inch tail.*

WEIGHT: *6–14 pounds.*

HABITS: *After warning predator, will emit strong, long-lasting musk. Does not hibernate, but becomes lethargic in northern regions.*

HABITAT: *Almost anywhere.*

FOOD: *Insects, mice, rats, shrews, chipmunks, young birds, eggs, chickens, turtle eggs.*

BREEDING: *1 litter of 3–8 per year. Gestation about 60 days.*

ENEMIES: *Coyotes, badgers, eagles, owls, bobcats.*

LIFE SPAN: *10–12 years in captivity.*

The striped skunk discharges its scent only as a last resort after it has warned the enemy. First it lowers its head, growls, stamps the ground with its forepaws, and arches its back as shown here. Finally it twists its body sidewise into a U-shape so the target is both within line of sight and line of fire.

Found in almost every type of land habitat over most of North America from southern Canada to northern Mexico, the striped skunk is the best-known member of the skunk family, familiar by name if not by sight. In some areas it is known as a wood pussy, in others as a polecat, although it is in no way related to the European polecat. Closer to the mark is its generic name *Mephitis,* noxious vapor. Our word skunk comes from its Algonquin Indian name *seganku*.

For an animal that is so well known, the skunk is strangely misunderstood, misrepresented, and maligned. We often hear about a skunk killing chickens, raiding the nests of ground-nesting birds, and blinding other animals with its scent. All these incidents can, and sometimes do, happen. But it is unfair to condemn all skunks for the actions of an erring few.

I have known many farmers who never passed up an opportunity to kill a skunk. Yet this animal is just about the best wildlife friend the farmer has. While the skunk is a carnivore, the bulk of its diet consists of insects. The skunk might be called nature's vacuum cleaner, because it does such a thorough job of seeking and destroying insect pests. When working over a pasture field, the skunk overturns every stone to root out and eat the beetles hidden beneath. Thousands of small, cone-shaped holes reveal where the skunk has dug out insects that have burrowed into the earth.

The skunk also feeds on mice, young rats, shrews, chipmunks, and other smaller mammals, as well as on birds' eggs and young. By eating snapping turtle eggs, the skunk actually helps our duck population and gives further evidence of its great value to man. A single snapping turtle may wipe out an entire brood of ducks by pulling them underwater to drown and eat them.

In turn, the skunk is preyed upon by a number of natural enemies, including the coyote, bobcat, badger, eagle, and great horned owl, which preys on it regularly. I have never encountered one of these owls that did not reek of its skunk supper.

The scent glands of the skunk are better developed than those of any other member of the weasel family. Through ducts controlling two glands under its tail, the skunk discharges the scent, usually in a fine spray. The skunk can accurately reach its enemy's eyes at distances up to about eight feet. A few drops of scent may be atomized so that they thoroughly saturate hundreds of square yards, particularly on a foggy night. The skunk uses its scent sparingly and does not discharge it when the tail is lowered. There is no truth in the saying that a skunk will not spray if lifted off the ground by its tail. Too many persons have learned this lesson the hard way.

The scent is a defensive weapon used by the skunk as a last resort, but never without ample warning. At the approach of a persistent intruder, the skunk expresses alarm by lowering its head and growling. It stamps on the ground with first one forepaw, then the other, or rakes at the grass with its long claws, elevating its tail until just the tip hangs down. Arching the tail over its back, the skunk twists its chunky body sideways into a U-shape, so that its target is within its line of sight as well as in the line of fire. Only then does the skunk discharge its amber-colored fluid. The skunk produces about one-third liquid ounce of musk per week, sufficient for perhaps five consecutive discharges.

Skunks are most careful about getting the scent on their own fur and do not use it when fighting among themselves. To some humans and animals the scent, composed of mercaptan (a suphurous compound), is nauseous and causes vomiting. It may cause severe burning of the skin or eyes, and temporary blindness may result. Water is the best treatment for the eyes. An old rural remedy for clothes contaminated by skunk scent was to bury them. A better one is to make a smudge fire by placing green conifer branches in the flames. I have found tomato juice more effective than vinegar, while others prefer gasoline, ammonia, or chloride of lime. Skunk musk leaves a long-lasting odor. Some dogs, even when exposed to the outside elements, still retain a skunk smell for several weeks after their encounter. Damp or rainy weather makes the scent even more pungent.

In the southern part of its range, the skunk remains active all year, while in the northern regions it dens up for long periods. It does not really hibernate, but becomes lethargic. Unlike most of the weasels, this skunk often becomes fat and sluggish. Several skunks may den up together to take advantage of mutual body heat. The male is much more active in winter than the female, and in nightly forays may cover six to eight times its summer range of one-half to one mile from its den. Any secluded ground cavity, perhaps an abandoned woodchuck burrow, makes a good skunk den and nest when lined with dried leaves or grasses. This skunk enjoys the works of man and often takes up residence under a house or farm building, but can be discouraged from doing so by a sprinkling of moth balls or naphthalene flakes around the area.

The male usually mates with several females during the late winter breeding season. The average litter of three to eight young is born after a gestation period of about sixty days. At birth, the black-and-white striped pattern shows through clearly on the babies' pinkish skins. Starting from a white line up the nose to a white skull cap, two white stripes of varying width and length run down the black back to the tail.

Baby skunks have well-developed coats of black fur by the time they are about three weeks old and their eyes open. At five weeks of age, they are big enough to follow single file after their mother on her nightly forays for food. By fall most of the young will have wandered away on their own, either to seek out their own dens or to stay in the general area and den up with the mother. Skunks are ready to breed when they are a year old.

Because the striped skunk is not a climber like its energetic spotted cousin, it is less likely to raid chicken coops. Most states foolishly allow skunks to be trapped all year long. Skunk hair is quite coarse. The blacker the pelt, the more valuable it is to the trapper. The skin of a skunk with just a patch of white on the head, known as a star skunk, commands the highest price. Even the skunk's odor-producing musky secretion is deodorized and used in the manufacture of perfume. The wood pussy is an excellent mouser and, when caught young and de-scented, makes a playful and affectionate pet. A captive skunk may live for ten to twelve years.

Badger

(Taxidea taxus)

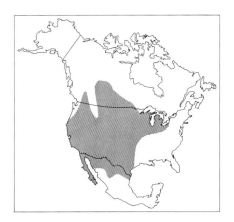

SIZE: 30 inches, including 5-inch tail.

WEIGHT: 15–25 pounds.

HABITS: Monogamous; digs for food. Does not hibernate, but sleeps below frost line in winter.

HABITAT: Prairies and high plains.

FOOD: Rodents of all kinds, especially ground squirrels; snakes, insects, birds, eggs, carrion.

BREEDING: 1 litter of 3 (average) per year. Delayed implantation; gestation 183–365 days.

ENEMIES: Wolves, bears, mountain lions.

LIFE SPAN: 12 years in captivity.

With its powerful short legs and strong claws, the badger is an expert digger in pursuing burrowing animals. This tunneling ability is also a useful defense against wolves, bears, or mountain lions.

During a recent wildlife filming trip, I camped with my family in Glacier National Park in Montana. High on my photographic want list was a badger. I had seen several of these low-slung animals in the distance, but had no luck with photographs. Late one afternoon I returned—tired, dirty, and disgusted—to camp following a futile, daylong camera chase after the elusive mountain goat. My wife couldn't wait to tell me about a thrilling experience she'd had that morning. It seems that a squat, long-haired animal with black and white stripes on head and cheeks had decided to dig a tunnel about six feet from the entrance to our tent. It remained for several hours, paying scant attention to the campers as they came running up to photograph it from every angle. That's right—the moment my back was turned, a badger had come visiting. Luckily for my disposition, I got my chance to photograph one later on.

This member of the weasel family inhabits the prairies and high plains of midwestern and western North America from southern Canada to northern Mexico. Wisconsin is known as the Badger State in honor of this scrappy resident. Badger fur is grizzled, sandy-brown in color, rather stiff, but long and dense. Cheeks, chin, and belly are creamy white. In addition to black patches over the nose and in front of the ears, a white stripe runs from the badger's nose over its forehead and tapers into its shoulders. Most likely the badger's name, from the French *bageard*, "one with the badge," refers to these markings. Male and female are identical in size and coloring.

An adult badger is about thirty inches long, including five inches of stubby tail. It stands perhaps ten inches high at the shoulder and weighs from fifteen to twenty-five pounds, although its bulky hair makes it appear much larger. The badger shuffles along on the flat of its feet. Because so much of its time is spent in tunnels, this animal can run backward almost as fast as it can forward.

Rodents of all types, especially the small ground squirrels, provide the mainstay of the badger's diet. These rodents usually escape by seeking refuge in their underground burrows, but the badger is not so easily thwarted. The powerful muscles of its short legs and long, strong claws of its black forefeet make this creature an expert digger. In fact, the badger can out-dig any of the burrowing mammals. A badger in pursuit of a meal digs as one possessed. The earth is loosened with the front feet and sent flying backward with the hind feet. Sod, dirt, and stones rain down in a steady stream until in minutes the badger is out of sight.

Much is made of the so-called hunting partnership between the badger and the coyote, in which the badger actually is more of a tool than a partner. Having discovered a badger trying to dig out a ground-burrowing creature, the coyote waits nearby. While the badger is busy digging in from the entrance to the burrow, its intended victim is likely to leave by another exit. As the rodent pops out, the coyote catches it before it reaches safety in another burrow. The trouble with this partnership is that the coyote never shares its catch with the badger.

Because it expends so much energy digging for food, the badger has a tremendous appetite. In addition to rodents, it eats snakes, insects, birds and their eggs, and even carrion. When more food is available than can be eaten at one sitting, the prudent badger buries it for retrieval at a later date.

The badger's tunneling ability is put to good use as a defensive measure in case of attack by an enemy too large to handle. A wolf, bear, or mountain lion can tackle a badger, but most other animals prefer to give this ferocious fighter a wide berth. The badger used to be taken alive and placed in a pit to fight dogs, but the dogs were unable to get a good hold with their teeth on the animal's long hair and loose skin. When angered or threatened, a badger digs out of sight, if possible. If cornered, it flattens itself against the ground, hissing loudly and baring its teeth, and sometimes discharges a strong scent from its musk glands.

This creature is not gregarious. Its preference for remaining by itself is a necessity, for too many badgers in one area would clean out the available food in jig time. Badgers mate in late summer or early fall, but the average litter of three blind but fully furred young is not born until the following spring. The den is a snug burrow deep in the earth at the end of a long tunnel. The nest usually is lined with soft, dry grasses. Occasionally, the monogamous male helps to rear the young, whose eyes remain closed for about six weeks. By the time the little ones are two months old, the mother is bringing back food for them to eat in an attempt to wean them. Shortly afterward, the young follow the mother about as she hunts for food, mainly at night. In late summer, the young leave the den and go their separate ways.

Although not a true hibernator in winter, the badger in the northern part of its range sleeps for long stretches in a snug burrow well below the frost line. Fat from gorging in the fall, the badger comes out to seek food only when it feels like it.

Because it never occupies a hole for long, the badger does a lot of digging. All its old diggings are revisited, for the badger knows that a variety of small mammals seek refuge in these holes. Many ranchers kill every badger they see, claiming that a horse or cow could break a leg by stepping into badger hole. This could happen, but seldom does. Meantime, the ranchers overlook the good the badger does in controlling the rodent population.

Man is the principal enemy of the badger, trapping it or flooding it out of its burrow. For years, before being displaced by synthetics, the best paint-brushes and shaving brushes were made of badger hair. Most of the famous old masters painted with badger brushes. A few coats still are trimmed with collars of badger fur. When taken young, a badger can be tamed and makes a playful pet. Its life span in captivity is about twelve years, a good deal longer than it would be in the wild.

Red Fox
(*Vulpes vulpes*)

SIZE: Body and head 30 inches; tail 14 inches. Female smaller than male.

WEIGHT: 8–10 pounds.

HABITS: Families live together in summer, split up in winter. Male does not den
up in winter.

HABITAT: Woodlands, treeless areas, brushy areas, suburbs.

FOOD: Pheasants, quail, grouse, ducks, rabbits, poultry, frogs, snakes, mice, rats,
fruits, berries, grain, grasses.

BREEDING: 1 litter of 6–8 per year. Gestation 56 days.

ENEMIES: Lynx. Young foxes are also preyed upon by owls, hawks, mountain lions,
wolves, and bobcats.

LIFE SPAN: 12–15 years.

The red fox has become the most numerous and widely distributed fox on the continent. In winter it does not den up, but sleeps out in the snow, with its bushy tail covering its nose.

In colonial days, gentlemen who wanted to fox-hunt as they had in England found that the native gray fox would not cooperate. The native red fox was not found south of New England nor east of Illinois. So red foxes were imported and they extended their range. When the native and imported interbred, the latter became assimilated and lost their identity to the former. Today, this species is the most numerous and widely distributed of the foxes. It is found over most of Canada and the greater part of northern United States. Within this range, the fox has adapted itself to a wide variety of habitats: open woodlands, treeless areas, the brushy borders of swamps, and suburban communities.

The alert expression characteristic of the red fox is enhanced by its long, sharp nose, erect, pointed ears, bright yellow eyes, and slight ruff on the cheeks.

The pupil of the eye becomes elliptical when it contracts, instead of round, as with the other wild dogs. Smaller than a coyote or small collie, the adult dog (male) weighs averagely eight to ten pounds, while the vixen (female) is not quite so large. Normally, its long, silky coat is bright yellow to deep rust in color, with white chin, throat, and underparts. Legs and feet are jet black. Other color forms found only in the north are black, silver, and cross (so-called after the dark, cross-shaped patch over the shoulders). In all color variations, the tail is white tipped. All forms may occur in a single litter, but in captivity they are not interbred—for example, silver foxes are only bred to silver foxes.

Red fox pups spend most of their daylight hours playing near the entrance to their den. As the pups grow older, the parents bring food that is still alive, teaching the young to kill for themselves.

In January the male begins to search for a mate, with whom it will remain for most of the year. Breeding takes place in February, and the young are born about fifty-six days later in a den prepared by the vixen. Because the fox seldom digs a den of its own unless the soil is soft and sandy, most dens are enlarged woodchuck burrows. They may be located along the edge of a field, on the top of a knoll, or out in the middle of a large, bare area. The fox likes to have a den location with a good view of the countryside. A red fox's den is recognizable from its mildly skunk-like odor.

Red fox litters average six to eight pups, fully furred but blind for the first nine days. They grow rapidly and crawl out of the den in about three weeks. With a telephoto lens on my camera, I have spent many enjoyable hours photographing the pups outside a fox den. If anyone disturbs the young or the den, the vixen moves the pups to another spot. Both parents bring food to the pups playing at the entrance to the den, where they spend most of the daylight hours. As the pups grow larger, they are brought some food that is still alive, so that they can learn to kill it for themselves. By summer, the young have begun to try their luck at catching their own food. I have often heard the parents on late summer nights barking back and forth as they taught the youngsters to hunt. With the coming of cold weather the family splits up, and the pups seek a range for themselves. The female remains within the home range, perhaps a mile or two from the den, and may be rejoined by the male for another year.

The adult red fox does not den up in cold weather, preferring to sleep curled up in a ball out in the snow, with its large, bushy tail serving as a blanket to cover its nose and the pads of its feet. Snow completely covers the fox at times. By sleeping out in the open, the fox eliminates the possibility of being attacked by a predator without warning. In areas where they are found, mountain lions, wolves, lynxes, and bobcats feed on young foxes. Owls at night and some of the larger hawks by day also may kill the pups. Occasionally, an adult fox bogged down in the deep northern snows is taken by the lynx, whose large foot pads enable it to move over the snow without sinking in deeply.

For centuries, from Aesop's fables to Joel Chandler Harris' tales of Uncle Remus and his friends, the intelligence and cunning of the fox have been celebrated in song, story, and folklore. The red fox is famed for the tricks and ruses it employs to fool a pack of hounds. While it has a top speed of almost thirty miles per hour and good endurance, it much prefers to use its brain instead of its muscle.

A friend of mine had an opportunity to observe one of these performances while hunting small game in New York on land owned by a fox hunting club. A red fox had been started and was running about a field-length ahead of the dogs, with horses and riders strung out farther behind. The fox dashed through a gateway in a fence row that was perhaps five feet high. Turning sharply, it ran along the bottom of the stonerow for about 200 feet, leaped lightly to the top of the fence, and, crouching low on its belly, crawled back toward the gate. By this time the hounds were pouring through the gateway, hard on the hot trail. When the last dog had passed through the gate, the fox jumped down on the far side of the fence and ran back across the field the same way it had come—straight through the middle of the thundering horsemen. By the time the dogs were called back from the spot where the fox had leaped up on the fence, the churning of the horses' hooves had destroyed the fox's scent trail. The fox, meanwhile, crossed a busy highway and sought refuge in the mountain beyond.

Some foxes become so knowledgeable about traps that it is next to impossible to catch them in one. They steal the bait, dig out and uncover the traps, and even turn the traps upside down, causing them to snap shut on the dirt.

Bounties, the payment of money by local governments to control the numbers of a specific species, have been offered since the first settlers came to this country. A bounty was first placed on the red fox because of its appetite. Sportsmen usually are against it for the simple reason that it eats pheasants, quail, grouse, ducks, and rabbits. Some foxes get into the habit of feeding on poultry, so farmers dislike the fox. Aided by its keen sense of smell, the fox takes whatever is easily caught, be it frog, tadpole, or snake, as well as vast numbers of mice and rats. In certain seasons, the fox eats fruits, berries, grain, and even grasses instead of meat. To the orchardist, the fox is invaluable, for every mouse or rabbit taken is one less pest to kill fruit trees by gnawing off the bark.

Many states still try to control the red fox with the archaic bounty system, in spite of the fact that it has not proved to be a successful method of control. Other states conduct predator control campaigns to seek out and destroy the individual fox guilty of doing damage rather than indiscriminately trying to eradicate all foxes.

At one time the soft, durable silver fox was one of the most valuable fur pelts in the world, some of the finest skins bringing as much as $1,500 at fur auctions. But fashion is fickle and tastes change. Only a handful of fox farms are in operation today. The price of the ordinary red fox pelt has dropped so low that many trappers take the fox just for the bounty and do not even bother to skin it. In captivity, a fox may live twelve to fifteen years, considerably longer than in the wild, where disease also takes its toll. In addition to encephalitis and distemper, outbreaks of rabies occur every nine or ten years. The bite of a rabid fox can cause death to livestock as well as to humans if rabies treatment is not given.

Gray Fox
(Urocyon cinereoargenteus)

SIZE: *40 inches, including 12-inch tail. Female slightly smaller than male.*

WEIGHT: *8–10 pounds.*

HABITS: *Runs to cover or climbs tree when pursued.*

HABITAT: *Woodlands and fields.*

FOOD: *Mice; rabbits; all kinds of small birds, mammals, reptiles, amphibians, fish, carrion, fruits, berries, grain, insects.*

BREEDING: *1 litter of 3–5 per year. Gestation about 2 months.*

ENEMIES: *Young foxes preyed upon by dogs, coyotes, wolves, bobcats, owls.*

LIFE SPAN: *10–12 years in captivity.*

The only fox capable of climbing, the gray fox can scramble up a tree as fast as any cat. When pursued by dogs, it prefers climbing or burrowing to running.

Because the gray fox has quite a lot of red hair, it is frequently confused with the red fox in one of its color phases, while its over-all salt-and-pepper coloration leads some persons to mistake it for the silver fox, another color phase of the red fox. The two species, however, are quite different and do not interbreed.

The gray fox is slightly smaller, shorter-legged, and more compact than the red fox. It has similar pointed facial features, but its ears are shorter, its face ruff is more prominent, and its pupils are round when they contract. This fox has red hair in its ruff, along its flank, on its legs, feet, and underparts. Its bushy tail is black tipped, with a ridge of stiff black hairs running along the top. In fact, the generic name *Urocyon* describes this fox as *oura*, big-tailed, *kyon*, dog. A full-grown male has an overall length of about forty inches, of which twelve inches is tail, stands approximately fifteen inches high at the shoulder, and weighs between eight and ten pounds. The female is slightly smaller.

While many trappers consider the red fox much more intelligent than the gray fox, this is purely a matter of opinion. It is misleading to generalize about species, because every creature is an individual. I have encountered gray foxes as smart as any red fox could ever be. Although the gray fox is smaller than the red, it almost always comes up the winner in any clash between the two. Clashes are not too frequent, as the two species prefer slightly different territories.

It is easy to distinguish between the tracks of the two foxes, because the gray has much larger toe pads than the red. Being a more northerly animal, the red fox has more hair between its small pads, and this almost obliterates the pads from the tracks. The gray fox is primarily a southern animal, inhabiting Central America, Mexico, and all of southern United States. As our climate moderates, it has been steadily expanding its range northward until it is now common throughout most of the United States to the Canadian border, with the exception of the northern plains and Rocky Mountain area.

Unlike its red relative, the gray fox does not like to run. It prefers to live in more inaccessible cover. When pursued by dogs, this fox seeks a woodchuck's burrow, a cavity or den in the rocks, or climbs a tree. It is the only member of the dog family capable of climbing. Sometimes called the tree fox, the gray can scramble up a tree as fast as any cat. The gray fox also is more nocturnal than the red fox and has a yapping bark.

This fox breeds a little earlier than the red, starting in January. About two months later three to five pups are born in a rocky den or hollow log or tree. Both male and female are devoted parents and provide food, care, and instruction to the young. The little ones are fully furred but blind for the first nine days. They nurse for about two months, although the parents start them on solid food when they are six weeks old and big enough to be taught how to hunt and to escape from their enemies. In addition to man and his dogs, these include coyotes, wolves, bobcats, and even the great horned owl. The male leaves the family first, the female remaining with the young until fall, when all go their separate ways.

Mice and rabbits are the mainstays of the gray fox's diet, although it will consume almost anything edible. All types of small birds, mammals, reptiles, amphibians, fish, carrion, fruits, berries, grain, and insects are grist for its mill. The fox occasionally kills moles and shrews, but does not eat them and leaves them lying around untouched. Both these little mammals have an odor that makes them repulsive to most meat-eaters, yet predators cannot seem to resist the temptation to hunt them. Every time the fox eats a mouse, it is actually helping the farmer, although most farmers overlook this. The gray fox takes chickens less often than the red fox. For one thing, the red fox lives in close proximity to a farm, while the gray prefers to live in wilder, more dense brushy cover.

Gray fox fur is so coarse that it has little value, being used mostly for trimming coats rather than for fine furs. This fox makes a good pet if caught young, although like most wild animals, it is inclined to become snappish after the first year. A captive gray fox has been known to live for over ten years.

Arctic Fox
(Alopex lagopus)

SIZE: 30 inches, not including tail. Female smaller.

WEIGHT: 10–12 pounds.

HABITS: Often follows bear or wolf for share of its kill. After eating, sleeps in snow until hungry.

HABITAT: Above timberline, circumpolar regions.

FOOD: Arctic lemmings, shore birds, waterfowl, small mammals, berries, fruits, carrion.

BREEDING: Average annual litter of 6–7. Gestation 2–3 months.

ENEMIES: Arctic wolves.

LIFE SPAN: 7 years wild; 14 in captivity.

Except for its black eyes and nose, the arctic fox is almost invisible in the snow. Its staple food is the arctic lemming, which has a four-year cycle of abundance. The fox is so dependent on this food source that its population rises and falls with that of the lemming.

Drifting silently along, its pure white coat blending into the snow-covered landscape, the arctic fox seems to be almost a figment of imagination. If it were not for its black nose and eyes, it would be almost invisible. Living above the timberline in a harsh circumpolar land that is snow-covered most of the year, the arctic fox needs this camouflage in order to survive. In spring, when the weather moderates and bare earth can again be found, the fox sheds its winter coat until fall and dons its summer coat of brownish fur. The arctic fox also has a blue phase, found in just a fraction of the white fox litters. In winter, the blue fox has a dark bluish-gray coat; in summer it turns into a pale bluish-gray. Through selective breeding, fur ranchers were able to build up the numbers of blue fox in captive litters, and the raising of blue foxes was formerly an important industry in the north.

The staple food of this fox is the arctic lemming, which has four-year cycles of abundance. When lemmings are plentiful, the foxes wax fat, living is easy, and the females produce big litters. When the lemming population declines, the fox population dips. During these starvation periods, the arctic fox migrates far south of its usual range in an attempt to find food. Some foxes survive, but many die.

Living is easy for the fox in summer, when the arctic region teems with all types of wildlife. Clouds of shore birds, waterfowl, and many small mammals are found on the seacoasts and along the tundra. Various berries and fruits grow in profusion under the almost constant sun. It is winter that brings hard times, when the flocks of birds have departed southward, the berries and fruits have been eaten or lie buried under the snow, and the sun appears for only a few hours a day. At this season the arctic fox is primarily a scavenger, feeding on anything edible that it can find. Some foxes spend the entire winter following the giant polar bear to feast on the remnants of its kill. The bear ordinarily kills more than it can eat and seldom stays in one spot long enough to devour all the food. As the bear is forced to stray miles from land out onto the ice pan in search of food, the fox follows along. Sometimes bear and fox spend months adrift on an ice floe, perhaps twenty miles from shore. The bear is unwilling to share its food, but has little choice. The fox is much faster and more agile than the bear, and can easily outrun it if necessary. Hardship for the fox arises when the bear swims from one floe to another. Although the fox can swim, it prefers not to.

Sometimes the fox follows the arctic wolf to feed on remains of the kill it leaves behind. This is risky business, because the wolf is so much larger and faster that it will run down the fox, kill and eat it if it gets the chance. Often the arctic fox finds a seal or walrus carcass washed up on the beach. This is a perfect source of food. This far northern fox is not a quarrelsome creature; when a food supply of this size is found, all the foxes in the area gather to feast. Once over a hundred arctic foxes were seen feeding on a whale carcass that had been beached. That was enough food to last them throughout the entire winter.

After filling its belly, the fox digs a hole in the soft snow, crawls inside, curls up into a ball, and sleeps until it is hungry again, paying no attention to the cold. Drifting snow soon covers it completely and the snow itself is an excellent type of insulation. As a further adaptation to the extreme cold, the arctic fox has a short face, short, well-rounded ears, long winter fur, and a heavy covering of stiff hairs on its paws. Its scientific name means the fox with hare feet.

When about ten months old the fox is ready to mate. The breeding season starts in late February or March, and the young are whelped in May. The female usually digs a den in the soft sand of a riverbank or along the coast.

At birth the six or seven young of the average litter are blind, covered with a dark coat of fine down, and weigh about two ounces each. With both parents providing for the pups, food usually is no problem. While the parents are absent, preying on other small game, their own young may become the victims of wolves, bears, eagles, owls, and even an occasional red fox.

After a month's time, the young are able to leave the den for a short period each day to join their parents in the luxury of a sun bath. The adults keep the pups in line by giving short, sharp warning barks. The family members stay together until fall, when they split up. This fox pairs up for the season and may have the same mate in successive years. When full-grown, the male measures about thirty inches in length, stands nine to eleven inches high at the shoulder, and weighs ten to twelve pounds. Although actually smaller in size than the red fox, the arctic fox looks heavier owing to its dense, woolly coat.

Before the drop in the price of fox pelts, in the mid-1940s, there were many fox farms in the Pribilof Islands off the coast of Alaska. Some ranchers let the foxes run loose on one island, while others kept theirs in pens so that selective breeding could be practiced. The life span of a fox in captivity is about fourteen years, in the wild about seven years. At present most fur farms have gone out of business, because the animals have eaten up all the profits. Blue fox pelts that perhaps would have brought as much as $300 each thirty years ago now go for $10 to $25 each. These prices reflect the fact that most long-hair furs have gone out of fashion. The price of this fur has also worked a hardship on the Eskimos, who bartered for much of their trading material with the fox pelts that they had trapped.

Because it does not have much contact with man, the arctic fox is one of the most trusting of wild mammals. It frequently scrambles out of its den to watch an occasional human go by. At night the fox and its fellows sit on the edge of light thrown by a campfire to study the strange intruders in their homeland.

Gray Wolf
(Canis lupus)

SIZE: *Up to 64 inches, including 16-inch tail. Female smaller than male.*

WEIGHT: *150 pounds.*

HABITS: *Mates for life. Pups stay with family for 1 year.*

HABITAT: *Open country and forests.*

FOOD: *Almost any kind of meat from mouse to caribou, elk, or moose; insects, berries, vegetation, fruits.*

BREEDING: *Annual litter of 4–6. Gestation 63 days.*

ENEMIES: *No natural predators.*

LIFE SPAN: *15 years.*

The gray wolf's thick fur coat may vary from jet black to pure white. A strong animal of high endurance, it can lope along for hours at twenty miles per hour. At top speed it can run twice that fast.

One of the most spine-tingling, hair-raising sounds you can hope to hear is the gray wolf's long mournful wail emanating from the darkened forest in the Canadian wilderness. Although it can't help but make you edge nervously closer to the campfire, there is nothing to fear from the animal hidden in the primeval gloom. The gray wolf will not kill a human being. Having been subjected to constant persecution and harassment, the wolf is familiar with the authority of a high-powered rifle. Fear of man always makes the wolf bolt.

In Europe, it was a different story. There the wolf has long had a reputation for ferocity. Some wolves terrorized whole districts; Aesop recounted the tale of the Greek shepherd boy, who called all the farmers from their fields merely by shouting, "Wolf! Wolf!"

The gray wolf, also called the timber wolf, has been driven out of all but a few areas of North America. It is found in some sections of Michigan, Minnesota, and the Rocky Mountains. Even in Canada and Alaska, its last strongholds, its numbers are greatly reduced. A smaller relative, the red wolf (C. niger), inhabits a small section of Oklahoma and Texas.

Although smaller than the Ice Age ancestor whose fossil remains were discovered in California's La Brea tar pits, the wolf is the largest of our present-day wild dogs. A full-grown male measures up to sixty-four inches in length, including a full, sixteen-inch tail, stands twenty-seven inches high at the shoulder, and weighs as much as 150 pounds. The female is smaller. The wolf has a broad nose pad, rounded ears, and slanted eyes. In color, it varies from almost jet black to the pure white of the arctic wolf; different colors may occur in the same litter. Thick fur protects the wolf from the cold, and broad feet give it good footing on hard-packed snow. Endurance, not speed, is the secret of the wolf's success. With tail held high, it can travel for hours on end at a fast dog-trot, and its bounding, twenty-mile-an-hour lope really eats up the miles. The wolf's track is angular like the coyote's rather than oval like that of most other canines.

Intelligent and faithful, the wolf is thought to mate for life. The solicitude of the female wolf is symbolized in the tale of Romulus and Remus, the founders of Rome, who were nursed by a she-wolf. The female first breeds when she is two or three years old, probably in February or March. She then prepares a den for the young on a bluff or knoll. Such heights are ideal, because they provide a good lookout over the surrounding countryside. Frequently chosen are high riverbanks that offer the advantage of soft soil for digging.

Four to six blind, fuzzily furred pups are born after a sixty-three-day gestation period. In about nine days their eyes open, and they are nursed for about two months. All the love, care, and protection possible are lavished on the pups. Not only do both parents bring food, but an unattached uncle or aunt as well occasionally cares for the young. As soon as they are strong enough, the young accompany their parents on training forays to learn how to hunt, swim, and protect themselves. The wolf is a tremendous feeder, consuming one-fifth of its weight in nourishment. It eats almost any kind of meat, from the tiny mouse up to the caribou, elk, and giant moose, as well as insects, vegetation, and fruits. The wolf family customarily stays together for about a year, so that the young are fully capable of caring for themselves by the time they leave in the early spring. The packs of wolves described as hunting together usually turn out to be entire family groups. One such group may hunt, almost always at night, on regular runs covering territory of more than a hundred square miles.

At the time of the coming of the white man, the wolf was found over most of North America. One of the first things the early settlers did was to start a war to the finish with the wolf. Now that this animal has been almost wiped out, the end of that war is in sight.

One of the most controversial issues in wildlife management over the years has been the effect of predation on species that are of particular interest to sportsmen. Studies made by such biologists as Drs. Adolph and Olaus J. Murie, Harold E. Anthony, and others have given conclusive evidence that the wolf is not wiping out any game species. Only now are we learning what the Eskimos and Indians have known all along: that the wolf actually improves its prey species by killing off the old and the weak. The wolf kills by a process of natural selection. It attacks a herd of animals by first making a wild dash toward it. If all the animals gallop away, the wolf ends the chase. If, on the other hand, one animal falters and falls behind, the wolf falls upon it, snarlingly tearing open its throat, and then gorges on the flesh. Sometimes newborn animals fall victim to the wolf before they have a chance to grow and prove themselves, yet those that survive pass on the genes that are needed to maintain the species.

It is not commonly appreciated that normal predation strengthens the prey animal. Many species have been exterminated by man, however, directly through killing or indirectly through alteration of the habitat or introduction of a foreign species of predator. In the United States a more enlightened policy is now in effect. Bounties and predation control campaigns are not implemented unless it can be proved that the increased wolf population in an area seriously threatens the other animal species. The cyclical wolf population peaks about every fifteen or twenty years.

Wolves must be controlled in areas where man is trying to raise livestock, for these domestic animals have lost their native agility and ability to defend themselves, and so they easily fall victim to predators. As farms and ranches pushed the bison off the open range, the wolf turned to prey on cattle, sheep, and horses. Some of the large timber wolves of the western states became legends in their own lifetimes, having cost ranchers vast sums of money in livestock killed. Custer, one of the most notorious of the predators, did $25,000 worth of damage and avoided capture for ten years with a bounty of $500 on its head. A number of noted hunters carved out careers for themselves just by killing such wolves for the bounty. The Indians demonstrated their admiration of the wolf's intelligence, strength, and cunning by using its name in various combinations for their warriors.

Northern trappers and hunters have found the long-haired wolf fur excellent for trimming the hoods of parkas. Trichinosis, rabies, and mange are among the troubles that may befall the creatures that survive man's guns, traps, and poison.

Coyote
(Canis latrans)

SIZE: 4 feet, including tail. Female about ⅘ as large as male.

WEIGHT: 25 pounds.

HABITS: Runs up to 40 miles per hour. Sometimes hunts in packs. Packs yelp in chorus in response to high-pitched sounds.

HABITAT: Forests and prairies.

FOOD: Deer, rabbits, rodents, birds, fish, insects, game mammals, carrion, berries, fruits, domestic livestock.

BREEDING: Annual litter of 8–10. Gestation 64 days.

ENEMIES: No natural predators.

LIFE SPAN: 15 years in captivity.

Few wild animals are capable of catching the coyote, which runs at forty miles per hour. Because of its craftiness, this animal has long been an important trickster in the folklore of the western Indians.

The weird, wild singing of the coyote is unmistakable. Many sounds, including those made by man, will set off a chorus of coyotes. Low-pitched notes do not affect the coyote, but high-pitched notes set off an immediate response. This is true of most members of the dog family. While on an expedition to the Rocky Mountains early in the 19th century, American naturalist Thomas Say heard the coyote yelping and gave the animal its Latin name meaning barking dog.

In forested regions, the coyote is often referred to as the brush wolf; in plains country, it is called the prairie wolf. Actually, the coyote has a narrower nose pad than the wolf and carries its bushy tail down instead of straight out. The average male coyote weighs around twenty-five pounds, with the female perhaps five pounds lighter, and measures about four feet long from nose tip to tail tip. It has a pointed muzzle, long, erect ears, and an alert expression. Its coat varies from grayish to tawny in color, with darker shadings on the back, lighter underparts, and rusty legs, feet, and ears.

The coyote has always been an inhabitant of the western plains and foothills of North America. The Spaniards, who were the first white men to become acquainted with this animal, named it *coyote*, a corruption of the Aztec name *coyotl*. *Muy coyote* is an expression used in Mexico to describe a demonstration of great shrewdness and cunning. In filling the vacuum left by the eradication of the gray wolf, the coyote has proved to be exceptionally resourceful, intelligent, and adaptable.

Steadily, the coyote has extended its range northward and eastward until at present it is fairly numerous in the Adirondack Mountains, an area where previously it was unknown. This has happened because New York is in the midst of a great population shift. Many of its people are moving to other states, leaving the substandard marginal farms on which they or their parents were raised and letting them revert to the wild and become overgrown with brush. This food supply attracts deer, which in turn attracts the coyote, replacing the deer's former natural predators, now exterminated from the region.

From Michigan the coyote spread into Canada, moved eastward through Ontario, then southward over the icy St. Lawrence into New York and New England. Recently, a coyote was killed just a few miles from my home in New Jersey. Many of the eastern coyotes have mated with feral dogs, producing offspring (called coydogs or doyotes) that usually are larger, more vicious, and more destructive of game than either of the parents. A number of other eastern coyotes were imported as pets, escaped, and reverted to the wild. They became established in Florida in this fashion.

Fleet of foot, as becomes an animal native to the open prairies, the coyote can travel at a speed of forty miles per hour and is one of the few mammals capable of catching a jack rabbit. The clever coyote sometimes hunts cooperatively, each member of the team taking turns in running a faster prey in circles. Even the swift pronghorn is caught in this manner. The coyote is quick to take advantage of a situation, as in its so-called partnership with the badger. On discovering a badger digging out a ground squirrel or prairie dog, the coyote lingers nearby, ever alert to catch the rodent if it should elude the hardworking badger.

The coyote, like the wolf, probably mates for life. The breeding season begins in January, at which time the coyote becomes even more vocal than usual. About sixty-four days later, the blind, fully furred young are born in a den dug in a sandy bank or enlarged from a fox, skunk, or badger burrow. Coyotes have exceptionally large litters, the record being eighteen pups, while the average is eight to ten. The young coyotes are nursed about six weeks, then they are fed on meat brought by the male and partially digested, then regurgitated, by the female. Rodents are carried back to the den by the parents so that the pups can play with live food and tear it apart themselves. This training fosters the hunting instinct so necessary to the young when the time comes for them to go out on their own. The entire family stays together at least until early fall, by which time the young have been taught how to provide for themselves. After the young go off, the parents remain together.

Rabbits and rodents make up three-fourths of the coyote's diet. This animal also feeds on birds, fish, insects, some big game, carrion, and whatever berries and fruits are available, showing a particular preference for watermelon. Now and then, the coyote preys on domestic livestock. This prompted western stockmen in 1875 to undertake unremitting warfare against the wily animal. Enlightened studies have proved, nevertheless, that this senseless killing is detrimental to the stockmen's interests. Not only does the coyote conserve grass and grain by controlling harmful rodents, but it also is an important scavenger of carrion. As these facts are appreciated, more and more stockmen are giving protection to the coyote. The individual coyote that destroys livestock is eliminated rather than the whole species. Many western stockmen today do not allow government trappers to trap coyotes on their land.

Few wild creatures are capable of catching an adult coyote. Bears, wolves, lynxes, bobcats, and golden eagles may take an occasional young coyote. Rabies, distemper, and parasites take their toll, but man is the chief enemy. Because its pelt never has been worth more than a few dollars, the coyote has not been trapped extensively just for its fur. Most pelts that reach the market are the result of coyotes having been taken in areas where they are not protected or where a bounty has been placed on them. When taken young, a coyote makes an interesting pet. In captivity, it may live fifteen years.

The craft and cunning of the coyote were highly valued by the western Indians, who depicted it as an important trickster in much of their folklore. According to one Indian legend, the coyote will be the last animal on earth. One thing is certain, we shall be the losers if the singing of the coyote is no longer heard in the star-studded night.

Jaguar

(Felis onca)

SIZE: 6½ feet, including 2-foot tail.

WEIGHT: 250–275 pounds.

HABITS: Unlike other cats, enjoys swimming. Probably mates for life.

HABITAT: Jungles, thickets, or deserts.

FOOD: Birds, reptiles, fish, wild mammals, livestock.

BREEDING: Litter of 2–3 born every other year. Gestation 4 months.

ENEMIES: Crocodiles, alligators.

LIFE SPAN: Up to 22 years.

The largest and fiercest American cat, the jaguar is more closely related to the African leopard than to the American mountain lion. But while the leopard's spots are solid and round, many of the jaguar's are squarish in shape and encircle lighter "rosettes."

The jaguar is the largest, fiercest, and most powerful of the native American cats, more closely related to the lions, tigers, and leopards of Asia and Africa than to the American mountain lion. South of the border, it is known as *el tigre*, while the South American Indians call it *jaguara*, said to mean "meat-eater that overcomes its prey in a single leap."

Almost as restricted in its distribution as the jaguarundi, this big cat is comparatively rare in the United States, where it is found only in a few sections of Arizona, New Mexico, and Texas. To the south, its range extends as far as Paraguay. The largest concentration of jaguars occurs in the damp, tangled jungles of Brazil's Amazon basin. Equally at home in desert regions, it prefers dense thickets.

This big cat's beautiful tawny yellow coat and white underparts are marked with black spots. Unlike the smaller leopard, with its solid black spots, the jaguar has many spots, or "rosettes," enclosed within black circles. The jaguar's principal spots are squarish in shape, while the leopard's are more circular. This spotted coat makes an effective camouflage, especially important for a predator that stalks its prey. The compactly built jaguar gives the appearance of great strength. Its legs are much heavier than the mountain lion's or the leopard's, and have a rounder appearance. A full-grown jaguar measures about six and a half feet from nose tip to tail tip, and stands approximately twenty-eight inches high at the shoulder. Its top weight is 250 to 275 pounds.

It was probably the jaguar's size and strength that impressed the Aztec Indians of Mexico and their forerunners. They worshiped the jaguar as an earth god, with the power to cause eclipses by swallowing the sun, and formed special jaguar cults. Many objects recovered from pre-Conquest archeological sites depict this animal.

It is the jaguar's size, too, that gets it into trouble. For one thing, it is large and dangerous enough to constitute a top-notch trophy for any sportsman. Most sportsmen prefer to hunt game that will be a challenge and that perhaps can also hunt them. For another, the jaguar's large size requires it to eat a lot of food and at frequent intervals. It takes birds, reptiles, fish, and whatever mammals happen by. Sometimes these mammals are livestock. Although principally a ground hunter, the jaguar climbs well, pursuing game into the trees or waiting on a limb to drop down on any unsuspecting peccary or deer.

Unlike most other members of the cat family, except the jaguarundi, the jaguar actually enjoys swimming. It spends hours at a time playing and lazing about in the forest pools and rivers. Folklore has it that the jaguar attracts fish by twitching its tail as a lure above the surface of the water. Should any of its four-footed prey attempt to escape by plunging into the water, this spotted cat follows right in after it. Often at night, a jaguar coughs or grunts in an effort to startle the prey into disclosing its position by moving about.

Jaguars probably mate for life, and the den is a hollow log or in a heavy tangle of brush. Four months after a January breeding, two or three blind young are born. Occasionally, one is completely black in color. The babies grow rapidly and in six weeks reach the size of a domestic cat. Six-month-old jaguars are out with the parents every night, learning at firsthand the art of catching and killing their prey. When they are a year old, the young are large enough to go out on their own. By the time they are three years old, they are full-grown and capable of breeding. Because the young remain with her so long, the female commonly breeds only once every two years.

Few enemies, with the exception of a large crocodile, alligator, or man, are rash enough to take on an adult jaguar. Battles between a jaguar and the huge anaconda have been recorded, but in most cases the cat has been more than a match for the snake. Poisonous snakes and "civilized" man are instinctively feared and avoided. It may be that the jaguar can sense the destructive power of firearms, for there have been instances of attacks made on Central and South American Indians armed only with bows, arrows, and lances. Cornered or wounded, a jaguar is indeed a foe to be respected.

Ocelot
(Felis pardalis)

SIZE: 4 feet, ⅓ of which is tail.

WEIGHT: 25–35 pounds.

HABITS: Agile climber and swimmer, active chiefly at night. Probably mates for life; frequently travels in pairs.

HABITAT: Forests.

FOOD: Birds, birds' eggs, rats, mice, snakes, iguanas, coatis, deer fawns, livestock.

BREEDING: Twin cubs born in September or October.

ENEMIES: No natural predators.

LIFE SPAN: Unknown.

The ocelot's handsome coat is a masterpiece of camouflage to conceal the animal in its natural surroundings. The buff-colored back and sides and whitish underparts are marked with black stripes, spots, and streaks.

Most people have never heard of an ocelot, let alone seen one. Its Latin name means leopard-like cat, an apt description of this beautiful animal. The ocelot's handsome buff-colored coat and whitish underparts are marked with black stripes, spots, and streaks. The stripes occur mostly on the head and neck, and the entire coat is a masterpiece of camouflage to conceal the animal in its natural surroundings.

A resident of tropical America, the ocelot is found in the United States only in areas of thickets and heavy brush along the Texas-Mexican border. An adult measures about four feet in length, about one-third being tail, and stands roughly eighteen inches high at the shoulder. Its weight varies between twenty-five and thirty-five pounds, with only the male attaining the maximum weight.

The ocelot is an exceptionally agile climber and swimmer, and is active chiefly at night. Much of its time is spent in the trees, where it hunts for food. Stretched out on a sun-dappled limb, the ocelot in its spotted coat remains invisible to its prey as long as it remains motionless. Birds, birds' eggs, and nestlings make up a large part of this cat's diet; rats, mice, and other small rodents also are taken. Snakes are commonly encountered, both poisonous and non-poisonous species probably being killed for food. Although I have never actually seen an ocelot kill a snake, I have often watched a domestic cat do so. Swift as the snake's strike is, the cat's movements are faster. In the tropics, the ocelot often kills iguanas, agoutis, monkeys, and even coatis. A deer fawn as well as a weakened adult sometimes is pulled down for food. A successful depredation against livestock may become a habit as the ocelot develops a taste for poultry, pigs, lambs, calves, and even small dogs.

Raids on livestock create trouble for the ocelot, as the owners lose no time in trying to hunt it down with dogs. When cornered, this cat puts up a spirited fight and gives a good account of itself. If it is trapped or treed, it does not hiss and growl as the bobcat does, but usually remains quiet.

Ocelots probably mate for life, for they customarily travel in pairs. The den may be any protected hollow, such as a cave, hollow tree, or dense thicket, lined with soft material provided by the female. The twin cubs are born in September or October. Although fully furred, they are helpless, and their eyes are closed for at least the first nine days. The cubs continue to nurse for about two months even though they already have been started on meat. Food is provided by both parents.

The ocelot is not hunted for its fur, which brings only a modest price on the commercial market. If taken young, it is readily tamed. It is one of the gentlest of felines and does not become vicious like other cats. Pet ocelots are not uncommon; one was featured in the "Honey West" television series. Long Island ocelot fanciers hold an annual club banquet for owners and their pets.

Mountain Lion
(Felis concolor)

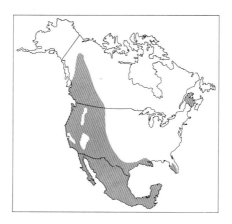

SIZE: *Up to 9 feet, including 3-foot tail. Female smaller than male.*
WEIGHT: *175–200 pounds.*
HABITS: *Furtive, nocturnal habits. Has screaming mating call. Often kills prey by dropping on it from tree or rocky ledge.*
HABITAT: *Mountains, swamps, thick woodlands.*
FOOD: *Deer, domestic livestock, other mammals, birds.*
BREEDING: *Litter of 2–5 born every other year. Gestation about 3 months.*
ENEMIES: *No natural predators.*
LIFE SPAN: *20 years in captivity.*

The mountain lion usually kills a deer by stalking it on the ground. Sometimes it will drop on it from a tree or rocky ledge. Seven to ten pounds are eaten at a time. Then the lion will cover the vicitim with grass and debris, saving it for a future meal.

The only lion native to the New World is known by so many different names it is difficult to realize that they all belong to the same animal. Among the names are mountain lion, panther, painter, puma, catamount, cougar, and American lion. It is sometimes called the screamer because the mating call of the lovesick cat sounds like a woman screaming in mortal terror. Even the name mountain lion is something of a misnomer, for this big cat inhabits swamps and thick woodlands as well as mountainous regions.

When the white man arrived in the Americas, the mountain lion had an extensive range and was found throughout most of what is now the United States. In the seventeenth century, colonial legislatures put a bounty on the big cat, setting off a war of extermination that has continued to the present day. Little by little, the mountain lion's numbers dwindled. In spite of the fact that it has the widest distribution of any native New World mammal—from British Columbia to Patagonia, at the tip of South America—this lion is found only in a few isolated pockets within that range. The Florida Everglades, the Canadian province of New Brunswick, Rocky Mountains, and Sierras still provide a refuge for the big cat.

Yet even in these areas the mountain lion is seldom seen, owing to its furtive, nocturnal habits. I have talked with men who have lived all their lives in mountain lion country, who have seen tracks and other signs of the animal's existence, and still have never seen a lion except when it was treed by dogs. Anyone who sees a mountain lion in New Jersey, Pennsylvania, Maryland, or any of our other densely populated eastern states either possesses an overactive imagination or simply does not know how a mountain lion looks. The animal simply does not exist in that part of the country.

The graceful mountain lion has a tawny yellow coat with white underparts, a characteristically cat-like head, and small, rounded ears. A large specimen measures nine feet overall, one-third being the dark-tipped tail. Standing twenty-six to twenty-nine inches high at the shoulder, the lion weighs about 175 to 200 pounds. The female is smaller in size and weight. As this big cat walks, its low-hanging belly sways from side to side. This slack-bellied appearance is characteristic of every mountain lion I have seen. While this animal is the second largest (after the jaguar) of the native North American cats, it is less than half the size of the African lion.

Most young mountain lions are born in April or May, although the adults seem to be capable of breeding at any time of year. Adults living in the south breed before those in the north, where the weather is colder and there is less food available during the early months of the year. Because the male may kill the young after they are born, he is driven from the cave or rock ledge den by the female, who gives birth to two to five kits about three months after mating.

Mountain lion kits have spotted coats and comparatively short, ringed tails; they do not resemble their parents until they are six months old. Their eyes, sealed at birth, open on the ninth day. The young spend a great deal of time playing and wrestling about. All play is a conditioning for later life, and the kits carefully stalking their mother's twitching tail someday will use the same skills to secure their food.

By the time young mountain lions are two months old they follow the mother when she hunts. This saves a lot of time and effort, for the little ones can chew off their meals from a freshly killed carcass. Deer are the mainstay of the mountain lion's diet, although the lion eats any bird or animal it can catch. The lion usually kills a deer by dropping on it from a tree or rocky ledge, which may be as high as twenty feet above the victim. Sometimes the lion stalks the deer closely, then makes a furious charge, often covering twenty feet in a single bound. Leaping upon the startled deer, the big cat breaks its neck either by a hammer blow with its paw or by pulling the deer's neck backward until it snaps, or the lion may bury its claws into the deer's shoulders and kill it by biting down through the neck.

After the kill, the lion usually tears out the entrails. Seven to ten pounds of meat are eaten at a time. If the young accompany the mother, they fall upon the carcass and chew off as much as they can hold. When all have eaten their fill, the female covers the carcass with grass, sticks, and other debris in order to hide it from other meat-eaters. The lion returns to its kill for perhaps another meal or two, then abandons it to go out and make a fresh kill. Except when it is starving, this lion does not eat carrion. Two to three big kills a week are needed to feed a single lion. It does not hibernate, but must hunt all winter long, ranging over a wide territory of some thirty to fifty miles.

Gradually, the young lions learn to hunt and to make their own kills. Their training period may take as long as eighteen months, during which time they remain with their mother, who breeds only every two years. At three years of age, a mountain lion is considered full-grown and capable of breeding. The life span of this big cat in captivity is about twenty years; in the wild, it is considerably less.

Because of its size and strength, the mountain lion has no real enemies except man. Popular notions to the contrary, this lion is not considered dangerous to man, and authenticated records of its having killed a human being are rare. Nevertheless, the lion is still being hunted for bounty or sport. Its pelt has no commercial value. Dogs are used to tree the lion, which can be brought down from its refuge easily with a light carbine shot. The taste of mountain lion meat is said to resemble a combination of veal and lamb.

Killing a mountain lion that preys on domestic livestock can be condoned, but the centuries-long effort to exterminate all of these big cats has seriously upset the balance of nature in certain areas. Where the lion cannot find deer, it preys upon livestock; where the lion has been wiped out, deer compete with range cattle for forage. In the Kaibab Indian Reservation in Arizona, for example, after the mountain lion was exterminated, the deer population increased at such a rate that it outgrew its food supply. Forest and topsoil were permanently damaged, and deer by the thousands died from starvation. The fact that the big cat now is protected in our national parks indicates a growing awareness of the vital role played by predatory animals in maintaining natural controls.

Jaguarundi
(Felis eyra)

SIZE: 4 feet, including long, slender tail.

WEIGHT: Up to 20 pounds.

HABITS: Furtive, glides easily beneath branches or among bushes.

HABITAT: Dense thickets.

FOOD: Fish, ducks, small birds, birds' eggs, rabbits, mice, rats.

BREEDING: Little known about breeding habits. Litter of 2–3 born at a time.

ENEMIES: Few predators can catch the adult. Hawks, owls, coyotes, bobcats eat young.

LIFE SPAN: 8–10 years.

In the United States, the jaguarundi is found only in the dense thicket country of the south Texas coast and along the Rio Grande. With its short limbs, it glides easily beneath branches or scrambles to safety in the bushes.

If you want to stump your friends, ask them about the jaguarundi, or eyra, as it is often called. They won't be able to tell you much about it, because this slender-bodied, low-slung feline is the least known of all our native American cats.

In spite of its name, this animal has nothing to do with the jaguar. With its long body and tail, small head, and short legs, the jaguarundi looks more like a weasel than a cat. In Mexico, it is called the otter cat, because of its marked resemblance to the otter. The jaguarundi, furthermore, shows none of the reluctance to enter the water and swim customarily encountered among other members of the cat family.

The jaguarundi has two color phases: a bluish-gray and a red. Its short hair has no commercial value. At one time, it was thought that the two different colors represented different species, but this has been discounted. Young of both colors may be found in the same litter. Unlike the jaguar and ocelot, which inhabit the same areas, the jaguarundi is not spotted. An adult is larger than a house cat, measuring almost four feet from the tip of its nose to the end of its long, slender tail. It stands about ten to twelve inches high at the shoulder, and may weigh up to twenty pounds, although it rarely does.

In the United States, this creature has the most restricted range of any member of the cat family. It is found only in the dense thicket country of the south Texas coast and along the Rio Grande. The body build of the jaguarundi is ideally adapted to the type of country it inhabits. Long legs would be a handicap to moving about in impenetrable thickets. With its short limbs, the jaguarundi can glide beneath the branches or easily scramble up into the bushes if necessary.

Owing to its furtive manner and restricted range, very little is known about the breeding habits of this cat. Very likely breeding takes place at any time of the year, as is usual in hot climates. The den is located in a hollow tree, under a tangle of roots, or in a fissure in the rocks. Two to three young are born at a time, fully furred, but with their eyes closed. In about nine days, when their eyes open, the babies begin to crawl about.

Fish, ducks, small birds and their eggs, rabbits, mice, and rats form the bulk of the jaguarundi's diet. The tangled growth in which this animal lives, on the other hand, protects it from most of its enemies, including man. Few predators can catch an adult jaguarundi, although hawks, owls, coyotes, and bobcats eat the young when they can find them.

Man threatens the jaguarundi because he is steadily destroying its habitat. With bulldozers, cultivators, and other machines, man is tearing the Texas thicket apart, burning the brush, and creating new farmland and citrus groves. Nothing is as fatal to a wild creature as the complete destruction of its home.

Lynx

(Lynx canadensis)

SIZE: *3 feet, including short tail.*

WEIGHT: *15–30 pounds.*

HABITS: *Nocturnal. Mates for life. Primarily a ground hunter, but frequently drops on prey from trees.*

HABITAT: *Brush or woodlands.*

FOOD: *Varying hares, grouse, red squirrels, other game.*

BREEDING: *Litter of 2–4 born in spring. Gestation 2 months.*

ENEMIES: *No natural predators.*

LIFE SPAN: *10–12 years.*

A creature of the north country, the lynx is found throughout Canada, wherever there are varying hares. These two animals are so closely linked that the lynx's population depends on the abundance of the varying hare, which rises and falls over a ten-year cycle.

The elusive lynx often is confused with its cousin the bobcat, which it closely resembles. Both have short bodies, long, heavy legs, and face ruffs. They are the only native American cats with short tails. The lynx can be identified by its longer ear tufts and by its completely black tail tip.

This cat measures approximately three feet long overall, stands about two feet high at the shoulder, and weighs between fifteen and thirty pounds. Its pale gray or buff coat is streaked with brown. Hair from its face ruff hangs down along its lower cheeks like old-fashioned muttonchop whiskers. With its large, furred feet serving as built-in snowshoes, the lynx is able to walk over soft snow without sinking in too deeply.

The lynx is a creature of the northland. Its range, far more restricted than the bobcat's, extends from Alaska to Newfoundland. It is found wherever there are trees and brush and wherever the varying hare, or snowshoe rabbit, makes its home. The varying hare is the mainstay of the Canada lynx's diet. So closely are these two mammals linked that the lynx population depends upon the cyclical abundance of varying hares. The hare cycle takes about ten years to complete. When the varying hare is plentiful, the lynx is also; when the hare is scarce, lynx numbers decline. The lynx cycle, however, usually is one year behind the hare cycle. Although the lynx eats an occasional grouse, ptarmigan, red squirrel, or other game, it cannot catch enough to offset the shortage of hares.

The female lynx makes her den in a rock cave or hollow log. As soon as breeding is completed, the male leaves. After a gestation period of about two months, the female gives birth to two to four kittens in late spring. The young are fully furred, but their eyes remain sealed for about ten days. Like most of the wild felines, the father helps in providing food for the young. For about three months the family stays together in the den, then the young lynxes are ready to follow the mother as she tries to instruct them in the art of catching their own food. Their first prey are the mice that abound in the leaf litter of the forest floor. Only after the young become sufficiently skilled will they be able to catch a varying hare for themselves.

Although the lynx is primarily a ground hunter, it frequently climbs trees to drop down on an unsuspecting hare passing beneath. This big cat's generic name, *Lynx*, comes from the Greek and refers to its sharp eyesight. Like other wild felines, the lynx is most active at night.

I shall never forget the first time I saw a wild lynx. It was in 1959, in Quebec, Canada. Returning to camp at dusk, I was driving down a lumber company's dirt road when a large lynx bounded across the road in front of my truck and went down into the ditch on the other side. I jammed my foot hard on the brake, stopped the truck, and ran back to get a closer look. When I reached the spot where I thought the lynx had crossed, the big cat suddenly jumped back onto the road and stood looking at me. Its eyes glowed in the semidarkness and its stumpy tail jerked nervously. I waited, motionless, holding my breath. Then the lynx finished its scrutiny and bounded lightly back into the brush.

Most creatures have a healthy respect for the sharp claws and teeth of a full-grown lynx, but owls, eagles, wolves, or wolverines sometimes take a young one. Man is the lynx's principal enemy, trapping the cat for its long, rather soft fur that is made into collars on cloth coats. Europe is the chief commercial market for most lynx pelts.

Bobcat
(Lynx rufus)

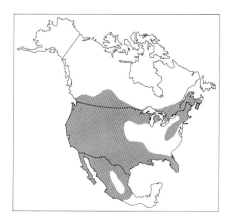

SIZE: *3 feet, including tail.*
WEIGHT: *15–30 pounds.*
HABITS: *Nocturnal, furtive, excellent hunter.*
HABITAT: *Forests, mountains, swamps, deserts.*
FOOD: *Small birds and mammals, deer and fawns.*
BREEDING: *Litter of 2–4 born in spring. Gestation about 50 days.*
ENEMIES: *No natural predators.*
LIFE SPAN: *Up to 15 years in captivity.*

The powerful bobcat uncoils like a steel spring to leap at its prey. To make the kill it is equipped with razor-sharp claws and strong pointed teeth.

This bobtailed American cat is one of our most beautiful—and most lethal —wild mammals. It is equipped with razor-sharp claws, needle-like teeth, and the wiry strength to make good use of these weapons. The man who can lick his weight in wildcats, as bobcats sometimes are called, is a man indeed. If he were to survive such an encounter, I am willing to bet that he would not be the same man, or at least would not look like the same man, as before the fray.

A mature bobcat is about the same size as a lynx; in some areas it is known as the bay lynx. The largest specimen on record weighed forty pounds. The bobcat's ears are inconspicuously tufted, although its face ruff is as prominent as that of the lynx. Only the top of its stubby tail is marked with distinctive black and white rings and black tip.

Widely distributed throughout most of North America, this cat has adapted so well to civilization that it actually is extending its range and increasing in numbers. The bobcat is equally at home in deep forest, mountainous terrain, swamp, or desert. The color of its coat changes to meet the requirements of the region where it lives: a desert-dweller has the lightest and palest coat, while a woodland-dweller has the darkest.

Bobcats prowl today in the suburban areas surrounding huge metropolitan cities. Several of my friends have reported seeing these cats in Palisades Park, which lies across the Hudson River from New York City, and it is not unlikely that representatives of California's large bobcat population frequent the outskirts of Los Angeles. Yet so wary and furtive are these wild cats that they are seldom seen nor is their existence suspected.

All a bobcat wants is to be left alone, to have a mate, and to be able to secure enough food for survival. Its diet consists of all the small birds and mammals that share its habitat. The bobcat also kills weak fawns and old deer and thus helps to maintain a natural control over deer population and selection. An extremely efficient hunter, the bobcat, like all felines, hunts by sight and usually at night. A territory of five or six miles is covered in its slow, careful roaming; at the slightest movement, it pounces on its prey. At other times it picks out a spot near a game trail, where it sits and waits to ambush its prey.

By day or night, camouflaged by its black-spotted, pale brown or reddish-brown coat, the bobcat is all but invisible. As the intended victim approaches, the cat's only sign of life is a tensing of the muscles and an involuntary, nervous twitching of the stubby tail. It bides its time until the prey can be caught by a direct leap or in one or two bounds. Within that distance almost nothing escapes the lurking bobcat, which uncoils like a steel spring. The bobcat is a good climber and frequently catches its prey by dropping onto it from an overhanging tree limb.

A hollow log, cave, or rocky ledge is the favored location for a bobcat's den. There two to four young are born in late spring after a gestation period of about fifty days. The newborn kits have full coats of spotted fur, but their eyes do not open until they are nine days old. To celebrate that occasion they try to crawl from the safety of the den. This really is the only time a bobcat is subject to predation, when some of the larger mammal and bird predators may kill and eat the helpless young. Such predation can only take place in the mother's absence as she would fearlessly fight off any attackers.

As soon as the young are large enough to be weaned, the mother brings in birds, rabbits, mice, squirrels, and other small game for them to play with and eat. Sometimes the prey is brought in alive, so that the young can further their hunting education by killing it themselves. When the kits are old enough to follow, the parents take them into the field to teach them to hunt for themselves. In the fall the young are ready to go out on their own. The parents may stay together or split up and go their separate ways. In captivity a bobcat may live to be fifteen years old, but in the wild its life span is considerably shorter.

The bobcat's unpredictable disposition does not make it a popular candidate for domestication. The nineteenth-century naturalist John James Audubon described a two-week-old specimen as "a most spiteful, growling, and snappish little wretch." On the other hand, this wild cat is a ferocious fighter, often taking on enemies twice its size. Because few predators will tangle with a bobcat, its chief enemy is man. Its strikingly marked pelt has little market value, so the bobcat—when it can be found—is killed for bounty or sport.

7

❧ ❧ ❧

Pinnipedia—

Fin-Footed Mammals

The eared seal family (Otariidae), to which sea lions belong, the fur seal family (Phocidae), and the walruses (Odobenidae) are all meat-eaters. Until recently, they were considered to be members of the order Carnivora. Now, however, they have their own classification, for they resemble each other much more than they resemble the rest of the carnivores.

Members of the order Pinnipedia have streamlined bodies, short fur or hair, flipper-shaped forelimbs, and paddle-shaped hind limbs. This modification of the limbs helps the pinnipeds move in the water, but hampers them on land. Most pinnipeds come ashore only to breed and to give birth to their single offspring per year. Males usually are much larger than the female.

Pinnipeds have special physiological adaptations to their life at sea. Their eyes and nose close underwater. The lungs are longer and larger than those of land mammals of similar weight. Instead of breathing rhythmically, the pinnipeds breathe rapidly, then hold their breath for ten to twenty minutes. Special valves or muscles close down when these mammals submerge, slowing the flow of blood to the extremities, while at the same time permitting it to flow freely to the brain and heart. In a dive, the heartbeat slows to about one-tenth of capacity. Pinnipeds can also tolerate larger amounts of carbon dioxide in their lungs than can other mammals.

Sea Lion
(Zalophus californianus and
Eumetopias jubata)

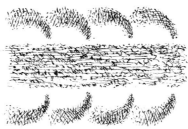

SIZE: *California—Male 7½ feet; female 6 feet. Northern—Male over 11 feet; female 8–9 feet.*

WEIGHT: *California—Male up to 600 pounds; female about 200 pounds. Northern —Male more than 2,000 pounds; female about 750 pounds.*

HABITS: *Both species spend most of life in water. Excellent swimmers, dive to depths of 700 feet.*

HABITAT: *Surf and rocky coastal areas.*

FOOD: *Fish. Northern prefers trash fish; California, squid.*

BREEDING: *1 pup born in July. Gestation 342 days.*

ENEMIES: *Sharks and killer whales.*

LIFE SPAN: *19 years.*

Two California sea lions poke their sleek black necks above the ocean surface. Because they are more agile and more intelligent than seals, these playful animals are often trained as circus performers.

If the sea lion isn't the most frustrated of all mammals, it should be, for it never receives credit for anything it does. All its glory goes to the seal instead. Yet one never sees a trained seal perform in a circus or zoo. The star juggler and horn player is always a California sea lion (Z. *californianus*) that has been mislabeled.

Sea lions differ visibly from seals in two ways: their ears are external, and they have the ability to turn their hind flippers forward. This latter characteristic enables sea lions to be much more active and agile than seals. Sea lions, for example, can sit erect while seals are forced to lie prone. Because of their agility and superior intelligence, sea lions are trained as performers and seals are not.

Sea lions are called marine mammals because, although they do come out on land, by far the greatest portion of their lives is spent in the water. Like all mammals, they breathe air and must come to the surface to renew their oxygen supply. Truly superb swimmers, sea lions have been known to dive

Although it dives to depths of 700 feet, the sea lion must come to the surface to breathe. The external ears on the side of the animal's head are a reliable clue that it is not a seal.

to depths of 700 feet. Recent studies have revealed that the eyes of these animals, which feed at night, are sensitive to extremely low light intensities and are suited for use at night and in deep water. It has even been suggested that, with their vocal ability and well-developed hearing, the sea lions may be able to catch their prey in the darkness by a kind of built-in sonar or echo-ranging sense.

Two different species of sea lion are found along the Pacific coast of North America: the California (*Zalophus*, from *zale*, of the surf, and the *ophion*, a fabulous sea beast) and the Northern (*Eumetopias jubata*). The California sea lion population numbers between 50,000 and 100,000; the Northern, approximately 150,000.

The more southerly species is the California sea lion, which ranges along the coast of California throughout most of the year. This is the animal that has made Seal Rocks at San Francisco famous as a tourist attraction. It is gregarious and fun-loving, the perfect circus performer. Adults have a characteristic honking bark. Sometimes called the black sea lion, this animal's short, light brown hair appears to be jet black when wet. The bull (male) has a distinctive small mane of hair that starts between the eyes, goes up over the top of the head, and down to the neck. An adult bull weighs up to 600 pounds and measures seven and a half feet in length, while the female averages about 200 pounds and measures six feet in length.

The Northern sea lion lives off the Alaskan shore in summer and the California coast in winter, where it shares the surf and rocks with the smaller California species. One such haunt is the Point Lobos State Reserve near Carmel. To the Spanish who came to the area, the sea lions were *lobos marinos*, sea wolves. A big bull weighs more than 2,000 pounds and measures over eleven feet in length. The cow is eight or nine feet long and weighs about

750 pounds. This heavyweight does not bark like the California species, but emits a bellowing roar. It is sometimes known as the Steller's sea lion, after Georg Wilhelm Steller, the first naturalist to see and describe it for science. Steller accompanied Vitus Bering on that explorer's voyage to the Alaskan coast in 1741.

Sea lion hides are used for leather, although they are not nearly so valuable as the pelt of the fur seal. Sea lions, however, are rich sources of oil—which almost proved to be their undoing. Once hunted close to extinction, sea lions now are protected by law and are making a steady comeback. Illegal attacks still are made upon them occasionally by fishermen, who view the sea lions as direct competition for commercial fish. Studies have shown this attitude to be false, although the California sea lion occasionally damages fishnets. Sea lions do eat fish, but the large Steller's prefers trash fish that are neglected by the fishermen, while the California sea lion's taste runs to squid.

Once sea lions also were killed for their stiff whiskers, which the Chinese found excellent for cleaning the stems of opium pipes. The sea lions can be protected against man, but their natural enemies, the sharks and the killer whales, still take a heavy toll.

After spending the winter at sea, the bulls come onto land about July. They heave themselves up out of the water and immediately establish individual territories on the sea beaches. Then the cows appear. Each cow gives birth to her single pup within a few days of coming ashore. The little fellow is precocious and can move about within an hour or so. Its large blue eyes, which turn brown a few weeks later, take in a world that seems to be populated only by sea lions.

The females are ready to breed right after the birth of their pups. The ensuing battles between the males are fierce and bloody, as the bulls tear long gashes in each other's hides with their long canine teeth. Each bull tries to control as large a harem as possible. Dividing their time between breeding with the cows and fighting with the lesser males that continually try to entice away stray females, the big bulls go long periods without sleep or food. At such a pace, it is not surprising that they lose weight rapidly.

During this time the pups feed upon the exceptionally rich milk of their mothers, doubling their weight within a month or two. Even though it will spend most of its life in the ocean, the pup is afraid of water at first and must be taught to swim by the mother. Gradually the pup gains confidence and soon is bounding around in the surf like a rubber ball.

As summer draws to a close, the sea lions return to the sea. By gorging themselves on their rich seafood diet, the animals quickly regain strength and sleekness. Soon the Steller's sea lions begin their winter migrations southward, leaving the northern sea beaches in the custody of a few wheeling, screaming gulls.

8

❧ ❧ ❧

Artiodactyla—Even-Toed Hoofed Mammals

The bear and wolverine walk on the soles of their feet, the dog and cat walk on their toes, while the deer and other hoofed mammals walk on their toenails.

All of the wild species of hoofed mammals living in North America are even (*artios*)-toed (*daktylos*), or split-hoofed. Most of these animals have four toes on each foot; the two outside toes are up on the back of the foot and are known as dewclaws. The peccary has only one dewclaw on each of its hind feet. When the animal is walking in soft, deep mud, the dewclaws spread out and help support the body weight; otherwise, they are seldom used.

The North American artiodactyles represent four of the nine living families: peccary (Tayassuidae), deer (Cervidae), pronghorn (Antilocapridae), and bison, goats, and sheep (Bovidae). Some species graze, others browse, and all but the peccary are vegetarians. With the exception of the peccary, they have a gristly pad in the top of the mouth instead of upper front, or incisor, teeth. All, except the peccary, have a four-compartment ruminant stomach. This permits the hoofed mammal, which is preyed upon by the carnivores, to spend a short time actually feeding and a much longer period masticating the food in the safety of protective shelter. In the largest section of the stomach, the rumen, the food that has been gathered is moistened by stomach juices and softened. When the animal is ready to complete the digestive process, some of the softened food or cud is regurgitated into the mouth and chewed. The cud is again swallowed, passing into the second part of the stomach, the reticulum. From there it passes into the third section, the omasum, then into the fourth section, the abomasum, and finally into the intestines.

Most of our artiodactyles are referred to as big game, and because the male's antlers or horns make such splendid trophies, they are hunted avidly. Male deer have antlers, which are solid, and are shed (usually in late fall) and regrown (in spring) every year. Antlers are fed by an exterior network of blood vessels, called velvet, which dries up when the antlers reach their full development in September and is rubbed off against saplings and brush by the deer. Deer use their antlers chiefly to fight rivals during the mating season.

Male and (to a lesser extent) female pronghorns, bison, goats, and sheep have horns, which they use for defense as well as for mating battles. The hollow horns grow over bony cores and are nourished by an internal network of blood vessels. They are not shed, but continue to grow year after year. The sole exception to this rule is the pronghorn, the only true-horned mammal that sheds the outer sheath annually.

Collared Peccary
(Tayassu tajacu)

SIZE: *About 38 inches.*
WEIGHT: *35–45 pounds.*
HABITS: *Uses musk scent for identification or to warn of danger. Lives in herds, most active in cool hours of morning and evening.*
HABITAT: *Brush and scrub country.*
FOOD: *Fruits, nuts, leaves, berries, melons, insects, reptiles, birds, small mammals.*
BREEDING: *Twins born in average litter. Birth any time of year. Gestation 4 months.*
ENEMIES: *Red wolves, jaguars, ocelots, coyotes, bobcats.*
LIFE SPAN: *Up to 15 years.*

The collared peccary is named for the yellowish collar that encircles its neck and shoulders. Like the domestic pig, the peccary grunts softly while feeding and roots up food from the earth with its long snout.

The collared peccary, or javelina, is a pig-like native of the United States that inhabits the brush and scrub country of Texas, New Mexico, and Arizona. It is quite common all the way down into South America. Not to be confused with this animal is the European wild boar (*Sus scrofa*), which has been introduced into several of our mountainous eastern states.

This species of peccary derives its name from the whitish or yellowish collar encircling its neck and shoulders. Roughly the size of a springer spaniel, it is about thirty-eight inches long and stands perhaps sixteen inches high at the shoulder. A full-grown peccary weighs up to forty-five pounds. Its dense, bristly, dark grayish-black or grizzled-brown hair stands out from the body, making the animal look larger than it really is. Unlike the domestic pig, the peccary's ears stand erect and its hind feet have only a single dewclaw quite high up on the inside.

Both male and female look alike and have a large musk gland above the short, almost invisible tail. The peccary, sometimes called a musk hog, uses this scent as a means of identification for marking bushes and shrubs. Scent also is discharged in time of danger to warn the rest of the herd.

The peccary is not a cud-chewer, but uses its typically swinish, elongated snout to root up tubers and other food from the earth. It eats fruits, nuts, leaves, berries, melons, insects, reptiles, and any ground-nesting bird or small mammal it can discover and catch. A favorite fruit is prickly pear, spines and all.

Finding water is a problem in the regions inhabited by the peccary. Paths chopped in the mud by countless sharp hoofs radiate from every waterhole, whose location is well known. Aware that the waterholes are ideal for waylaying a peccary, predators frequent them in their hunting. The red wolf, jaguar, and ocelot are the chief enemies, while a coyote or bobcat occasionally takes a young peccary.

Peccaries grunt softly while feeding, thus assuring the herd that all is well. When danger threatens, a deep alarm note is sounded, the musk is ejected, and the herd dashes off together. Although peccaries try to run from danger if possible, they fight well when forced to give battle.

Tough, vicious, and courageous, a peccary is capable of inflicting considerable damage with its slightly curved tusks. Because there is strength in numbers, this animal lives in herds. An attack on one peccary is considered an attack on all. The entire herd wheels and charges into battle with shrill squeals of rage and a popping together of tusks. Peccaries have been known to rout such dreaded killers as the jaguar. On some occasions, hunters have been treed for considerable periods of time by a herd of angry peccaries.

The peccary is most active in the cool hours of the morning and evening, sensibly preferring to spend the heat of the day bedded down under a thicket. If a cave can be found, the peccary may use it for winter quarters, emerging only long enough to feed. Mine tunnels are favorite refuges, and miners welcome the peccary because of its penchant for rattlesnakes. Like the domestic hog, the peccary seems to be immune to the bite of the rattler. It was thought that the domestic pig's fat prevented the snake's venom from getting into its bloodstream. Because the peccary never becomes as fat as the pig, it is now believed that the entire swine family possesses a built-in immunity to the poison. Also in the peccary's favor is its cleanliness; it takes frequent dust baths to rid itself of parasites.

Before giving birth, which may occur at any time of year about four months after conception, the female retires to a burrow, cave, a hollow log, or some other sheltered spot where additional protection can be given to the young. The average litter consists of twin light-colored piglets with dark stripes running down their backs. The piglets run about a few hours after birth and in two days follow after the mother. When two months old, they are weaned and begin to root food for themselves.

Occasionally the peccary raids a farmer's fields and manages to inflict considerable damage in a short time. The other side of the coin is that the peccary in search of food actually benefits the soil by turning it over and aerating it.

The collared peccary is hunted on a small scale for its succulent meat, its hide, which is manufactured into gloves, bags, shoes, and other pigskin articles, and for its bristles, which are used for brushes. As a result of protective regulations, the peccary population is holding its own and currently numbers around 125,000.

Elk
(Cervus canadensis)

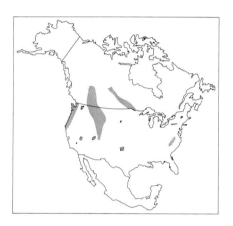

SIZE: *Bull 8 feet in length; cow smaller.*
WEIGHT: *Bull 600–800 pounds; cow 300 pounds lighter.*
HABITS: *Bull in prime in October, challenges others for supremacy. Winner mates with harem of cows.*
HABITAT: *Prefers forest clearings.*
FOOD: *Snowbrush, willows, pines, poplars, wheat grass, brome grass, fescues.*
BREEDING·   *Single calf born in spring. Gestation 250 days.*
ENEMIES: *Occasionally attacked by wolves or mountain lions.*
LIFE SPAN: *18–20 years.*

The bull elk's antlers may measure four feet across and five feet high when full grown. Indians called the elk wapiti, meaning white deer, after the light patch on the animal's rump.

The elk is a large American deer, second in size only to the moose. Although we are accustomed to thinking of this large animal as an inhabitant of the Rocky Mountain region, it was at one time common throughout most of northern and eastern United States. Such place names as Elkton, Elkhart,

Elk Gardens, Elk River, Elkhorn City, and Elk Park testify to its former abundance in the east.

The term elk is really a misnomer. It was given to this animal by the early settlers, who thought it was a variety of moose. In reality, it is more closely allied to the European stag. This is hardly surprising, as our elk originated in Asia and during the Pleistocene epoch spread eastward into North America. In Siberia today there is a form of stag almost identical with the American elk. A more accurate name is *wapiti*, a Shawnee Indian word meaning white deer, probably in reference to the animal's yellowish-white rump patch.

A full-grown bull elk measures about eight feet long, stands about four and a half feet high at the shoulder, and weighs between 600 and 800 pounds. The cow is smaller and some 300 pounds lighter. The animal's reddish-brown body terminates in a distinctive yellowish-white rump patch and small white tail. The neck is chestnut-brown, with a mane in males. This lighter shading above rather than below is unusual, reflecting the elk's preference for forest clearings, where the light falls from above. Cow elk do not have antlers, but the bull's large, spreading set may branch out as much as four feet across and five feet high along the beam.

During the breeding season in October the adult bull elk is in his prime—truly one of our most magnificent and awe-inspiring mammals. At this time the bull gathers harems of as many cows as can be controlled. The frosty air is filled with bugled challenges and the resounding crash of antlers as rivals fight for the right to mate with the cows. Once the battle is joined, it becomes a pushing and shoving contest, as each combatant strives mightily to throw his opponent off balance. Each protagonist tries to drive its antlers into the other's body, if the opportunity presents itself. The vanquished animal, lucky to escape alive, is more than willing to leave the cows to the victor. Younger bulls, not yet strong enough to challenge the herd master, keep circling around the fringes of the herd in an attempt to lure one of the cows away.

As winter approaches and the breeding season wanes, the elk forsake the high mountain meadows for the valleys in search of food, sometimes migrating long distances. Gathering in large herds, the elk browse on snowbrush, willow, pine, and poplar. Unlike other deer, they paw aside the snow with their forefeet in order to find such vegetation as wheat grass, brome grass, and fescues. It is during this time of year that the bulls' splendid antlers are shed or drop off. The shed antlers of elk and other mammals seldom last long after they reach the ground, because rodents and carnivores chew on them to obtain the calcium and phosphorus they contain.

With the passing of winter and the arrival of warmer weather, the cows return to the summer feeding grounds in the mountains before giving birth to their young. They are also eager to be rid of the hordes of biting flies, ticks, midges, and mosquitoes that infest the lowland area. The bulls follow along at

During breeding season, the bull gathers a harem of cows and challenges rival bulls for mating rights. Here a bull is shown with a herd of cows and calves.

a more leisurely pace. A single spotted calf is born after a gestation period of about 250 days. It weighs around fifty pounds and is able to walk a few hours after birth. In two or three days' time, the calf follows the mother as she grazes. The calf, too, is grazing by the time it is a month old, and weans itself in another month or so.

In the fall, when the thin summer coat is exchanged for dense, heavy, winter hair, the calf loses its spots. A young elk grows rapidly, acquiring about two-thirds of its growth by wintertime. The antlers of the young bull begin to develop at the start of its second year; the young cow breeds in the third year.

Approximately twenty years is the potential life span of this large animal.

Bears sometimes kill a calf, but seldom molest a full-grown elk. The coyote, bobcat, and similar smaller predators also attack calves, but frequently are driven off by the sharp, slashing front hoofs of a band of cows. The adult elk has little to fear from predators, with the exception of an occasional wolf or mountain lion. The elk also is a good deal faster than its enemies, often reaching speeds of up to thirty-five miles an hour. When not in a hurry, this animal usually travels at a trot, a gait it can keep up for hours and over long distances. Only when hard pressed does it break into a gallop. When running, the elk carries its head back, so that nose and eyes are horizontal to the ground. This awkward, nose-in-the-air position has evolved through thousands of years, during which the big bull elk has had to tilt its head up and place its antlers along its back to travel through dense forests. Although the cow does not have antlers, it also carries its head in the same position. The elk can jump as well as run, clearing high hurdles of fallen trees with little effort. One elk is recorded to have jumped over a seven-foot six-inch fence.

Like the bison, elk were so numerous many years ago that they were easy targets for the guns of the early colonists and for the settlers who followed. Between 1815 and 1910, the elk population dropped eighty per cent, to around 50,000. Before game laws were introduced and enforced, many elk were killed for their hides, flesh, and their two canine teeth, which were highly regarded by the Benevolent and Protective Order of Elks and widely used as watch charms. Man still is the most important predator, and hunting is allowed in many states, although herds in some areas are protected. Today there are about 167,600 elk in the United States.

Two of the best-known herds of elk are those in Yellowstone National Park and in the National Elk Refuge at Jackson Hole, Wyoming. The herd in Jackson Hole is supplied with winter feed, the one in Yellowstone is not. In Yellowstone good management procedure of herd reduction is practiced, making certain that the elk population does not outgrow the capacity of the land to support it. The controversy currently raging there is whether the government representatives should reduce the herd or whether the sportsmen should, by being allowed to hunt in the park. Because the park was set up as a sanctuary, my feeling is that its status should be respected. If animals must be removed, the game biologists should do the job.

A number of eastern states are experimenting with the reintroduction of elk. Virginia has been so successful that some of its counties now have a limited hunting season. Many factors must be considered before any mammal can be introduced into an area. In the case of the elk, tracts of timber must be large enough to allow the elk to live relatively unmolested from daily contact with man. There also must be sufficient natural food of the proper type, so that the elk will not be competing with deer and other mammals already present on the range.

Mule Deer

(Odocoileus hemionus)

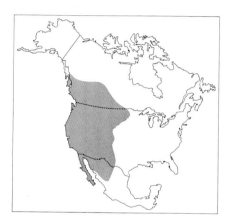

SIZE: *Buck 72 inches; doe smaller.*

WEIGHT: *Males reach 400 pounds.*

HABITS: *Runs up to 35 miles per hour. Mating battles infrequent; buck mates with harem of does.*

HABITAT: *Woodlands and brush.*

FOOD: *Leaves and twigs of oak, bitterbush, sagebrush, serviceberry; bluegrass, wheat grass, brome grass, fescues.*

BREEDING: *Twins or triplets born in June. Gestation 210 days.*

ENEMIES: *Mountain lions, coyotes, bobcats, bears.*

LIFE SPAN: *7 years. Can live up to 15 years.*

The mule deer is named for its oversized ears which resemble those of a mule. Its blunt, forked antlers are easily distinguished from the whitetail's, which are pointed and branch off a single main beam.

Numbering about 2,500,000, the mule deer is not so plentiful as its whitetail relative, because its range is much more restricted. The mule deer is a western species and is distributed on both sides of the Rocky Mountains from Canada to northern Mexico. While preferring the forested areas of higher elevations, it is also found in brushy and cactus country. Several varieties of mule deer may be seen in a number of western national parks.

This deer's general pattern is similar to the white-tailed deer's. Both belong to the genus that derives its name from *koilos*, hollow, and *odo*, toothed ones. There are, however, distinct differences between the two species. The mule deer's ears, for instance, resemble those of a mule—hence its name—and seem much too large for its head. Larger, stockier, more heavy-set than the whitetail, a big mule deer buck may stand forty-two inches high at the shoulder, measure seventy-two inches in length, and weigh close to 400 pounds. The doe is smaller.

Another distinguishing feature is this deer's short, black-tipped or black-topped tail. The tail is much shorter than the whitetail's and is not displayed so often or as jauntily. Unlike the whitetail's antlers, which have points (tines) all branching off a single main beam, the mule deer's antlers are forked and give it the appearance of carrying four slingshots on its head. The average adult mule deer buck has ten points on its antlers—two sets of Ys and a single point on each beam.

While not so graceful a runner as the whitetail, the mule deer is faster, sometimes attaining speeds up to thirty-five miles per hour for short distances. It covers the ground in bounding leaps, keeping all four feet together as though jumping on a pogo stick. Despite its awkward appearance, this deer has little trouble clearing high hurdles and disappearing behind heavy cover. It is less inclined than its white-tailed relative to enter the water.

More gregarious and migratory than the whitetail, the mule deer also mates later. At the end of the rutting season, with the air holding more than a hint of snow and cold, the deer moves down from the highlands into the protected valleys. The buck seems to prefer to bluff its rivals rather than fight them, so mating battles on the whole are scarce. Still the buck manages to collect a harem of does.

The leaves and twigs of oak, bitterbush, sagebrush, and serviceberry become important sources of food in winter, because this deer does not paw down through the snow to get at the grasses buried beneath. To find food, it feeds on windswept slopes; some mule deer have been known to make migrations as far as 150 miles in order to reach such areas.

By December, when the bucks begin to lose their antlers, the deer start to herd up in large numbers. Winter is the time of greatest hardship; starvation takes a heavy toll, and the weakened deer are also more vulnerable to predation. Although mountain lions are the chief enemy, they are becoming so scarce that coyotes, bobcats, and bears probably kill more mule deer nowadays. Parasites and disease also take their toll of deer.

When the new green shoots start to sprout in the early spring, the deer are tempted to linger as long as they can in the valleys. At last they head for their summer homes in the high mountain meadows, where bluegrass, wheat grass, brome grass, and the fescues are among the wide selection that awaits them. The bucks are growing a new set of antlers, and the does prepare for the birth of their young, which are born in June. Twins are the usual number, but triplets occur where the doe has access to a plentiful food supply. Spotted at birth, the fawns weigh about six pounds. They are able to walk soon after birth, but the mother does not allow them to do so. Within a week's time, the fawns are strong enough to follow the doe and stay at her side almost constantly. Sometimes a golden eagle attacks the fawns, but is driven away by the mother whenever possible. Does have even been seen using their sharp hoofs to beat off attacking coyotes desirous of adding young venison to their diets.

By early fall, the fawns are weaned. With the approach of cold weather, the fawns shed their spotted coats, and the adults exchange their reddish summer

In addition to her long ears, the mule deer doe has an oversized, stocky body. But she is faster than her more graceful relative, the whitetail.

coats for dense winter coats of gray, but retain their white rump hair and tail with black tip.

Often a pest on agricultural land, the mule deer also competes with the elk for food. This does not seem to have any effect on its numbers, however, and it is a prized game animal in western United States. Hunters improve the health of the herds by harvesting about 630,000 deer annually. This reduction helps to keep the herd in balance with its range and with the available food. The deer actually is its own worst enemy, because it reproduces in such numbers that it soon consumes all available food and destroys its own range if not controlled.

Whitetailed Deer
(Odocoileus virginianus)

SIZE: Buck 34–40 inches high at shoulder and 4–5 feet long. Doe smaller.

WEIGHT: Average buck 125–175 pounds; occasionally up to 400 pounds.

HABITS: Runs up to 28 miles per hour and leaps over fences 8 feet high. Strong swimmer; has keen senses of hearing and smell.

HABITAT: Open, well-watered woodlands.

FOOD: Leaves, twigs, brush, vines, fruits, berries, fungus.

BREEDING: 1–4 born at a time. Gestation 6½ months.

ENEMIES: Dogs, coyotes, wolves, mountain lions, bobcats, lynxes.

LIFE SPAN: 20 years.

The whitetailed deer is one of few wild animals that has profited by man's activity. Its numbers have increased with the reduction of its natural predators and the clearing of deep forests. Above, a whitetail doe.

Our number-one big game animal, the much-admired whitetailed (or Virginia) deer gets its name from the white underside of its twelve-inch tail, which is displayed like a flag when the deer is alarmed or dashes off. The topside of the tail has a broad gray or brown stripe down the center and is bordered with white.

A full-grown whitetail buck (male) stands about thirty-four to forty inches high at the shoulder and measures four to five feet in length. It weighs averagely between 125 and 175 pounds, although exceptionally large bucks have weighed over 400 pounds. The doe (female) is smaller. Two dwarf subspecies are the Coues deer (*O. v. covesi*) of the Arizona desert and central Mexico and the collie-sized Key deer (*O. v. clavium*) of the Big Pine Key area in southern-most Florida. Once in danger of extinction, the tiny Key deer's survival was assured by the establishment in 1961 of the National Key Deer Refuge.

The whitetail is the most widely distributed and most numerous species of deer in North America, ranging from southern Canada throughout eastern and central United States into Mexico and thence southward. Although most big game animals have been drastically reduced in number by man, the white-tail has actually profited from human activity. Our present national herd of whitetailed deer is estimated to exceed 5,000,000 animals, far more deer than we have had at any time in the country's history. This increase has come

The buck's antlers sweep backward, then forward, sometimes to a length of more than thirty inches on each side. The antlers are shed during the winter.

A whitetail doe nurses her twins among the trees and foliage of the woods. The fawns' white spots serve as protective camouflage.

through the reduction of the deer's natural predators, the improvement of its habitat, better laws and stricter enforcement, and the rapidity with which whitetails reproduce.

The whitetail is an animal of open, well-watered woodlands, not of the deep forest. Its principal food consists of leaves, twigs, and brush, whose growth man stimulated when he cut down the virgin forest. Given a plentiful supply of food, the whitetail increased in numbers, in size, and in antler development. Good antler development proves that the deer is living in harmony with the land. Anything less than a beautiful set of branching antlers indicates either that there is not enough natural food for the deer or that there are too many deer for the available food.

You cannot tell a deer's age by the number of tines, or points, on its antlers. All you can usually tell from the antlers is that the deer is a buck; sometimes not even this is true, because about one out of every 18,000 deer is an antlered doe. During its first summer, a young buck develops little knobs on the top of its head in the center of the hair swirls that it has from birth. Beginning in the second year, the whitetail's antlers usually start to develop in mid-April, and by August the buck should have wide, spreading antlers.

A large whitetail buck with a good set of antlers is an impressive sight. The antlers start backward, then sweep forward, with single tines rising straight up from the main beam. Some of the world's record heads have main beams over thirty inches in length on each side. The older the buck, the heavier the beam of its antlers becomes. The antlers are shed during the winter.

Shy and solitary most of the year, the whitetail buck grows bold during the breeding season, which starts in November, and readily locks horns with rivals for the favors of the doe. The buck breeds at the age of two, usually with several does, but does not gather a harem. About half the does breed in their first year.

In the northern part of its range, winter spells hardship for the deer. Food usually is in short supply, and the bitter weather forces the animals to seek shelter from the cold, piercing wind. The deer yard up (gather) in swamps, gullies, and draws, where they trample out a network of trails. So many deer in such a small area rapidly deplete the food supply. The young of the previous summer are hit hardest, as they are too small to compete with the older, larger deer.

Spring commonly finds these areas littered with the bleaching bones of deer that died of starvation. More often than not the surviving animals are so weakened that they are particularly vulnerable to predation. Next to man, the deer's most feared predator is the free-running dog. Even well-fed dogs that are docile at home all day may be deer killers by night. Coyotes, wolves, mountain lions, bobcats, and lynxes take deer whenever possible, although the coyote and bobcat do not actually kill many deer. Deer use the sharp, cloven hoofs of their forefeet to strike down or fight off predators.

Fawning takes place about six and a half months after mating. A young doe usually has an initial single birth, with twins thereafter. Triplets are fairly

A whitetail fawn jumps over a log. The fawns lose their spots in September when they are three or four months old.

common, quadruplets are rarer, but I know of three instances of quintuplets. A newborn doe weighs about four and a half pounds, a buck about five and a half pounds. Within ten minutes of birth, the fawns are able to walk about and nurse. After licking the little ones dry, the mother leads them to a place of safety, where they can remain hidden while she goes out to feed. The fawns' white-spotted coats serve as protective camouflage as they rest under the sun-dappled foliage, and their location is kept secret by the mother, who returns only to nurse them and then leaves the area so that her body scent will not be detected.

A frightened fawn makes a bleating sound much like a lamb's, to which the doe responds instantly. I have called deer to me by imitating the blatting sound used by adult deer when calling to one another. A frightened adult deer snorts explosively by expelling its breath through its nostrils.

The fawns follow the doe within a week or two after birth and soon begin to eat vegetation. This will include almost every type of brush, vine, fruit, berry, and fungus, with a special partiality for red maple, white cedar, and hemlock. In September the fawns lose their spots, for they now are large enough to outrun almost all their enemies and no longer need to depend on camouflage. The adults shed their bright red summer coats for somber-hued winter coats of grayish-brown (the Coues deer wears its dark coat all year round).

The whitetail can reach speeds up to twenty-eight miles per hour and can leap over fences eight feet high. Its most common defense is to dash off wildly until it reaches cover. Then it stops running and quietly sneaks away. Alerted by its remarkably keen senses of hearing and smell, a deer often remains motionless in the forest, allowing danger to walk right past. Frequently the deer attempts to escape by taking to the water. Whitetails are strong swimmers and, buoyed up by their air-filled coats of hollow hairs, have been found crossing miles of open water at speeds of up to four miles per hour.

Aside from its great esthetic value, the whitetail has had an even more important economic and sporting value. To the Indians and early colonists, it was a basic source of food, clothing, and shelter. Moccasins, blankets, and tepees were among the articles made from its skin. Its tendons were used for thread and fishing lines, its bones for needles, scrapers, and ornaments. As early as 1639, Rhode Islanders enacted game laws for deer conservation, but in succeeding years overhunting led to the animal's extermination in some areas. Reintroduced and protected, it became so abundant that limited hunting once more was permitted.

Most states open the deer hunting season soon after the animal's breeding season is under way. To a large extent, today's hunters take deer for sport rather than for food, yet thousands of tons of venison yearly are eaten throughout the nation. Deer hunting has become big business. New York alone garners $56,000,000 annually from Nimrods stalking the agile whitetail.

Moose
(Alces alces)

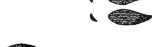

SIZE: 10 feet long; 7 feet high at shoulder. Antlers spread 4–5 feet, record of
81-inch spread.

WEIGHT: 1,200–1,400 pounds average. Cow 300–400 pounds lighter.

HABITS: Grazes on knees to reach short plants. Excellent swimmer, wades in lakes
to feed on water plants or escape flies and mosquitoes.

HABITAT: Dense forests bordering shallow lakes.

FOOD: Leaves and twigs of willow, aspen, maple, birch, balsam, water weeds and
plants.

BREEDING: 1–3 calves per birth. Gestation 240–270 days.

ENEMIES: Wolves, bears, coyotes, wolverines, cougars.

LIFE SPAN: 20 years.

In fall the bull moose's antlers grow to a spread of four to five feet. Yet the moose maneuvers them skillfully through heavy cover and underbrush without making a sound.

The early French explorers and trappers in Canada called the moose *l'original*, because they had never seen anything that looked quite like it. Nothing does look like a moose, which happens to be the largest member of the deer family.

This ungainly creature gives the impression of being a combination of several different animals, looking as though it had been put together from an assortment of leftover parts. Measuring perhaps ten feet in length, it stands taller than a horse, or about seven feet high at its humped shoulders. From heavy fore-quarters the body tapers back to seemingly weak hindquarters, terminating in a three-inch tail. An overhanging muzzle gives the moose's face a mule-like appearance. The dewlap, or bell, of skin and hair hanging under the throat is found primarily on the bull, although a cow occasionally has one.

There are about four different subspecies of moose in North America, which vary only in size. All are dark brown to black in color. Some of the big Kenai (*A. gigas*) bulls of Alaska weigh as much as 1,800 pounds, but the average weight for this animal is from 1,200 to 1,400 pounds. The cow usually is 300 to 400 pounds lighter.

With its wide flat antlers looking like giant hands held palm up, a huge bull moose is a truly majestic sight in the fall. A four to five-foot spread of antlers is average, with the current world's record being a spread of about seven feet. How a big bull maneuvers its massive antlers between the trees I have never been able to figure out. Yet the moose can sneak through heavy cover and underbrush that man cannot penetrate, and does so without making a sound. At other times, it crashes through the forest sounding like a run-away steamroller.

Like its elk and deer relatives, the moose originated in Asia and came to North America during the late Pleistocene epoch, perhaps a little less than 1,000,000 years ago. A northern animal, the moose ranges from Alaska across Canada and into the wilderness areas of Idaho, Wyoming, Montana, Minnesota, Michigan, and Maine. Its habitat is dense forest bordering shallow lakes.

The name moose was the English colonists' approximation of the Algonquin Indian word *musee*, meaning twig-eater. The leaves and twigs of willow, aspen, maple, birch, and balsam are particularly favored by the moose, a gourmand that consumes forty to fifty pounds of browse per day. Sometimes the browse is so high up that the moose stands on its hind legs to reach it or pushes the trees, if they are small enough, to the ground with its chest. Because its neck is so short, the moose must get on its knees to graze on short plants in summer. It feeds in the cool hours of early morning and late afternoon, its ears continually flopping back and forth to pick up any unlikely sound. The moose has keen senses of hearing and smell. Because its eyesight is only fair, it has difficulty in detecting danger unless a suspicious object moves.

The moose uses its long legs to good advantage. In summer it frequently wades about in a lake feeding on succulent water weeds and plants. It also wades out into deep water to escape the black flies and mosquitoes that make life a torment during June and early July. A strong swimmer, the moose often takes to the water to escape danger and to travel from one area to another. Sometimes when a calf is tired, it will place its forelegs on its mother's neck and be towed in that fashion.

Moose have a rather restricted range, except in the breeding season, when

With its long legs, the moose wades out into deep water to escape flies and mosquitoes and to feed on succulent water weeds and plants.

Dripping water from her neck, a cow moose cools herself while she feeds in the water of a northern lake.

the bulls travel considerable distances. They usually trot when going from place to place in a hurry, covering the ground at a faster clip than most racing harness horses. A few moose have been domesticated and taught to pull sulkies or to race at tracks. In Canada, Scandinavia, and Siberia, efforts have been made to train moose as dray animals without much success. These awkward animals gallop, but infrequently, perhaps because their gallop is slower than their trot. I saw a moose galloping purposefully along a beach in the wilds of Quebec Province, slip off a sandbar and tumble head over heels into deep water. It was a very surprised moose, indeed, that rose to the surface of that lake.

Legs and sharp cloven hoofs are used to good effect in fighting and in protection against wolves, bears, and the occasional coyote, wolverine, and cougar. In winter the moose is able to wade through deep snowdrifts and to pack down trails when the herd yards up for protection, gathering near close-growing trees. At one time it was thought that deep snow was a hazard to the moose. On the contrary, recent investigations proved that snow is essential to the animal's survival. The moose can winter in snow too deep for the elk. The soft drifts provide a blanket of insulation: sinking down into the snow affords the moose protection from the winter's bitter cold and biting winds; it prevents the loss of body heat and puts less strain on the body, thus enabling the animal to subsist on less food.

Only during the fall rutting, or breeding, season can the moose be considered dangerous to man. At this time the bull challenges any and all comers to battle, using its antlers in fighting other bulls for the favors of the cows. Now and again the antlers of moose protagonists may become locked and the animals may die of starvation. As the breeding season usually coincides with the hunting season, most hunters in moose areas are well armed. To bring a moose into gun range, they employ hunting methods learned from the Indians. Using a roll of birchbark shaped like a megaphone, the hunter imitates the guttural grunt of a bull to challenge the animal he is trying to call, or he may imitate the mooing call of a lovesick cow to lure a big bull into the area. During this season, the bull may stay for ten to fourteen days with a cow and her offspring of the previous year, then seek another cow.

Early in the following May, the cow drives the yearlings away and proceeds to a secluded place for calving, while the bulls move to the uplands. The first birth is a single calf; thereafter twins are usual and triplets are a rarity. The newborn calves are a rich russet brown color, have no spots, and stand about three feet high. In ten to twelve days' time they follow the mother and soon trail her to the higher elevations, where the bulls already have congregated. In the first summer the young bulls have a button, or knob, on their heads. The second year they usually have long spikes. From that time on, the antlers commonly develop heavy palms with many points, or tines. In late November or December the antlers are shed. A moose is in its prime between six and ten years of age, and may live for another ten years beyond that.

The moose has never been widely distributed in North America south of the Canadian border, so it conflicts little with man, yet along the southernmost fringes of its range, its numbers have been reduced. Throughout most of its range, however, the moose may be hunted on a limited basis as a result of improved game law enforcement and protection. In Newfoundland the introduced moose population has increased so dramatically that the province now has the best moose hunting east of Alaska.

There are probably 200,000 moose in North America today, but no figures on the yearly kill are available. Moose meat, which tastes like good beef, still is an important food item for the Indians and trappers who live in the areas where moose are found. These people take more moose than the sportsmen do, and there is no way of keeping track of the numbers they kill. I know of one small band of Indians in Canada who killed and ate thirteen moose in a single summer season.

Pronghorn Antelope
(Antilocapra americana)

SIZE: Buck 4 feet long, 3 feet tall at shoulder. Doe smaller.

WEIGHT: Up to 125 pounds.

HABITS: Sheds outer sheath of horns each fall. Runs up to 70 miles per hour. Often races cars or moving trains.

HABITAT: Scrub and desert grasslands.

FOOD: Sagebrush, rabbit brush, snowberries, saltbush, grama grass, wheat grass.

BREEDING: 1–3 (usually 2) born in spring. Gestation 240 days.

ENEMIES: Coyotes.

LIFE SPAN: Average up to 15 years.

In late summer, pronghorn bucks grow restless and often fight for control of the harem. They breed during October and November.

It is estimated that more than 40,000,000 pronghorns roamed the plains from southern Canada to northern Mexico when the first white man arrived in the New World. In numbers they rivaled the American bison, whose grazing grounds they shared. In the latter half of the last century there was a massive reduction in the numbers of bison and pronghorns. [Within a matter of fifty years, both animals were almost exterminated.] The slaughter began when the rifle was taken west. By 1920, the pronghorns' numbers had dwindled to 26,000, and the animal was protected in all states. With the introduction of wise game management policies in the 1930s, the pronghorn population increased, until today it numbers about 200,000. On a recent trip west, the swift-running pronghorn was the most common wild mammal seen.

The pronghorn is not really an antelope at all, being more closely related to sheep than to the so-called true antelope of the Old World. This last surviving member of the Antilocapridae family is an exclusively North American mammal, found nowhere else in the world. The prongbuck, as it is sometimes called, inhabits sagebrush areas of open, rolling plains. When forced to cross a river, the prongbuck swims well.

The forward-jutting prong, or tine, on the curve-tipped horns give this animal its name. The prong resembles the hilt or guard on a knife and serves in the same capacity. Both sexes have horns, but the doe's (female's) seldom extend beyond the long, pointed ears. The record length for a set of buck horns is nineteen inches. The pronghorn is the only horned mammal that sheds the outer sheath of its horns each year, in the fall. Growing up and down from the permanent core tip, the new sheath is complete in the mature buck by July.

Unlike the other even-toed hoofed mammals, the pronghorn lacks dewclaws and has only two hoofs, or toes, on each of its four feet. The sharp hoofs are used advantageously in winter to paw away snow in search of vegetation.

Graceful and slim-bodied, a mature pronghorn buck measures about four feet in length, stands perhaps three feet high at the shoulder, and reaches a

The pronghorn buck has a rich, russet-tan coat with a white rump and underparts and broad black bands on the throat and face. It is the only mammal that sheds the outer sheath of its horns every year.

top weight of around 125 pounds. It is beautifully marked, with a rich, russet-tan coat, white flanks, rump, and underparts, and broad black bands on the throat and face. The somewhat smaller doe lacks all or most of the black head markings. To withstand the biting cold and winds of prairie winters, nature has provided the pronghorn with a dense coat of hair having long, hollow, outer guard hairs for insulation and a thick, woolly undercoat for warmth. Seen close up, the hair resembles the bristles on an oversized scrub brush.

Sometimes referred to as the heliographer, the pronghorn has the ability to flash danger signals with its white rump patch, the hairs of which are short in the center and long at the sides. When alarmed or frightened, the pronghorn raises the hairs and turns them outward, almost doubling the size of the rump patch until it resembles a great white rosette. The sun reflected off these hairs sends bright flashes that are visible to the members of the herd across the flat plain miles away. The animal also discharges a musk that can be detected from a distance of up to 500 yards. Alerted, the herd gathers at a central point and moves off to safety at an even gait.

The pronghorn's large black eyes with wide-angle range of vision give the animal the exceptionally keen eyesight required to survive on the open prairies. Hunters sometimes take advantage of this creature's natural curiosity by waving a white flag or handkerchief to decoy it into gunshot range. Unable to identify the waving flag, and secure in its ability to outrun danger, the pronghorn moves in ever closer until the hunter springs to his feet and tries to shoot the animal before it dashes off. This trick does not work as well nowadays as formerly because the pronghorn has become much more wary.

Strong leg bones and a large windpipe that makes for easy breathing permit the pronghorn to reach speeds of up to seventy miles per hour for short distances. Being a horizontal rather than a vertical jumper, the pronghorn can jump between or dash under the strands of barbed wire fencing without a break in its stride. This swiftest of North American mammals seems to take great pride in its running ability, frequently pacing alongside a moving car or train until, with a dazzling display of acceleration, it cuts directly across the vehicle's path. Although most would-be predators are easily outrun, high speeds can be maintained only for three or four miles before exhaustion sets in. The coyote, the pronghorn's number one enemy, usually has to prey on the old, sick, or very young members of a herd. Occasionally, a coyote may run a healthy pronghorn in a circle, then rest while another coyote takes over. This continues until the exhausted victim drops.

With the approach of the breeding season in late summer, the buck grows restless. It has a peculiar habit of making sudden jumps from a standing position to the left or right. Fights between bucks are common, as each individual gathers together a harem of all the does it can control. Breeding takes place during October and November.

Winter finds the gregarious pronghorns gathering in herds that may number in the hundreds. In some northern states, they migrate several hundred miles to areas where driving winds have swept away the snow exposing the plants they feed upon. In the southern part of their range, they stay within an area of ten to fifteen square miles. Sagebrush, rabbit brush, snowberry, saltbush, grama grass, and wheat grass are favored foods at all times of the year. The pronghorn does not damage the range, even though it may share grazing grounds with sheep and cattle for short periods or compete with livestock for water.

When spring arrives the bucks reform into small herds, while the does go off by themselves to give birth to their young—usually twins, after a single first birth, and occasionally triplets. Able to walk almost immediately after birth, the kids in a week's time can outrun a dog. If a coyote or golden eagle should attempt to get the young, the doe attacks unhesitatingly with her sharp hoofs and strong forelegs. In July, does and young start to congregate in small bands. The kids call to their mother on a high-pitched, quavery note; the adults respond with an explosive snort. Soon the kids are nibbling on vegetation. At three months of age, they have acquired adult coats and about two-thirds of their growth. Pronghorns seem to suffer little from diseases and are comparatively free from parasites. Their average life span is around fifteen years.

The pronghorn does not do as well in captivity as the bison, its companion of the plains, because it requires more space and greater freedom. In addition to the pronghorn's great esthetic appeal, it is valued by man for its tender meat and fine trophy head. Although protected in a number of national parks and refuges, notably Sheldon National Antelope Refuge in Nevada and Hart Mountain National Antelope Refuge in Oregon, open seasons permit the hunting of pronghorns in several states. Entire herds have been trapped and shipped to Louisiana, South Carolina, and Florida as part of a continuing experiment with non-native animals conducted by state game management officials. If the animals do well and thrive in their new habitat, the plan is to make them available to hunters.

Bison
(Bison bison)

SIZE: *10 feet long, 6 feet tall at top of shoulder. Cow smaller.*

WEIGHT: *Record is 3,000 pounds.*

HABITS: *Herd animal. Bulls wage furious battles for favors of cows.*

HABITAT: *Government ranges or private herds.*

FOOD: *Grama grass, dropseed grass, buffalo grass, bluestem.*

BREEDING: *Single calf born in May.*

ENEMIES: *Former predators, grizzly bear and lobo wolf, now almost extinct. Protected by government from hunters.*

LIFE SPAN: *15 years in wild, almost 40 years in captivity.*

Wild bison, which once numbered in the millions, are no longer seen roaming the prairies in the United States. Today they are found only in private herds or on government ranges.

Robert Ripley, of "Believe It or Not" fame, once remarked that Buffalo Bill never killed a buffalo. Ripley was right. In North America, we have bison, not buffalo. The latter name properly belongs to the African buffalo (*Syncerus caffer*) and water buffalo (*Bubalus bubalis*) of southeast Asia, members of a quite different group of bovines which the bison was thought to resemble.

There are no wild bison in North America any more. Today the animals are fully protected and are found only on government ranges or in private herds. But this was not always so. At the time of the coming of the first white men to the New World, it is estimated that perhaps 60,000,000 to 70,000,000 bison inhabited central North America from the Appalachian Mountains to the Cascade Range and Great Slave Lake in Canada to northern Mexico. Bison were found in many eastern forests (in Pennsylvania as late as 1799). But by 1820 they had been exterminated east of the Mississippi River.

Most abundant on the central prairies and western plains, the bison was the staple of life to the plains Indians. It provided them with meat, hides for clothing and shelter, bones for awls, sinew for thread. Before the Spaniards brought the horse to the New World, the Indians hunted the bison on foot. Covered with the skins of wolves, whom the bison did not fear, the early Indian hunters crept close enough to the huge beasts to kill them with bows and arrows. The Indians also held drives, where they stampeded herds of bison over cliffs. Sometimes they trapped the animals by setting fire to the prairies. The horse gave the red men greater mobility in pursuing their prey.

The early white settlers also hunted bison for food. The supply was believed to be inexhaustible. Second Lieutenant George S. Anderson, assigned to the 6th Cavalry at Fort Hays, Kansas, described the scene as late as 1871: "For six days we continued our way through this enormous herd, during the last three of which it was in constant motion across our path. . . . it is impossible to approximate the millions that composed it." And yet disaster had already overtaken the bison by the 1870s. Ranchers and farmers, busy dividing up vast acreages for their own use, could not tolerate the huge beasts that broke down fences and paid little attention to the works of man. Market hunters killed bison by the thousands for their tongues, which sold for 25 cents apiece. They were butchered by the millions for their hides, and their bones were sent east to be converted into fertilizer.

The extent of the massacre is revealed in the company records of the Northern Pacific Railroad, which in 1882 shipped 200,000 bison hides to market, but only three years later had no bison cargo at all. This slaughter was approved by the U.S. Government because it effectively destroyed the food supply of the Crow, Blackfoot, and Sioux Indians, who were making a last desperate attempt to hold onto their lands, coveted by the white man.

By the late 1880s the bison had been pushed close to the edge of extinction. Conservationists undertook the tremendous job of alerting and educating the public to fight for the animal's survival. Largely through the efforts of the American Bison Society, the New York Zoological Society, and President Theodore Roosevelt, Congress was persuaded to save the bison from extermination. Gradually the herds were built up, and today we have about 5,000 bison. These can be seen in their natural environment in such places as the National Bison Range in Montana, Wichita Mountains Wildlife Refuge in Oklahoma, and Yellowstone National Park in Wyoming.

The bison is the largest land mammal in North America. Some exceptionally heavy bulls (males) have weighed over 3,000 pounds. This wild cattle measures perhaps ten feet in length and stands about six feet high at the top of the huge shoulder hump that prompted Spanish explorers in the southwest to call it the crooked-back ox. Shaggy brown hair covers the bison's entire body in winter, but in summer the hindquarters appear to be almost hairless. So well protected is the bison by the long hair on its massive forequarters, neck, and head that it is the only mammal to face a storm head on. Other hoofed mammals turn their rumps to the gale's fury and drift before it. Both sexes have horns, the cow's being more slender and curved than the bull's. The cow also is smaller and lighter in color. The woodland bison (*B. b. athabascae* Rhoads) of western Canada is larger and darker than the plains bison. Canada has about 40,000 wood bison, and the number is increasing. These may be seen at Wood Buffalo National Park in Alberta and in the wild in the Northwest Territories.

The largest animal in North America, the bison bull weighs up to 3,000 pounds. Shaggy brown hair covers its entire body in winter, but in summer the hind quarters appear to be almost hairless.

The cares of the world seem to have settled on the bison as it walks with slow, measured step and head bent low, its short beard giving the great beast an air of thoughtful wisdom. All this changes in a twinkling when the bison's keen hearing and smell alert it to danger. When angry or frightened, the bison paws the earth with its forefeet, showering dirt in all directions. Raising high its short, tufted tail, head lowered, and chin drawn in, the bison bellows its disapproval. When this big animal charges or runs from danger, it moves its bulk with amazing swiftness. Its large heart and huge lungs enable the bison to run at speeds of up to forty miles per hour for hours on end.

The bison has always been a herd animal, preferring to be in the company of its own kind. Old bulls are the exception. These old fellows separate from the herd and lead a solitary existence, or group together with two or three others. They may seek this solitary life voluntarily, or may be forced from the herd by younger, stronger bulls.

Before the white man's arrival, the huge bison herds migrated every fall hundreds of miles to the south, where ample food was easily found. The move north began in the spring, when supplies of succulent grama grass, dropseed grass, buffalo grass, and bluestem were assured. Nowadays, when they are restricted in their movements and forced to remain on the northern ranges, the bison paw the snow aside with their hoofs to reach the grasses beneath. They feed mostly in the early morning and evening. Water is necessary, but the bison can go much longer than domestic cattle without it.

Bison generally breed when they are three years old. The breeding season, commencing in July and August, is punctuated by furious battles between bulls for the favors of the cows. The head-on collision between a pair of bulls reminds one of two locomotives crashing together. The bulk of the shock is taken on the heavy boss of hair and bone rather than on the sixteen to twenty-inch horns, with which each rival tries to gouge the other's unguarded parts. So great is the bison's strength that a single animal is capable of lifting a horse and rider on its horns and carrying them several hundred feet before throwing them down.

A single calf is born in May. Twins are a great rarity. In two or three days the calf is able to follow the mother as she moves with the herd, and the two remain together through the next winter. Before they became extinct, the plains grizzly bear and lobo wolf were the bison's most important natural enemies, preying on calves and on aged and sickly adults. Deep-drifting snows, river crossings, prairie fires, and marshy ground also took a toll of the huge herds, yet nothing made a real dent in their numbers until the white man appeared. The bison's life span of about fifteen years in the wild increases to almost forty years in captivity.

The bison received belated recognition as the symbol of the Old West by being one of the few native animals to appear on United States postage stamps —the 4-cent Trans-Mississippi issue of 1898 and the 35-cent regular issue of 1932. It also appeared on the reverse side of the Indian head nickel. With the disappearance of that coin from common use, few of us have any opportunity to see even a representation of what was once our most common hoofed animal.

Bighorn Sheep
(Ovis canadensis)

SIZE: *Ram 3½ feet high at shoulder, 7 feet in length. Horns (uncurled) can be 48 inches long. Ewes smaller.*

WEIGHT: *Up to 300 pounds.*

HABITS: *Grazes higher pastures in summer, lower ground in winter. Rams battle for favors of ewes.*

HABITAT: *Mountains.*

FOOD: *Sagebrush, fescue grass, wheat grass, bluegrass.*

BREEDING: *Single lamb or occasional twins born in spring. Gestation 150 days.*

ENEMIES: *Eagles, wolves, coyotes, mountain lions.*

LIFE SPAN: *12–14 years.*

The bighorn ewe, above, has horns to help her protect her young. Yearly growth rings on the horns indicate the animal's age.

In Wyoming several summers ago I tried to photograph some bighorn sheep up above the 10,000-foot mark, on top of Mount Washburn. The force of the wind had stunted and twisted the few trees growing below the crests. Grasses grew in profusion, and the bald tops made an excellent pasture. I located some ewes (females) feeding on the lee side of the mountain out of the force of the wind, and after a great deal of maneuvering, was able to take a few photos of them before they decided they had posed long enough. Over the side of the mountain they bounded, with such speed and recklessness that I expected at any moment to see at least one of them go tumbling head over heels into the valley below. Nothing of the kind happened, for the animals' black, sharp-edged, cushioned hoofs act like suction cups and provide a firm foothold on even the most precipitous slopes. About the only time bighorns lose their footing is when a rock slide or avalanche sweeps down upon them. When this happens, the animals do not utilize their horns to break their fall, as is sometimes claimed.

The horns of an adult bighorn ram (male) represent without a doubt the most sought-after big-game prize in North America. Curling out, backward, and then forward, these massive horns may measure more than forty-eight inches along the outside of the curve and have at the base a circumference of over sixteen inches. The heavy yearly growth rings show up prominently among the lesser ridges, making the horns accurate indicators of age. Being true horns, they continue to grow for the entire life of the animal, about twelve to fourteen years. The tips of the horns commonly are frayed or broomed from countless battering battles or from having been used to scrape away snow to secure the grass beneath. The ewe also has horns, narrow spikes that make good fighting weapons when needed in defense of the young.

When full-grown, the sturdy bighorn stands about three and a half feet high at the shoulder and measures seven feet in length. A really big ram weighs 300 pounds. The grayish-brown coat, with white underparts and circular white rump patch, provides the sheep with extremely effective camouflage in its rocky habitat. A subspecies, known as the desert bighorn, inhabits the dry, barren lands of the southwest. Although paler and smaller than the mountain sheep, its horns are equally impressive. Two northern forms are the white Dall sheep (*O. dalli*) of Alaska and the black Stone's sheep (*O.d. stonei*) of British Columbia.

Sheep are sociable animals, and as a rule members of the herd coexist peacefully. They are creatures of regular habits and lead quiet lives. Rising early to feed, they retire to chew their cuds, feed again in the late afternoon, and turn in early for the night. Sagebrush, fescue grass, wheat grass, and bluegrass are among the most sought-after foods. This sheep takes some water and also swims well. One member of the herd always stands guard, on the lookout for danger, while the other animals feed. Living among the mountain peaks with the predatory eagle, the bighorn's extraordinarily keen eyesight stands it in good stead.

During the breeding season, in November and December, the rams drop their sociability. Having rejoined the herd after a summer absence, they engage their rivals in battle for the favors of the ewes. Two competitors stand side by side, then, as if on command, they separate and stalk off in opposite directions. When they are about twenty to thirty feet apart, the rams suddenly rear up on their hind feet, whirl about, and rush at each other like express trains, grunting, snorting, and even grinding their teeth. With a resounding chock, the two heads crash together. The force is enough to crush the skull or break the neck of a lesser animal. Occasionally, rams are killed, but more often the battering merely leaves them dazed. Shaking their heads, they go at it again and again, until one is proved the victor or both break away. The victor, if there is one,

A frolicsome animal, the bighorn lamb spends much of its time gamboling about on the mountain top it inhabits. Its cushioned hooves act like suction cups to provide a firm foothold on the rocky slopes. Above, a lamb pauses in front of the camera.

gathers together a small herd of ewes and proceeds to defend them against all comers.

Winter forces the sheep to lower ground. Sometimes they have to cross a valley or even another mountain peak to seek food. At such times they are more susceptible to predation than when they are safely scrambling among the peaks of their home range. Wolves, coyotes, and mountain lions take a sheep when the rare opportunity presents itself. Disease and parasites, however, are far deadlier enemies.

At the end of the gestation period, in the spring, the ewe leaves the herd and seeks out a rocky outcropping or ledge. Such a spot provides a better defensive position against predation. The eagle is the chief offender, and at the first sight or sound of one, the ewe stands astride her young, protecting them with her own body.

Single lambs are the rule, although there are occasional twins. At birth the lamb is gray, with a dark stripe running down the middle of its back. It walks within an hour and grows rapidly, nursing almost every hour. In a week or so, ewe and lamb return to the herd. All the lambs join forces, dashing and gamboling about and running up to the top of large boulders, where they play a version of "King of the Mountain." Every once in a while some of the mothers enter into the frolic, with both ewes and lambs bleating in much the same fashion as domestic sheep. The rams in the meantime have separated from the herd to set up bachelor quarters. During the summer, all the sheep look as though they are wearing badly motheaten fur coats, for their dense winter coats are now shedding and the long, dead hair sloughs off in patches.

Although widely distributed throughout the western mountain regions from British Columbia to northern Mexico, the bighorn has been greatly reduced in numbers. Because there are only about 12,000 of these sheep left in the west, they may be hunted only in a few states and on a limited basis. They are hunted primarily for sport, as the stiff-haired skins have little commerical value. To obtain a set of horns, the hunter is required to have strong legs, keen eyesight, be an excellent marksman, and have infinite patience. Not all hunters are sportsmen. Poachers sometimes lie in wait for the animals at waterholes, then take only the heads, leaving the carcasses to be picked clean by vultures.

Many studies and experiments are being carried out to increase the number of bighorns. Among the best places to catch sight of these elusive, agile sheep are the Rocky Mountain National Park in Colorado, Glacier National Park in Montana, and Grand Teton National Park in Wyoming.

Mountain Goat
(Oreamnos americanus)

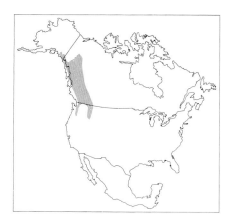

SIZE: *Billy 60–65 inches long, 40 inches high at shoulder. Nanny smaller.*

WEIGHT: *200–300 pounds.*

HABITS: *Sure-footed in jumping around mountain rocks. Herds post sentinels to warn of danger.*

HABITAT: *High mountains.*

FOOD: *Grasses, sedges, lichens.*

BREEDING: *1–2 kids born in spring or early summer. Gestation 147 days.*

ENEMIES: *Golden eagles occasionally prey on kids. Mountain lions, wolves, lynxes attack when goats descend to lower altitudes in winter.*

LIFE SPAN: *10 years.*

In winter the mountain goat grows a dense, shaggy coat to protect it from the cold. Deep snows force it down from the mountain peaks to seek food on lower ground.

In spite of its goat-like appearance and name, the mountain goat is not a goat but an antelope relative of the Alpine chamois. This sure-footed animal inhabits some of the most inhospitable terrain in North America; the upper slopes of mountains from Alaska into Oregon, Idaho, and Montana. Its Latin name is derived appropriately from Oreas, the spirit of the high mountains.

Sharing its rocky crags with the free-flying eagle, the mountain goat has found a segment of the landscape not coveted by man. Considering that the first goat skins were obtained in 1805 by members of the Lewis and Clark expedition, it is easy to predict what the fate of the mountain goat would have been had man coveted the peaks. These lofty heights also provide the goat with protection from almost all natural predators. Only the golden eagle, which makes off with an occasional kid, can be considered as preying on the mountain goat. No other predator is willing to enter its mountain fastness in summer to hunt it.

I well remember a day I spent climbing after mountain goats in Glacier National Park. Having spotted the animals from the road, I verified them with my binoculars—they were feeding on a high ridge above the Going to the Sun Highway. Packing cameras, tripod, telephoto lenses, and other photographic paraphernalia, I started up. The face of the mountain was just sheer enough to make me want to lean in, especially with all that gear packed on my back. Up, up, I went, and so did the goats, moving ever higher above me as they jumped nimbly from rock to rock. After about two and a half hours, I reached the top. There was not a goat in sight. A flat spine, about fifty feet wide, ran

These sure-footed mountain goat kids grow up on the upper slopes of America's highest mountains, far from any predator except the golden eagle.

along the top of the mountain, dropping on the far side in a precipice. Evidently the goats had gone down the ridge.

After resting for about twenty minutes, I began my climb down. The descent took me about an hour. When I reached the bottom, I looked up. There, standing about 500 feet above the spot where I had first seen them, were the goats.

I attempted another, easier climb in the afternoon, but had to give up when only part way. The altitude and terrific exertion were simply too much for me. Back in camp that night, I wrote in my log: "Too big a mountain, too small a man."

Nothing, apparently, is too big for the mountain goat. It scrambles up and down mountainsides that would tax the ability of a fly, finding footholds that cannot be seen by the person watching below. Rash young goats dash right up to the edge of an abyss, looking as though they are sure to lose their footing and go hurtling over the brink. Instead they stop, peer over the chasm, then calmly lie down on the edge and chew their cuds. Mountain goats' black, cloven hoofs are especially designed to provide a sure-grip, nonslip hold on the rocks. The hoofs, which splay widely, have a hard outer edge and soft, cuplike center portions.

The mountain goat has a compact, chunky body set on short legs. It moves at a stiff-legged, deliberate, sedate gait that gives it an air of dignity. This dignified bearing is further enhanced by the chin beard worn by both sexes. Both the billy (male) and nanny (female) have short, smooth, black horns, but the male's are much larger and better developed, curving back to a length of ten or more inches. Both also have scent glands at the base of the horns. An adult billy goat measures about sixty to sixty-five inches in length and up to forty inches high at its humped shoulder. Weights vary between 200 and 300 pounds, with the female being smaller in size and lighter in weight.

With the approach of cold weather the goat begins to acquire its heavy winter coat, a four-inch layer of soft woolen underfur beneath six to eight inches of guard hairs. The coldest, most piercing wind that shrieks around the peaks cannot penetrate this dense, shaggy, almost pure-white coat. Thus camouflaged, the goat blends into the snowy landscape that is so much a part of its habitat.

The breeding season starts in November and is marked by the aggressive behavior of the males, which have rejoined the herd. The billies rub the base of their horns against any shrubs in the area, releasing an oil scent attractive to the females. Fights between males are frequent, and sometimes serious injuries are inflicted with the dagger-like horns. After mating, the herd stays together for the remainder of the winter, sometimes taking shelter in caves. Deep snows force the goats down from the mountain peaks to seek food. At this time, they may be preyed upon by mountain lions, lynxes, and wolves.

In late spring or early summer, the nanny goat selects a secluded spot for the birth of her young. One kid is the usual number, but twins occur quite frequently. The kids weigh about seven pounds at birth and are able to run around when about a half-hour old. After a few days of isolation, the nanny takes the young down to join the herd. The kids call with a plaintive bleat, and the adults give an occasional grunt, but usually are silent. During the summer, most of the adult males separate from the main herd.

What the goat finds to eat in its barren world puzzles me. High above the tree level, even the grasses, sedges, and lichens are scarce. Yet apparently the goat finds them in sufficient quantities so that it is not tempted to forsake the peaks for valley woodlands, except in winter or to visit mineral licks. Generally, a solitary sentinel stands guard over the feeding herd, alert to any sign of danger. Unlike the bighorn sheep, however, the mountain goat is more dependent upon its sense of smell than on its senses of sight and hearing. This goat is unique among horned mammals for its habit of regularly sitting on its haunches when watching an object that has aroused its curiosity.

Avalanches and rock slides probably take a heavy toll. This goat is subject to many diseases and parasites. Its average life span is about ten years. Man does not constitute too great a hazard to the mountain goat simply because more effort is required to get up into goat country than most hunters are willing to expend. Additionally, its horns are not sufficiently spectacular nor is its flesh sufficiently tasty to be prized. At one time the Indians of British Columbia killed many of these goats for their fine underwool, which was spun into cashmere-quality Chilkat blankets, but today this production is restricted. Nevertheless, this goat is becoming increasingly rare. Most of the 8,000 mountain goats in existence are found in the national parks.

9

❦ ❦ ❦

Edentata—

Toothless Mammals

The tropical anteaters, armadillos, and sloths all belong to the ancient order of edentates—literally, *e*, without, *dentates*, teeth. Only the anteaters, however, are wholly toothless. No edentates have front teeth (canines and incisors), and even when teeth are present, they are extremely simple. Many members of this order have long, sticky tongues to assist them in gathering the insects that are the principal portion of their diet.

Almost 70,000,000 years ago, during the Paleocene epoch, the first edentates appeared on earth. During the Pleistocene, about 1,000,000 years ago, they reached their maximum development with the now long-extinct Glyptodont, which measured fourteen feet in length and stood five and a half feet high. This New World order may have had its beginning in the Southern Hemisphere, with certain species working their way northward. At any rate, the only member of this order found in the United States is the nine-banded armadillo.

Nine-Banded Armadillo
(Dasypus novemcinctus)

SIZE: 28 inches, including 12-inch tail.

WEIGHT: Up to 15 pounds.

HABITS: Nocturnal, spends most of day underground. Crosses rivers by crawling on bottom or floats on top by inflating intestines.

HABITAT: Deserts or shrubby, shaded areas.

FOOD: Ground insects.

BREEDING: Normally 4 in litter, born March or April. Cell division about 100 days after mating; young born 120–150 days later.

ENEMIES: Foxes, coyotes, peccaries, bobcats, dogs.

LIFE SPAN: Up to 4 years.

When threatened by a predator, the armadillo tries to scoot into a thicket or dig itself out of sight. If unable to get away, it flops down on its side and curls up within its thick shell.

In 1870 the armadillo entered the Rio Grande valley of Texas from the south. No one knows what prompted this move or its expansion farther north in the years following. It wandered into Arkansas, Oklahoma, and Louisiana, and became established in Florida when some pet armadillos transported there effected an escape in 1924. The only limiting factor to the expansion of the armadillo into more northerly states is cold weather, which kills off the surface insects and freezes the ground so hard the animal cannot dig for food.

In addition to warm weather and desert regions, the armadillo likes shrubby, shaded areas. It avoids the heat by spending the daylight hours underground. The burrows dug by the armadillo often benefit rabbits, opossums, and other small mammals, which take them over as living quarters.

The armadillo's Latin name describes it as hairy footed, *dasypus*, and nine-girdled, *novemcinctus*. To American naturalist John James Audubon, this unusual creature resembled "a small pig in the shell of a turtle." Its bony plates reminded the Spanish explorers of their own armor, and they gave it the name of *armadillo*, "little armored one."

Although the armadillo wears its armor for protection, it does not clank around in it like a knight of old. This is because the overlapping scales that make up the armor consist of modified skin rather than hard shell, as in the case of the lobster and other crustaceans. Brownish-gray to almost black scales cover the body, tail, legs, and top of the head. The nine hinged bands girdling the midsection of the body enable this armadillo to bend its body, although not in a compact ball as is possible with some of the South American species. Only the soft, leathery belly is unprotected.

All four toes on its forefeet and five toes on its hind feet are armed with long, strong claws. These are not used for fighting, but for digging up insects and excavating burrows. The armadillo's teeth are small, rootless, and continuously growing. A full-grown armadillo is about the size of a house cat, perhaps twenty-eight inches long, including a twelve-inch tail, and weighing up to fifteen pounds. Both male and female look alike and have a life span of not more than four years.

If threatened by such predators as the fox, coyote, peccary, bobcat, dog, or man, the armadillo's best hope is escape. It can move with surprising speed. Sometimes when startled, it bounces straight up in the air, then scoots for the nearest bush or thicket, or dives into its burrow. Given half a chance, the armadillo can dig itself completely out of sight in less time than it takes to talk about it. Only when cornered does it flop down on its side and curl up.

John James Audubon described the armadillo as "a small pig in the shell of a turtle." Nine hinged bands gird the animal's midsection.

This tactic is not always effective, for dogs often flip an armadillo over on its back and attack the unprotected underparts.

To cross a narrow stream or river, the armadillo holds its breath and walks along the bottom. If the river is too wide to be crossed in this fashion, the armadillo surfaces, gulps in air to inflate its intestines, and completes its journey buoyed up by its built-in waterwings, holding its slender, pink-tipped nose above water like the periscope of a submarine.

The armadillo usually mates in August, but the young are not born until the following March or April. This animal is unusual in that the female always gives birth to four young, all of which are of the same sex. The identical quadruplets result from the division of a single fertilized egg into two cells, each of which again divides.

Born in an underground burrow, the open-eyed young are covered with soft, bony scales, which do not harden completely until the animals are full grown. Shortly after birth, the young can move about. In about two months' time they are weaned to start feeding on insects, which make up the greater part of the armadillo's diet. Beetles, bees, wasps, ants (even the dreaded fire ants), caterpillars, grasshoppers, crickets, and termites are most frequently taken. By actual count, over 14,000 ants were consumed by an armadillo at a single meal. Tearing apart the anthills with their heavy claws, the armadillos use their long, sticky tongues to lap up their meal from the frantic insects milling about. The balance of their diet is made up of millipeds, snails, earthworms, fruits, berries, and an occasional crayfish, frog, or salamander.

Although the armadillo has been known to rob nests of ground-nesting birds, such instances are extremely rare. Instead of being harmful to the bobwhite quail, for example, the armadillo actually is helpful to it. Certain species of ants attack young quail, so that every nest of ants destroyed by the armadillo represents an added chance of survival for the quail.

The gregarious armadillo often feeds in small herds. Occasionally, using its tail as a support, it rears up on its hind feet, to get a better view of its surroundings. This position really doesn't help it much, because its eyesight is as poor as its hearing. On the other hand, its sense of smell is keen, and the armadillo shuffles along, snuffling noisily through its long, thin nose and making a soft grunting sound. For protection, the armadillo feeds under cover of darkness.

In some parts of its range, where it is known as the "poor man's hog," the armadillo is prized for its light, pork-flavored flesh. It is also hunted for its shell, which is made into baskets, lampshades, ashtrays, and other novelties for the tourist trade. The armadillo can be tamed sufficiently to accept food by hand, but it never becomes responsive enough to make a satisfactory pet. It is best kept in a concrete pen, because it easily claws up dirt floors and tears up wooden ones. In spite of the local hunting pressure being applied to the armadillo, it is slowly increasing in numbers and range.

Appendix A

Where to See Mammals

People often ask, "Where can I see the different mammals in their native habitat?" Watching mammals is much more difficult than watching birds because most birds are active all day long. Mammals, on the other hand, prefer the protective cover of darkness. Originally, many mammals were as diurnal as the birds, but pressure by man in the form of hunting and trapping forced them to change their habits in order to survive. Where they have complete protection, some mammals change back and can again be seen in the daytime.

The most difficult of all mammals to see are the carnivores, particularly the wild members of the cat family, which are so furtive and wary that even people living in areas they frequent seldom get more than an occasional glimpse of them. The members of the dog family, among the most intelligent of all mammals, also tend to avoid contact with man. There are always exceptions; recently a number of coyotes in several western parks, Yellowstone in particular, have become quite tame, to the point of accepting tidbits of food thrown to them. Some of the smallest carnivores are the most brazen. A weasel seems to fear nothing and often will stand right up to a man. By contrast its larger cousins, the marten and fisher, are very shy.

In areas where it is hunted, the black bear's native intelligence prompts it to avoid man. When it is given protection, the bear soon becomes a confirmed panhandler, much preferring to live off handouts and visits to the local dump than to make the effort of securing food on its own. These animals teach the same tricks to their offspring so that they, too, are dependent upon the dole. This situation delights tourists, who consistently disregard the signs telling them not to feed the bears. Every park superintendent knows that bears can cause him problems, but he also knows that bears attract more people than almost anything else the park has to offer.

Most of the hoofed game are comparatively easy to see. The only place where you can see bison is in preserves and parks. Scarce, except in the western parks, moose are increasing in numbers in the wilderness areas of Maine. Elk are more common, particularly in the western states, although some eastern states either have hunting seasons for elk or plan to in the near future. Mule deer are western creatures, while whitetailed deer are found almost all over the country. The whitetails are so common that they can be found about dusk in almost any farmer's field, and even in metropolitan areas deer constitute a hazard on the highways. I have seen as many as 183 deer in one hour's time within five miles of my home in New Jersey. Pronghorns are strictly western mammals, but are increasing to the point where they are commonly seen in the general countryside as well as in the parks. One of the most convenient spots to find collared peccaries is at the waterholes of the Arizona-Sonora Desert Museum in Tucson.

Bats can be found in the cities as well as in the rural areas. Their secretive nature prevents their being located in the daytime, when they try to hide in tiny dark crevasses.

The rodents' territorial ranges vary in size. Some of these animals are found from coast to coast, while the habitat of other species may be measured in miles. The best places to see gray squirrels are the city parks. There may be more squirrels and chipmunks, too, in the woodlands, but they will be wild and you will not see as many of them. Most of these creatures are extremely tenacious and are found on almost every spot of land not inhabited or used by man. Vacant lots in towns have mice, shrews, moles, rabbits, and so on. Any piece of land that man abandons is soon taken over and repopulated by wildlife.

If you have read this book carefully, you know in what areas the mammals described may be found. Except in zoos, you cannot expect to find an armadillo in Maine or a moose in Texas. In fact, this process of elimination is most helpful in identifying a mammal after you have located it. Before setting out to find wildlife, decide which mammal you wish to see. Determine its range from the maps and general description, then find out which parks, preserves, wild areas, or refuges lie within that area, and you will know where to start looking. Reread the descriptive text on the mammal telling the conditions under which it lives and where it makes its home—up in a tree, along rock ledges or water courses, and so on—and you will be able to narrow your search to a specific spot. Look for tracks and signs of the mammal. From then on, all it takes is patience—lots of patience. Don't hesitate to ask people living in the area concerning the whereabouts of the mammal you seek. Most people are willing to help, and they have the great advantage of knowing both the mammal and the area.

The best places to see wildlife in its natural environment are the National Parks and Wildlife Refuges. No hunting is permitted, and the wildlife soon comes to accept tourists and cameras as a part of its existence. State and provincial parks and refuges also are havens for wildlife. Only a few of the many areas with their special attractions can be listed here.

Abbreviations

FP = Forest Preserve
GP = Game Preserve
GR = Game Reserve
NF = National Forest
NM = National Monument
NMP = National Memorial Park
NP = National Park
NS = National Seashore
NWR = National Wildlife Refuge

P = Provincial Park
PF = Provincial Forest
SF = State Forest
SFGA = State Fish and Game Area
SP = State Park
SR = State Reserve or Reservation
WA = Wild or Wilderness Area
WLFR = Wildlife and Fish Refuge
WS = Wildlife Sanctuary

UNITED STATES

Alabama

WILLIAM B. BANKHEAD NF, Montgomery: Deer, bobcat, mink, muskrat, weasel, opossum.

GULF SP, Gulf Shores: Deer, raccoon.
TALLADEGA NF, Talladega: Deer, small mammals.
WHEELER NWR, Decatur: Small mammals.

Alaska
GLACIER BAY NM, Sitka: Black bear, mountain goat, wolverine.
KATMAI NM, Mount McKinley NP: Moose, lynx, wolf, wolverine.
KENAI NATIONAL MOOSE RANGE, Kenai: Moose, bear, lynx, wolverine, mountain goat, bighorn sheep (Dall), coyote, Arctic fox.

Arizona
CABEZA PRIETA GR, Yuma: Bighorn sheep, ringtail.
COCOCINO NF, Flagstaff: Elk, pronghorn antelope, deer, bear, mountain lion.
CORONADO NF, Arizona–New Mexico: Peccary, deer, bear, mountain lion.
GRAND CANYON NP: Pronghorn antelope, bighorn sheep, bobcat, mountain lion, badger, ringtail.
KOFA GR, Yuma: Bighorn sheep, ringtail.
ORGAN PIPE CACTUS NM, Ajo: Desert bighorn sheep, pronghorn antelope, whitetailed deer, mule deer, peccary.
SAGUARO NM, Tucson: Mule deer, coyote, peccary, bear.
TONTO NF, Phoenix: Elk, deer, bison, peccary, mountain lion.

Arkansas
BIG LAKE NWR, Manila: Muskrat, raccoon, mink.
HOT SPRINGS NP: Red and gray foxes, coyote, bobcat, small fur-bearers.
OUACHITA NF, Hot Springs: Deer, small mammals.
WHITE RIVER NWR, St. Charles: Whitetailed deer, black bear, mink, otter, raccoon.

California
CHANNEL ISLANDS NM, Santa Barbara and Santa Isabel Islands: Large sea lion rookeries.
LASSEN VOLCANIC NP, Mineral: Red fox, coyote, bobcat, mountain lion, bear, badger, marmot, small mammals.
POINT LOBOS RESERVE SP, Point Lobos: Sea lion.
POINT REYES NS: Sea lion herd, deer, rabbit.
PRAIRIE CREEK REDWOODS SP, Orick: Small herd of rare Roosevelt elk.
SEQUOIA NP and KINGS CANYON NP, Three Rivers: Bear, bighorn sheep, mule deer, small fur-bearers.
TULE ELK SR, Taft: Rare Tule elk.
TULE LAKE and LOWER KLAMATH NWR, Tulelake: Pronghorn antelope, mule deer, varying hare, jack and cottontail rabbits.
YOSEMITE NP: Mountain lion, bobcat, bear, coyote, badger, flying squirrel and other small fur-bearers.

Colorado
COLORADO NM, Fruita: Bison, elk, mule deer.
GRAND MESA–UNCOMPAHGRE NF, Grand Junction: Deer, elk, bear.
LA GARITA-SHEEP MOUNTAIN WA, Rio Grande, and SAN ISABEL NF, Gunnison: Bighorn sheep, elk.

Mesa Verde NP, Mesa Verde NP: Mountain lion, bobcat, coyote, gray fox, badger, ringtail.

Rocky Mountain NP, Estes Park: Elk, mule deer, bighorn sheep, mountain lion, marmot, beaver, prairie dog.

Roosevelt NF, Fort Collins: Elk, mule deer, bighorn sheep.

Connecticut
Cockaponset SF, Haddam County.
Macedonia Brook SP, Kent: Whitetailed deer, bobcat, raccoon.
Natchaug SF, Eastford County.
White Memorial Foundation, Litchfield: Game sanctuary.

Delaware
Trap Pond SP, Laurel.

Florida
Chassahowitzka NWR, Chassahowitzka: Deer, black bear, bobcat, raccoon, otter, mink.
Corkscrew Swamp WS, Immokalee: Black bear, otter.
Everglades NP, Homestead: Bobcat, mountain lion, black bear, whitetailed deer, opossum and other small fur-bearers.
Highlands Hammock SP, Sebring: Deer, armadillo, opossum.
Loxahatchee NWR, Dania: Bobcat, raccoon, otter.
Myakka River SP, Sarasota: Deer, raccoon, armadillo.
National Key Deer Refuge, Monroe County: Rare Key deer.

Georgia
Cloudland Canyon SP, Trenton.
Okefenokee NWR, Waycross: Black bear, bobcat, whitetailed deer, raccoon, otter, mink, fox, skunk.

Idaho
Clearwater NF, Orofino: Elk, deer, bear.
Heyburn SP.
Payette NF, McCall: Deer, elk, bighorn sheep, mountain goat.
Salmon NF, Salmon: Deer, elk, bighorn sheep, mountain goat, bear, mountain lion, pronghorn antelope.

Illinois
Buffalo Rock SP, Ottawa: Bison.
Pere Marquette SP, Grafton: Abundant wildlife.

Indiana
Brown County SP, Nashville: Game sanctuary.
Hoosier NF, Bedford: Whitetailed deer, coyote, fox.
Kankakee SFGA, Knox.
Pokagon SP, Angola: Deer, elk, bison.
Willow Slough SFGA, Enos: Small fur-bearers.
Yellowwood SF, Brown County.

Iowa
Lacey-Keosauqua SP, Keosauqua: Wildlife sanctuary.

Kansas
Kingman County State Lake, Kingman: Bison.
Meade County SP, Meade: Bison and elk preserve.
State GP, Garden City: Bison.

Kentucky
Kentucky Woodlands NWR, Golden Pond: Whitetailed deer, small fur-bearers.
Mammoth Cave NP, Mammoth Cave: Small mammals, many bats.

Louisiana
Delata NWR, Pilottown: Raccoon, mink, otter, muskrat.
Fontainebleau SP, Mandeville.
Lacassine NWR, Lake Arthur: Armadillo, muskrat, otter, mink.
Rainey WS, Abbeville: Nutria, muskrat, otter, whitetailed deer.
Sabine NWR, Sulphur: Armadillo, mink, muskrat.

Maine
Acadia NP, Bar Harbor: Bobcat, fox, beaver, porcupine, bats.
Baxter SP, Millinocket: Small mammals, deer
Katahdin State WS, Piscataquis County: Moose, bear, fisher, bobcat, deer.
Moosehorn NWR, Milltown: Deer, bear, otter and many other small mammals, rarely moose and lynx.

Maryland
Blackwater NWR, Cambridge: Muskrat.
Gambrill SP, Frederick.
Potomac SF, Oakland.
Savage River SF, New Germany.
Swallow Falls SF, Oakland.

Massachusetts
Arcadia WS, Easthampton: Muskrat, woodchuck, otter, red fox, red, gray, and flying squirrel.
Blue Hills Reservation, Milton.
Charles M. Gardner SP, Huntington.
Mount Greylock SR, North Adams.
Parker River NWR, Ipswich: Deer, fox, raccoon, mink, muskrat, skunk, opossum.
Pleasant Valley WS, Lenox: Deer, beaver colony, small mammals.

Michigan
Hartwick Pines SP, Grayling: Abundant wildlife.
Isle Royale NP, Houghton: Moose, coyote, varying hare, beaver.
Porcupine Mountains SP, Ontonagon: Wolf, bear, moose, elk, bobcat.
Seney NWR, Germfask: Bear, deer, otter, mink, beaver, muskrat.
Wilderness SP, Mackinaw City: Deer, bear, bobcat, wolf.

Minnesota
Itasca SP, Park Rapids: Specimens of almost every type of wild animal in state, including elk and deer.
Mud Lake NWR, Holt: Moose.
Scenic SP, Big Fork: Abundant wildlife.
Upper Mississippi River WLFR, Winona: Muskrat, raccoon.

Mississippi
De Soto NF, Laurel: Deer, raccoon, otter.
Holly Springs NF, Holly Springs: Deer, small fur-bearers.
Tishomingo SP, Tishomingo.

Missouri
Clark NF, Rolla: Whitetailed deer, small fur-bearers.
Mark Twain NF, Springfield: Deer, small mammals.

Montana
Anaconda-Pintlar WA, Beaverhead NF, Dillon: Abundant wildlife.
Custer NF, Red Lodge: Elk, bighorn sheep, mountain goat, pronghorn antelope, moose, deer, bear.
Glacier NP, West Glacier: Moose, elk, bighorn sheep, mountain goat, mule and whitetailed deer, bear, lynx, wolverine, coyote, beaver.
Bob Marshall WA, Flathead NF—Lewis and Clark NF: Outstanding population of large mammals.
National Bison Range, Molese: About 300–400 bison, elk, pronghorn antelope, deer.
Red Rock Lakes Migratory Waterfowl Refuge, Monida: Moose, pronghorn antelope, beaver, marmot, badger, otter, muskrat, ground squirrels.

Nebraska
Fort Niobara NWR, Valentine: Bison, elk, deer, beaver.
Nebraska NF, Lincoln: Largest mule deer herd in state, small fur-bearers.
Ponca SP, Ponca: Deer, fox, raccoon, opossum.

Nevada
Desert GR, Las Vegas: Bighorn sheep, pronghorn antelope, mule deer, many small mammals; Spring Mountains: small band of elk.
Humboldt NF, Elko: Abundant wildlife.
Sheldon Antelope Range and Sheldon Range, Washoe County: Large pronghorn antelope population.

New Hampshire
Mount Sunapee SP, Newport: Small mammals.
White Mountains NF, Laconia: Bear, deer, bobcat, small fur-bearers.

New Jersey
Killcohook NWR, Oceanville: Muskrat.
Lebanon SF, New Lisbon.
Norvin Green SF, c/o Ringwood Manor SF.

PENN SF, c/o Bass River SF.
STOKES SF, Branchville: Deer, small mammals.
WORTHINGTON SF, Columbia.

New Mexico
BITTER LAKE NWR, Roswell: Nutria.
CARLSBAD CAVERNS NP, Carlsbad: Bobcat, mountain lion, coyote, badger, ringtail;
    Bat Cave: millions of bats.
GILA WA, GILA NF, Silver City: Bobcat, mountain lion and other big game animals.
SAN ANDRES NWR, Las Cruces: Bighorn sheep, mule deer.
SANTA FE NF, Santa Fe.

New York
ALLEGANY SP, Red Lake.
ADIRONDACK FP, Albany: Bear, bobcat, coyote, fox, beaver, woodchuck, porcupine.
BEAR MOUNTAIN SP-HARRIMAN SP, Bear Mountain: Deer, bobcat, raccoon, opos-
    sum, muskrat, woodchuck, mink.
BUCKHORN ISLAND SP, Grand Island: Wildlife sanctuary.
CATSKILL FP, Catskill: Deer, bear, coyote, bobcat, fox.
WILLIAM T. DAVIS WILDLIFE REFUGE, Staten Island: Small mammals.
HIGH ROCK NATURE CONSERVATION CENTER, Staten Island: Muskrat, squirrel,
    chipmunk.
LETCHWORTH SP, Portageville.

North Carolina
CROATAN NF, New Bern: Deer, bear.
MATTAMUSKEET NWR, New Holland: Deer, fox, opossum, otter, mink.
MORROW MOUNTAIN SP, Albemarles.
MOUNT MITCHELL SP, Marion.
NANTAHALA NF, Franklin: Deer, bear.
PEA ISLAND NWR, Manteo: Otter.
PISGAH NF, Asheville: Deer, bear.
WILLIAM B. UMSTEAD SP, Durham.

North Dakota
LAKE METIGOSHE SP, Bottineau: Deer, small fur-bearers.
THEODORE ROOSEVELT NMP, Medora: Pronghorn antelope, bison, coyote, bobcat,
    badger, beaver.
SULLYS HILL NATIONAL GP, Fort Totten: Bison, elk, deer.

Ohio
HOCKING HILLS SP, Hocking SF, Logan: Almost every species of wildlife native
    to the Midwest.
JOHN BRYAN SP, Yellow Springs: Wildlife reserve.
LAKE HOPE SP, Zaleski SF: Deer, small mammals.
MOUNT GILEAD SR, Mount Gilead: Game sanctuary.
SHAWNEE SF, Portsmouth.
WAYNE NF, Ironton and Athens.

Oklahoma

Lake Murray SP, Tahlequah: Bison, pronghorn antelope, deer.

Platt NP, Sulphur: Bison, coyote, bobcat, prairie dog and other small mammals.

Wichita Mountains NWR, Cache: One of the finest mammal sanctuaries in the country; large bison herd, elk, pronghorn antelope, whitetailed deer, coyote, bobcat, badger, prairie dog.

Oregon

Cape Lookout SP, Tillamook: Sea lion.

Crater Lake NP, Medford: Bear, deer, beaver.

Ecola SP, Cannon Beach: Sea lion.

Hart Mountain National Antelope Refuge, Lakeview: Pronghorn antelope, mule deer, coyote.

Malheur NWR, John Day: Pronghorn antelope, mule deer, small fur-bearers.

Sea Lion Caves, Florence: Sea lion.

Siskiyou NF, Grants Pass: Mountain lion, bear, elk, deer.

Three Arch Rocks NWR, Oceanside: Sea lion.

Pennsylvania

Allegheny NF, Warren: Dear, bear, small fur-bearers.

Cook Forest SP, Cooksburg: Deer, bear; wildlife sanctuary.

Leonard Harrison SP, Wellsboro: Deer, small mammals.

Trexlar-Lehigh County GP, Allentown: Bison, elk, deer.

Rhode Island

Burlingame SP, Charlestown.

Great Swamp Wildlife Reservation, West Kingston: Deer, raccoon, opossum, fox, flying squirrel, otter, chipmunk.

Lincoln Woods SP, Lincoln.

South Carolina

Cape Romain NWR, McClellanville: Deer, otter, fox squirrel.

Carolina Sand Hills NWR, McBee: Bobcat, gray fox, beaver.

Francis Marion NF, Columbia: Deer.

Santee NWR, Summerton: Raccoon, otter.

Sumter NF, Columbia: Deer.

South Dakota

Custer SP, Hermosa: Deer, elk, mountain goat, bighorn sheep, large bison herd.

Wind Cave NP, Hot Springs: Bison, pronghorn antelope, elk, whitetailed deer, prairie dog towns.

Tennessee

Cherokee NF, Cleveland: Deer, bear.

Fall Creek Falls SP, Pikeville: Bear, deer.

Great Smoky Mountains NP, Gatlinburg, North Carolina-Tennessee: Bear, bobcat, deer, gray fox, beaver, varying hare.

Andrew Johnson GR, Newport: Deer.

Standing Stone SP, Livingston: Wildlife sanctuary.

Texas

ARANSAS NWR, Austwell: White-tailed deer, armadillo, peccary.

BIG BEND NP: Mountain lion, black bear, pronghorn antelope, mule and whitetailed deer, coyote, badger, ringtail, armadillo, peccary, jack rabbit.

LAGUNA ATACOSTA NWR, San Benito: Deer, peccary, coyote, bobcat, weasel.

MACKENZIE SP, Lubbock: Prairie dog towns.

SANTA ANA NWR, San Benito: Ocelot, jaguarundi, coyote, bobcat, weasel.

Utah

BEAR RIVER NWR, Bingham: Coyote, beaver, marmot, and other small mammals.

BRYCE CANYON NP, Springdale: Mountain lion, bobcat, badger, coyote, mule deer, jack rabbit.

HIGH UINTAS WA, Ashley NF, Vernal: Pronghorn antelope, elk, mule deer.

UINTA NF, Provo: Mount Nebo Recreational Area, large elk herd.

ZION CANYON NP, Springdale: Mountain lion, bobcat, bighorn sheep, mule deer, badger.

Vermont

ASCUTNEY SP, Ascutney: Bear, deer, small mammals.

GREEN MOUNTAIN NF, Rutland: Bear, bobcat, deer.

MONROE SP, Moretown: Game preserve.

MOUNT MANSFIELD SF, Stowe.

Virginia

CHINCOTEAGUE NWR, Chincoteague Island: Deer, red fox, raccoon, muskrat.

GREAT DISMAL SWAMP, Virginia-North Carolina: Bear, bobcat, fox.

JEFFERSON NF, Roanoke.

SHENANDOAH NP, Luray: Bear, deer, bobcat, opossum, fox and many other small mammals.

GEORGE WASHINGTON NF, Harrisonburg.

Washington

MOUNT RAINIER NP, Longmire: Mountain goat, elk, black bear, coyote, beaver, varying hare.

NORTH CASCADE WA, Mount Baker NF, Bellingham: Most of the big mammals of the continent are represented.

OLYMPIC NP, Port Angeles: Rare Roosevelt elk, mountain lion, black bear.

SNOQUALMIE NF, Seattle: Deer, bear, elk, mountain lion.

WILLAPA NWR, Ilwaco: Bear, deer, muskrat, raccoon.

West Virginia

BLACKWATER FALLS SP, Davis: Deer, bear, varying hare.

MONONGAHELA NF, Elkins: Deer, bear, small fur-bearers.

SENECA SP, Marlinton: Deer.

WATOGA SP, Huntersville: Large herd of deer.

Wisconsin

BLACK RIVER SF, Black River Falls: Deer.

HORICAN NWR, Waupun: Deer, muskrat, mink, raccoon.

NECEDAH NWR, Necedah: Deer, muskrat, raccoon, mink, beaver.
NICOLET NF, Rhinelander: Deer, bear.
PENINSULA SP, Ephraim: Deer and other game animals.

Wyoming
CLOUD PEAK WA, Bighorn NF, Sheridan: Large mammals.
DEVILS TOWER NM, Devils Tower Junction: Prairie dog town.
GRAND TETON NP, Moose: Bighorn sheep, moose, elk, mule deer, black bear, beaver; National Elk Refuge at Jackson Hole adjoins.
HOT SPRINGS SP, Thermopolis: Bison and elk.
YELLOWSTONE NP, Wyoming-Montana-Idaho, Yellowstone NP: Moose, elk, pronghorn antelope, bear, coyote, herd of about 900 bison.

CANADA

Alberta
BANFF NP, Banff: Moose, elk, mule deer, mountain goat, bighorn sheep, bear, mountain lion, wolverine, coyote.
ELK ISLAND NP, Lamont: Moose, elk, mule deer, herd of about 600 bison, wolf, coyote.
JASPER NP, Jasper: Moose, bear, mountain lion and many other large mammals.
WATERTON LAKES NP, Waterton Park: Adjoins Glacier NP, Montana; exhibition bison herd, mule and whitetailed deer, bear, mountain goat, bighorn sheep, elk, moose.
WOOD BUFFALO NP, Alberta-Northwest Territories, Fort Vermilion: Woodland and prairie bison.

British Columbia
GLACIER NP, Revelstoke: Most of large mammals except bighorn sheep.
KOOTENAY NP, Radium Hot Springs: Moose, elk, deer, mountain goat, bighorn sheep, bear, mountain lion, lynx.
MOUNT REVELSTOKE NP, Revelstoke: Most of large mammals except bighorn sheep.
YOHO NP, Field: Moose, elk, deer, mountain goat, bighorn sheep, bear, lynx.

Manitoba
RIDING MOUNTAIN NP, Wasagaming: Elk, moose, deer, exhibition bison herd, bear, wolf, coyote.

New Brunswick
FUNDY NP, Alma: Moose, bear, bobcat, red fox, lynx, muskrat, weasel.

Newfoundland
TERRA NOVA NP, Terra Nova: Moose, bear, lynx, beaver, red fox, weasel, rabbit.

Nova Scotia
CAPE BRETON NP, Ingonish Beach: Moose, deer, bear, lynx, red fox, rabbit and other small fur-bearers.

Ontario
ALGONQUIN P, Pembroke: Moose, deer, bear.

GEORGIAN BAY ISLANDS NP, Beausoleil Island: Deer, red fox, raccoon, beaver, mink and other small mammals.

QUETICO P, Nym Lake, Atikokan: Adjoins Superior WA, Minnesota; bear, deer, porcupine and other small mammals.

TIMAGAMI PF, North Bay.

Prince Edward Island

PRINCE EDWARD ISLAND NP, New London: Small mammals.

Quebec

CHIBOUGAMAU and MISTASSINI RESERVES, Roberval: Abundant wildlife.

GASPESIAN P, Gaspé: Moose, deer, bear.

LAURENTIDES P, Quebec: Elk.

LA VERENDRYE P, La Vérendrye Park: Moose, deer, bear, many small mammals.

Saskatchewan

CYPRESS HILLS P, Cypress Hills: Pronghorn antelope, elk, deer.

DUCK MOUNTAIN P, Grandview: Moose, elk.

MOOSE MOUNTAIN P, Carlyle Lake: Abundant wildlife.

PRINCE ALBERT NP, Waskesiu: Exhibition bison herd, moose, mule deer, elk, bear, wolf, coyote.

MEXICO

Guerrero

ACAPULCO, interior Sierra Madre range: Jaguar, bobcat, deer.

Hidalgo

LOS MARMOLES NP.

Jalisco

NEVADO DE COLIMA NP: Extinct volcano, over 14,000 feet.

Mexico

IXTACIHUATL-POPOCATEPETL NP, Mexico-Puebla: Surroundings of extinct volcanoes (Ixta, over 17,000 feet, and Popo, over 18,000 feet).

NEVADO DE TOLUCA NP: Extinct volcano, over 15,000 feet.

Nuevo Leon

CUMBRES DE MONTERREY NP: Dense coniferous woods.

San Luis Potosí

EL COGORRON NP.

Tlaxcala

LA MALINCHE (Matlalcueyatl) NP, Tlaxcala-Puebla: Over 14,000 feet high, coniferous woods.

Vera Cruz

CANON DE RIO BLANCO NP: Temperate forests.

COFRE DE PEROTE (Nauchampatepetl) NP: Surroundings of mountain (over 14,000 feet), coniferous woods.

PICO DE ORIZABA (Citlaltépetl) NP: Highest mountain country, over 18,000 feet.

Appendix B

Sources of Information

Information about state parks and forests may be obtained from the following agencies:

Alabama, Department of Conservation, Division of State Parks, Monuments and Historical Sites, State Administrative Building, Montgomery.

Alaska, Department of Natural Resources, Division of Lands, 344 6th Avenue, Anchorage.

Arizona, State Parks Board, State Capitol Building, Phoenix.

Arkansas, Publicity and Parks Commission, State Capitol Building, Little Rock.

California, Department of Parks and Recreation, Division of Beaches and Parks, 1125 Tenth Street, Sacramento.

Colorado, Park and Recreation Board, State Services Building, Denver.

Connecticut, State Park and Forest Commission, State Office Building, Hartford.

Delaware, State Park Commission, 3300 Faulkland Road, Wilmington.

Florida, Board of Parks and Historic Memorials, Florida Park Service, Tallahassee.

Georgia, Division of Conservation, Department of State Parks, 7 Hunter Street, S.W., Atlanta.

Idaho, Board of Land Commissioners, Department of Public Lands, State House, Boise.

Illinois, Department of Conservation, Division of Parks and Memorials, State Office Building, Springfield.

Indiana, Department of Conservation, Division of State Parks, State Office Building, Indianapolis.

Iowa, Conservation Commission, Division of Lands and Waters, East 7th and Court Avenue, Des Moines.

Kansas, Park and Resources Authority, 801 Harrison, Topeka. Forestry, Fish and Game Commission, Pratt.

Kentucky, Department of Parks, Capitol Annex, Frankfort.

Louisiana, Parks and Recreation Commission, Old State Capitol Building, Baton Rouge.

Maine, Park Commission, New State Office Building, Augusta. Baxter State Park Authority, P.O. Box 488, Millinocket.

MARYLAND, Board of Natural Resources, Department of Forests and Parks, State Office Building, Annapolis.

MASSACHUSETTS, Department of Natural Resources, Division of Forests and Parks, Bureau of Recreation, State House, Boston. Mount Greylock State Reservation Commission, 154 Pleasant Street, Dalton.

MICHIGAN, Department of Conservation, Parks and Recreation Division, Stevens T. Mason Building, Lansing.

MINNESOTA, Department of Conservation, Division of State Parks, 6 State Office Building, St. Paul.

MISSISSIPPI, Park Commission, 1104 Woolfolk Building, Jackson.

MISSOURI, Park Board, 1206 Jefferson Building, Jefferson City.

MONTANA, Highway Commission, State Parks Division, Highway Department Building, Helena.

NEBRASKA, Game, Forestation and Parks Commission, Division of State Parks, Lincoln.

NEVADA, Park Commission, State Capitol Building, Carson City.

NEW HAMPSHIRE, Department of Resources and Economic Development, Division of Parks, State House Annex, Concord.

NEW JERSEY, Department of Conservation and Economic Development, Division of Resource Planning, Forests and Parks Section, Trenton.

NEW MEXICO, State Park Commission, Santa Fe.

NEW YORK, Conservation Department, Division of Parks, Albany. Allegany State Park Commission, Red House. Palisades Interstate Park Commission, Administration Building, Bear Mountain.

NORTH CAROLINA, Department of Conservation and Development, Division of State Parks, Raleigh.

NORTH DAKOTA, State Historical Society of North Dakota, Liberty Memorial Building, Bismarck.

OHIO, Department of Natural Resources, Division of Parks, 1500 Dublin Road, Columbus.

OKLAHOMA, Planning and Resources Board, Division of Recreation and State Parks, 533 State Capitol, Oklahoma City.

OREGON, State Highway Department, State Parks and Recreation Division, 301 Highway Commission Building, Salem.

PENNSYLVANIA, Department of Forests and Waters, Division of State Parks, 408 Educational Building, Harrisburg.

RHODE ISLAND, Department of Public Works, Division of Parks and Recreation, State Office Building, Providence.

SOUTH CAROLINA, State Commission of Forestry, Division of State Parks, 506 Calhoun State Office Building, Columbia.

SOUTH DAKOTA, Department of Game, Fish and Parks, Division of Forestry and Parks, Pierre.

TENNESSEE, Department of Conservation and Commerce, Division of State Parks, 203 Cordell Hull Building, Nashville.

TEXAS, State Parks Board, P.O. Drawer E, Capitol Station, Austin.

UTAH, State Park and Recreation Commission, 19 West South Temple, Salt Lake City.

VERMONT, State Board of Forests and Parks, Department of Forests and Parks, Montpelier.

VIRGINIA, Department of Conservation and Economic Development, Division of Parks, 1106 Travelers Building, Richmond.

WASHINGTON, State Parks and Recreation Commission, 522 South Franklin Street, Olympia.

WEST VIRGINIA, Department of Natural Resources, Division of State Parks and Recreation, State Office Building, Charleston.

WISCONSIN, Conservation Department, Forests and Parks Division, Box 450, Madison.

WYOMING, State Parks Commission, Boysen Route, Shoshoni.

OTHER AGENCIES

NATIONAL FORESTS, Forest Service, U.S. Department of Agriculture, Washington, D.C.

NATIONAL PARKS, MONUMENTS, AND SEASHORES, National Park Service, U.S. Department of the Interior, Washington, D.C.

NATIONAL WILDLIFE REFUGES, Fish and Wildlife Service, U.S. Department of the Interior, Washington, D.C.

WILDLIFE SANCTUARIES, National Audubon Society, 1130 Fifth Avenue, New York, N.Y.

CANADA

PROVINCIAL PARKS, Canadian Government Tourist Office, Ottawa, Ontario; Provincial Parks Branch, Department of Recreation and Conservation, Victoria, British Columbia; Parks Division, Department of Lands and Forests, Toronto, Ontario; Parks and Reserves Branch, Department of Fish and Game, Parliament Buildings, Quebec, Quebec; Parks Branch, Department of Provincial Secretary, Regina, Saskatchewan.

NATIONAL PARKS, Canadian Government Tourist Office, Ottawa, Ontario; Natural and Historic Resources Branch, Department of Northern Affairs and National Resources, Ottawa, Ontario.

RESERVES, Parks Division, Department of Game and Fisheries, Ottawa, Ontario.

MEXICO

NATIONAL PARKS, Departamento de Zonas Protectoras, Vedas y Parques Nacionales, Recursos Forestales y de Caza, Secretaria Agricultura y Ganadería, Mexico, D.F.

Appendix C

Orders, Families, Genera,

and Species

North America has examples of eleven of the nineteen orders of mammals. Of these, nine are represented in this book by sixty-six species. The species discussed and illustrated are indicated by an asterisk.

ORDER AND FAMILY	GENUS AND SPECIES
MARSUPIALS: Order Marsupialia	
Opossums: Family Didelphiidae	
*Opossum	*Didelphis marsupialis*
MOLES AND SHREWS: Order Insectivora	
Moles: Family Talpidae	
*Star Nose Mole	*Condylura cristata*
*Common Mole	*Scalopus aquaticus*
Hairy-Tailed Mole	*Parascalops breweri*
Townsend Mole	*Scapanus townsendi*
Pacific Mole	*Scapanus orarius*
California Mole	*Scapanus latimanus*
Shrew-Mole	*Neurotrichus gibbsi*
Shrews: Family Soricidae	
Masked Shrew	*Sorex cinereus*
Mt. Lyell Shrew	*Sorex lyelli*
Malheur Shrew	*Sorex preblei*
Smoky Shrew	*Sorex fumeus*
Arctic Shrew	*Sorex arcticus*
Tundra Shrew	*Sorex tundrensis*
Unalaska Shrew	*Sorex hydrodromus*
Pribilof Shrew	*Sorex pribilofensis*
Merriam Shrew	*Sorex merriami*
Southeastern Shrew	*Sorex longirostris*
Long-Tailed Shrew	*Sorex dispar*
Gaspé Shrew	*Sorex gaspensis*

Trowbridge Shrew	*Sorex trowbridgei*
Vagrant Shrew	*Sorex vagrans*
Dusky Shrew	*Sorex obscurus*
Pacific Shrew	*Sorex pacificus*
Ornate Shrew	*Sorex ornatus*
Ashland Shrew	*Sorex trigonirostris*
Santa Catalina Shrew	*Sorex willetti*
Suisun Shrew	*Sorex sinuosus*
Inyo Shrew	*Sorex tenellus*
Dwarf Shrew	*Sorex nanus*
Northern Water Shrew	*Sorex palustris*
Alaska Water Shrew	*Sorex alaskanus*
Pacific Water Shrew	*Sorex bendirei*
Pygmy Shrew	*Microsorex hoyi*
Desert Shrew	*Notiosorex crawfordi*
Least Shrew	*Cryptotis parva*
*Short-Tailed Shrew	*Blarina brevicauda*

BATS: Order Chiroptera
  Leaf-Nosed Bats: Family Phyllostomidae

Leaf-Chinned Bat	*Mormoops megalophylla*
Leaf-Nosed Bat	*Macrotus californicus*
Hog-Nosed Bat	*Choeronycteris mexicana*
Long-Nosed Bat	*Leptonycteris nivalis*

  Plain-Nosed Bats: Family Vespertilionidae

*Little Brown Bat	*Myotis lucifugus*
Yuma Myotis	*Myotis yumanensis*
Mississippi Myotis	*Myotis austroriparius*
Gray Myotis	*Myotis grisescens*
Cave Myotis	*Myotis velifer*
Arizona Myotis	*Myotis occultus*
Keen Myotis	*Myotis keeni*
Long-Eared Myotis	*Myotis evotis*
Fringed Myotis	*Myotis thysanodes*
Indiana Myotis	*Myotis sodalis*
Long-Legged Myotis	*Myotis volans*
California Myotis	*Myotis californicus*
Small-Footed Myotis	*Myotis subulatus*
Western Pipistrel	*Pipistrellus hesperus*
Eastern Pipistrel	*Pipistrellus subflavus*
Big Brown Bat	*Eptesicus fuscus*
Evening Bat	*Nycticeius humeralis*
Silver-Haired Bat	*Lasionycteris noctivagans*
Hoary Bat	*Lasiurus cinereus*
*Red Bat	*Lasiurus borealis*
Seminole Bat	*Lasiurus seminolus*
Western Yellow Bat	*Lasiurus ega*
Eastern Yellow Bat	*Lasiurus intermedius*

Spotted Bat	*Euderma maculata*
Western Big-Eared Bat	*Corynorhinus rafinesquii*
Eastern Big-Eared Bat	*Corynorhinus macrotis*
Pallid Bat	*Antrozous pallidus*
Bunker Bat	*Antrozous bunkeri*
Free-Tailed Bats: Family Molossidae	
Florida Free-Tailed Bat	*Tadarida cynocephala*
Mexican Free-Tailed Bat	*Tadarida mexicana*
Pocketed Free-Tailed Bat	*Tadarida femorosacca*
Big Free-Tailed Bat	*Tadarida molossa*
Western Mastiff Bat	*Eumops perotis*
Eastern Mastiff Bat	*Eumops glaucinus*
PIKAS, HARES, AND RABBITS: Order Lagomorpha	
Pikas: Family Ochotonidae	
Pika	*Ochotona princeps*
Hares and Rabbits: Family Leporidae	
Arctic Hare	*Lepus arcticus*
Tundra Hare	*Lepus othus*
White-Tailed Jack Rabbit	*Lepus townsendi*
*Varying Hare	*Lepus americanus*
European Hare	*Lepus europaeus*
Antelope Jack Rabbit	*Lepus alleni*
*Black-Tailed Jack Rabbit	*Lepus californicus*
*Eastern Cottontail	*Sylvilagus floridanus*
Mountain Cottontail	*Sylvilagus nuttalli*
New England Cottontail	*Sylvilagus transitionalis*
Desert Cottontail	*Sylvilagus anduboni*
Brush Rabbit	*Sylvilagus bachmani*
Marsh Rabbit	*Sylvilagus palustris*
Swamp Rabbit	*Sylvilagus aquaticus*
Pigmy Rabbit	*Sylvilagus idahoensis*
GNAWING MAMMALS: Order Rodentia	
Squirrels: Family Sciuridae	
*Woodchuck	*Marmota monax*
*Yellow-Bellied Marmot	*Marmota flaviventris*
*Hoary Marmot	*Marmota caligata*
Olympic Marmot	*Marmota olympus*
Vancouver Marmot	*Marmota vancouverensis*
*Black-Tailed Prairie Dog	*Cynomys ludovicianus*
White-Tailed Prairie Dog	*Cynomys gunnisoni*
Townsend Ground Squirrel	*Citellus townsendi*
Washington Ground Squirrel	*Citellus washingtoni*
Idaho Ground Squirrel	*Citellus brunneus*
*Richardson's Ground Squirrel	*Citellus richardsoni*
Uinta Ground Squirrel	*Citellus armatus*
Belding Ground Squirrel	*Citellus beldingi*
*Columbian Ground Squirrel	*Citellus columbianus*

Arctic Ground Squirrel	*Citellus undulatus*
*Thirteen-Lined Ground Squirrel	*Citellus tridecemlineatus*
Mexican Ground Squirrel	*Citellus mexicanus*
Spotted Ground Squirrel	*Citellus spilosoma*
Franklin Ground Squirrel	*Citellus franklini*
Rock Squirrel	*Citellus variegatus*
California Ground Squirrel	*Citellus beecheyi*
Yuma Antelope Squirrel	*Ammospermophilus harrisii*
Whitetailed Antelope Squirrel	*Ammospermophilus leucurus*
San Joaquin Antelope Squirrel	*Ammospermophilus nelsoni*
Mohave Ground Squirrel	*Citellus mohavensis*
Round-Tailed Ground Squirrel	*Citellus tereticaudus*
*Golden-Mantled Ground Squirrel	*Callospermophilus lateralis*
*Red Squirrel	*Tamiasciurus hudsonicus*
Chickaree	*Tamiasciurus douglasi*
Spruce Squirrel	*Tamiasciurus fremonti*
Western Gray Squirrel	*Sciurus griseus*
*Eastern Gray Squirrel	*Sciurus carolinensis*
Arizona Gray Squirrel	*Sciurus arizonensis*
Tassel-Eared Squirrel	*Sciurus aberti*
Apache Fox Squirrel	*Sciurus apache*
*Eastern Fox Squirrel	*Sciurus niger*
*Southern Flying Squirrel	*Glaucomys volans*
Northern Flying Squirrel	*Glaucomys sabrinus*
*Eastern Chipmunk	*Tamias striatus*
Alpine Chipmunk	*Eutamias alpinus*
Least Chipmunk	*Eutamias minimus*
Yellow Pine Chipmunk	*Eutamias amoenus*
Panamint Chipmunk	*Eutamias panamintinus*
Colorado Chipmunk	*Eutamias qnadrivittatus*
Uinta Chipmunk	*Eutamias umbrinus*
Charleston Mountain Chipmunk	*Eutamias palmeri*
Red-Tailed Chipmunk	*Eutamias ruficaudus*
Gray-Necked Chipmunk	*Eutamias cinereicollis*
Townsend Chipmunk	*Eutamias townsendi*
Sonoma Chipmunk	*Eutamias sonomae*
Long-Eared Chipmunk	*Eutamias quadrimaculatus*
Merriam Chipmunk	*Eutamias merriami*
Cliff Chipmunk	*Eutamias dorsalis*
Beaver: Family Castoridae	
*Beaver	*Castor canadensis*
Mice, Rats, Voles, Lemmings: Family Cricetidae	
Native Mice and Rats: Cricetidae	
Northern Grasshopper Mouse	*Onychomys leucogaster*
Southern Grasshopper Mouse	*Onychomys torridus*
Eastern Harvest Mouse	*Reithrodontomys humulus*

Plains Harvest Mouse	*Reithrodontomys montanus*
Western Harvest Mouse	*Reithrodontomys megalotis*
Salt Marsh Harvest Mouse	*Reithrodontomys raviventris*
Fulvous Harvest Mouse	*Reithrodontomys fulvescens*
Pygmy Mouse	*Baiomys taylori*
Cactus Mouse	*Peromyscus eremicus*
California Mouse	*Peromyscus californicus*
Canyon Mouse	*Peromyscus crinitus*
Deer Mouse	*Peromyscus maniculatus*
Sitka Mouse	*Peromyscus sitkensis*
Oldfield Mouse	*Peromyscus polionotus*
*White-Footed Mouse	*Peromyscus leucopus*
Cotton Mouse	*Peromyscus gossypinus*
Brush Mouse	*Peromyscus boylei*
White-Ankled Mouse	*Peromyscus pectoralis*
Piñon Mouse	*Peromyscus truei*
Rock Mouse	*Peromyscus difficilis*
Golden Mouse	*Peromyscus nuttalli*
Florida Mouse	*Peromyscus floridanus*
Rice Rat	*Oryzomys palustris*
Hispid Cotton Rat	*Sigmodon hispidus*
Least Cotton Rat	*Sigmodon minimus*
Yellow-Nosed Cotton Rat	*Sigmodon ochrognathus*
Eastern Woodrat	*Neotoma floridana*
Southern Plains Woodrat	*Neotoma micropus*
White-Throated Woodrat	*Neotoma albiguea*
Desert Woodrat	*Neotoma lepida*
Mexican Woodrat	*Neotoma mexicana*
Dusky-Footed Woodrat	*Neotoma fuscipes*
Bushy-Tailed Woodrat	*Neotoma cinerea*
Southern Bog Lemming	*Synaptomys cooperi*
Northern Bog Lemming	*Synaptomys borealis*
Brown Lemming	*Lemmus trimucronatus*
Hudson Bay Collared Lemming	*Dicrostonyx hudsonius*
Greenland Collared Lemming	*Dicrostonyx groenlandicus*
Unalaska Collared Lemming	*Dicrostonyx unalascensis*
Mountain Phenacomys	*Phenacomys intermedius*
Ungava Phenacomys	*Phenacomys ungava*
Mackenzie Phenacomys	*Phenacomys mackenziei*
Pacific Phenacomys	*Phenacomys albipes*
Tree Phenacomys	*Phenacomys longicaudus*
British Columbia Red-Backed Vole	*Clethrionomys*
Wrangell Island Red-Backed Vole	*Clethrionomys*
Tundra Red-Backed Vole	*Clethrionomys rutilus*
St. Lawrence Island Red-Backed Vole	*Clethrionomys*
Boreal Red-Backed Vole	*Clethrionomys gapperi*
California Red-Backed Vole	*Clethrionomys occidentalis*

*Meadow Mouse (Vole)	*Microtus pennsylvanicus*
Mountain Vole	*Microtus montanus*
California Vole	*Microtus californicus*
Tundra Vole	*Microtus oeconomus*
Alaska Vole	*Microtus miurus*
Townsend Vole	*Microtus townsendi*
Long-Tailed Vole	*Microtus longicaudus*
Yellow-Cheeked Vole	*Microtus xanthognathus*
Yellow-Nosed Vole	*Microtus chrotorrhinus*
Richardson Vole	*Microtus richardsoni*
Prairie Vole	*Microtus ochrogaster*
Oregon Vole	*Microtus oregoni*
Sagebrush Vole	*Lagurus curtatus*
Pine Vole	*Pitymys pinetorum*
Florida Water Rat	*Neofiber alleni*
*Muskrat	*Ondatra zibethica*
Old World Rats and Mice: Family Muridae	
*Norway Rat	*Rattus norvegicus*
Black Rat	*Rattus rattus*
*House Mouse	*Mus musculus*
Mountain Beaver: Family Aplodontiidae	
Aplodontia	*Aplodontia rufa*
Jumping Mice: Family Zapodidae	
Meadow Jumping Mouse	*Zapus hudsonius*
Western Jumping Mouse	*Zapus princeps*
*Woodland Jumping Mouse	*Napaeozapus insignis*
Nutrias: Family Capromyidae	
*Nutria	*Myocastor coypus*
Porcupines: Family Erethizontidae	
*Porcupine	*Erethizon dorsatum*
Pocket Gophers: Family Geomyidae	
Northern Pocket Gopher	*Thomomys talpoides*
Pygmy Pocket Gopher	*Thomomys umbrinus*
Sierra Pocket Gopher	*Thomomys monticola*
Townsend Pocket Gopher	*Thomomys townsendi*
Valley Pocket Gopher	*Thomomys botlae*
Bailey Pocket Gopher	*Thomomys baileyi*
Giant Pocket Gopher	*Thomomys bulbivorus*
Plains Pocket Gopher	*Geomys bursarius*
Southeastern Pocket Gopher	*Geomys pinetis*
Mexican Pocket Gopher	*Cratogeomys castanops*
Pocket Mice, Kangaroo Mice, and Kangaroo Rats: Family Heteromyidae	
Mexican Pocket Mouse	*Liomys irroratus*
Wyoming Pocket Mouse	*Perognathus fasciatus*
Plains Pocket Mouse	*Perognathus flavescens*
Merriam Pocket Mouse	*Perognathus merriami*

Silky Pocket Mouse	*Perognathus flavus*
Apache Pocket Mouse	*Perognathus apache*
Arizona Pocket Mouse	*Perognathus amplus*
Little Pocket Mouse	*Perognathus longimembris*
San Joaquin Pocket Mouse	*Perognathus inornatus*
Great Basin Pocket Mouse	*Perognathus parvus*
White-Eared Pocket Mouse	*Perognathus alticolus*
Long-Tailed Pocket Mouse	*Perognathus formosus*
Bailey Pocket Mouse	*Perognathus baileyi*
Desert Pocket Mouse	*Perognathus penicillatus*
Rock Pocket Mouse	*Perognathus intermedius*
Nelson Pocket Mouse	*Perognathus nelsoni*
San Diego Pocket Mouse	*Perognathus fallax*
California Pocket Mouse	*Perognathus californicus*
Spiny Pocket Mouse	*Perognathus spinatus*
Hispid Pocket Mouse	*Perognathus hispidus*
Heermann Kangaroo Rat	*Dipodomys heermanni*
Morro Bay Kangaroo Rat	*Dipodomys morroensis*
Mohave Kangaroo Rat	*Dipodomys mohavensis*
Panamint Kangaroo Rat	*Dipodomys panamintinus*
Stephens Kangaroo Rat	*Dipodomys stephensi*
Giant Kangaroo Rat	*Dipodomys ingens*
Banner-Tailed Kangaroo Rat	*Dipodomys spectabilis*
Texas Kangaroo Rat	*Dipodomys elator*
Merriam Kangaroo Rat	*Dipodomys merriami*
Fresno Kangaroo Rat	*Dipodomys nitratoides*
Ord Kangaroo Rat	*Dipodomys ordi*
Pacific Kangaroo Rat	*Dipodomys agilis*
Santa Cruz Kangaroo Rat	*Dipodomys venustus*
Big-Eared Kangaroo Rat	*Dipodomys euphantinus*
Great Basin Kangaroo Rat	*Dipodomys microps*
Desert Kangaroo Rat	*Dipodomys deserti*
Dark Kangaroo Mouse	*Microdipodops megacephalus*
Pale Kangaroo Mouse	*Microdipodops pallidus*

MEAT-EATERS: Order Carnivora
Bears: Family Ursidae

*Black Bear	*[Euarctos] americanus*
Grizzly Bear	*Ursus horribilis*
Big Brown Bear	*Ursus middendorffi*
Polar Bear	*Thalarctos maritimus*

Raccoons, Coatis: Family Procyonidae

*Raccoon	*Procyon lotor*
*Coatimundi	*Nasua narica*

Ring-Tailed Cats: Family Bassariscidae

*Ringtail	*Bassariscus astutus*

Weasels, Skunks, etc.: Family Mustelidae

Marten	*Martes americana*

*Fisher	*Martes pennanti*
Short-Tailed Weasel	*Mustela erminea*
*Long-Tailed Weasel	*Mustela frenata*
Least Weasel	*Mustela rixosa*
*Mink	*Mustela vison*
Black-Footed Ferret	*Mustela nigripes*
*Wolverine	*Gulo luscus*
*River Otter	*Lutra canadensis*
Sea Otter	*Enhydra lutris*
*Spotted Skunk	*Spilogale putorius*
*Striped Skunk	*Mephitis mephitis*
Hooded Skunk	*Mephitis macroura*
Hognose Skunk	*Conepatus leuconotus*
*Badger	*Taxidea taxus*

Dogs, Foxes, Wolves: Family Canidae

*Red Fox	*Vulpes fulva*
Kit Fox	*Vulpes velox*
*Gray Fox	*Urocyon cinereoargenteus*
*Arctic Fox	*Alopex lagopus*
*Coyote	*Canis latrans*
*Gray Wolf	*Canis lupus*
Red Wolf	*Canis niger*

Cats: Family Felidae

*Jaguar	*Felis onca*
*Ocelot	*Felis pardalis*
Margay Cat	*Felis wiedi*
*Mountain Lion	*Felis concolor*
*Jaguarundi	*Felis eyra*
*Lynx	*Lynx canadensis*
*Bobcat	*Lynx rufus*

Seals and Sea Lions: Order Pinnepedia

Eared Seals: Family Otariidae

*California Sea Lion	*Zalophus californianus*
*Northern Sea Lion	*Eumetopias jubata*
Alaska Fur Seal	*Callorhinus ursinus*
Guadalupe Fur Seal	*Arctocephalus philippi*

Hair Seals: Family Phocidae

Harbor Seal	*Phoca vitulina*
Ribbon Seal	*Histriophoca fasciata*
Ringed Seal	*Pusa hispida*
Saddle-Backed Seal	*Pagophilus groenlandicus*
Bearded Seal	*Erignathus barbatus*
Gray Seal	*Halichoerus grypus*
Hooded Seal	*Cystophora cristata*
Elephant Seal	*Mirounga angustirostris*

Walruses: Family Odobenidae

Walrus	*Odobenus rosmarus*

Even-Toed Hoofed Mammals: Order
Artiodactyla
  Peccaries: Family Tayassuidae
    *Collared Peccary   *Tayassu Tajacu*
  Domesticated Pigs: Family Suidae
    European Wild Boar   *Sus scrofa*
  Deer: Family Cervidae
    *Elk   *Cervus canadensis*
    *Mule Deer   *Odocoileus hemnious*
    *Whitetailed Deer   *Odocoileus virginianus*
    *Moose   *Alces alces*
    Woodland Caribou   *Rangifer caribou*
    Barren Ground Caribou   *Rangifer arcticus*
    Greenland Caribou   *Rangifer tarandus*
  Pronghorn: Family Antilocapridae
    *Pronghorn Antelope   *Antilocapra americana*
  Bison, Goats, Sheep, Oxen: Family Bovidae
    *Bison   *Bison bison*
    Muskox   *Ovibos moschatus*
    *Bighorn Sheep   *Ovis canadensis*
    White Sheep   *Ovis dalli*
    *Mountain Goat   *Oreamnos americanus*
Sloths, Armadillos: Order Edentata
  Armadillos: Family Dasypodidae
    *Nine-Banded Armadillo   *Dasypus novemcinctus*
Dugongs and Manatees: Order Sirenia
  Manatees: Family Trichechidae
    Manatee   *Trichechus manatus*
Whales and Porpoises: Order Cetacea
  Balaen Whales: Family Balaenidae
    Atlantic Right Whale   *Eubalaena glacialis*
    Pacific Right Whale   *Eubalaena sieboldi*
    Bowhead Whale   *Balaena mysticetus*
  Gray Whales: Family Rhachianectidae
    Gray Whale   *Rhachianectes glaucus*
  Fin-Backed Whales: Family Balaenoptridae
    Fin-Backed Whale   *Balaenoptera physalus*
    Rorqual   *Balaenoptera borealis*
    Piked Whale   *Balaenoptera acutorostrata*
    Blue Whale   *Sibbaldus musculus*
    Hump-Backed Whale   *Megaptera novaeangliae*
  Sperm Whales: Family Physeteridae
    Sperm Whale   *Physeter catodon*
    Pygmy Sperm Whale   *Kogia breviceps*
  Dolphins and Porpoises: Family Delphinidae
    Spotted Dolphin   *Stenella plagiodon*
    Long-Beaked Dolphin   *Steno rostratus*

Common Dolphin	*Delphinus delphis*
Atlantic Bottle-Nosed Dolphin	*Tursiops truncatus*
Pacific Bottle-Nosed Dolphin	*Tursiops gilli*
Right Whale Dolphin	*Lissodelphis borealis*
Atlantic White-Sided Dolphin	*Lagenorhynchus acutus*
Pacific White-Sided Dolphin	*Lagenorhynchus obliquidens*
White-Beaked Dolphin	*Lagenorhynchus albirostris*
Atlantic Killer Whale	*Grampus orca*
Pacific Killer Whale	*Grampus rectipinna*
Grampus	*Gramphidelphis griseus*
False Killer	*Pseudorca crassidens*
Common Blackfish	*Globicephala ventricosa*
Pacific Blackfish	*Globicephala scammoni*
Short-Finned Blackfish	*Globicephala brachyptera*
Atlantic Harbor Porpoise	*Phocaena phocaena*
Dall Porpoise	*Phocaenoides dalli*
White Whale	*Delphinapterus leucas*
Narwhal	*Monodon monoceros*
Beaked Whales: Family Ziphiidae	
Baird Beaked Whale	*Berardius bairdi*
Sowerby Whale	*Mesoplodon bidens*
True Beaked Whale	*Mesoplodon mirus*
Pacific Beaked Whale	*Mesoplodon stejnegeri*
Goosebeak Whale	*Ziphius cavirostris*
Bottle-Nosed Whale	*Hyperoodon ampullatus*

Bibliography

This bibliography lists only the books that contain several or many mammals, since listing all the books that I consulted which are monographs or the life history of just one mammal would make this list too lengthy.

Anthony, Harold E., *Field Book of North American Mammals*. G. P. Putnam's Sons, New York, 1928.

_____ (tech. ed.), *Animals of America*. Garden City Publishing Co., Garden City, N.Y., 1937.

Barkalow, Frederich S., Jr., *A Game Inventory of Alabama*. Alabama Department of Conservation, Montgomery, Ala., 1949.

Bennitt, Rudolf, and Nagel, Werner O., *Survey of Game & Furbearers of Missouri*. University of Missouri, Columbia, Mo., 1937.

Booth, Ernest S., *How To Know the Mammals*. William C. Brown Co., Dubuque, Ia., 1949.

Bourlière, François, *Mammals of the World*. Alfred A. Knopf, New York, 1955.

_____, *The Natural History of Mammals: A Field Outline*. Alfred A. Knopf, New York, 1964. Rev.

Brooks, David M., *Fur Animals of Indiana*. Indiana Department of Conservation, Indianapolis, Ind., 1954.

Burt, William Henry, and Grossenheider, Richard Philip, *A Field Guide to the Mammals*. Houghton Mifflin Co., Boston, 1952.

Burton, Maurice, *Systematic Dictionary of Mammals of the World*. Thomas Y. Crowell Company, New York, 1962.

Cahalane, Victor H., *Mammals of North America*. The Macmillan Co., New York, 1947.

Carrington, Richard, *The Mammals*. Life Nature Library, New York, 1963.

Cockrum, E. Lendell, *Introduction to Mammalogy*. The Ronald Press Co., New York, 1962.

Cony, Charles B., *The Mammals of Illinois and Wisconsin*. Field Museum of Natural History, Chicago, 1912.

Cronan, John M., and Brooks, Albert, *The Mammals of Rhode Island*. Rhode Island Division of Fish and Game.

Dufresne, Frank, *Alaska's Animals and Fishes*. Binfords and Mort, Portland, Ore., 1946.

Gunderson, Harvey L., and Beer, James R., *The Mammals of Minnesota*. University of Minnesota Press, Minneapolis, Minn., 1953.

Hall, E. Raymond, *Mammals of Nevada*. University of California Press, Berkeley, Calif., 1946.

Hamilton, W. J., Jr., *American Mammals*. McGraw-Hill Book Co., New York, 1939.

————, *The Mammals of Eastern United States*. Hafner Publishing Co., New York, 1943.

Hamnett, William L., and Thornton, David C., *Tar Heel Wildlife*. North Carolina Wildlife Resources Commission, Raleigh, N.C., 1953.

Handley, Charles, Jr., and Patton, Clyde P., *Wild Mammals of Virginia*. Commission of Game & Inland Fisheries, Richmond, Va., 1947.

Hornaday, W. T., *The American Natural History*. Charles Scribner & Sons, New York, 1935.

Jackson, Hartley H. T., *Mammals of Wisconsin*. The University of Wisconsin Press, Madison, Wisc., 1961.

Jenkins, J. H., *The Game Resources of Georgia*. Georgia Game and Fish Commission, Atlanta, Ga., 1953.

Ligon, J. Stokley, *Wild Life of New Mexico*. New Mexico Department of Game and Fish, Santa Fe, N. Mex., 1927.

Louisiana Department of Conservation, *The Fur Animals of Louisiana*. New Orleans, La., 1931.

Miller, Gerritt S., Jr., and Kellogg, Remington, *List of North American Recent Mammals*. Smithsonian Institution, Washington, D.C., 1955.

Moore, Ruth, *Evolution*. Silver Burdett Co., Morristown, N.J., 1962.

Nelson, Edward William, *Wild Animals of North America*. National Geographic Society, Washington, D.C., 1930.

Palmer, E. Laurence, *Fieldbook of Natural History*. McGraw-Hill Book Co., New York, 1949.

Scheele, William E., *The First Mammals*. The World Publishing Co., Cleveland, Ohio, 1955.

Schwartz, Charles E., and Elizabeth R., *Wild Mammals of Missouri*. University of Missouri Press, Columbia, Mo., 1960.

Seton, Ernest Thompson, *Lives of Game Animals*. Charles T. Branford, Boston, 1953. 8 vols.

Shoemaker, Lois Meier, *Mammals of New Jersey*. New Jersey State Museum, Trenton, N.J., 1962.

Silver, Helenette, *A History of New Hampshire Game & Furbearers*. Survey Report No. 6. New Hampshire Fish and Game Department, Concord, N.H., 1957.

Stone, Witmer, and Cram, William Everett, *American Animals*. Doubleday, Page & Co., New York, 1902.

Walker, Ernest P., *Mammals of the World*. The Johns Hopkins Press, Baltimore, Md., 1964. 3 vols.

Index